"Very few of us get to become legends in our own lifetime, but Fred Frank is a deserving member of that elite club. He was also one of the geniuses behind the creation of many of the modern funding vehicles that made it possible to raise the amounts of money required for capital-intensive, high-risk endeavors. And yet he always made time to help those coming behind him: kind, humble, ever ready to share his wisdom. And he walked on water—but you have to read the book to find out about that."

—**Karen Bernstein,** co-founder, editor in chief, *Biocentury*

"Fred is an innovator and seasoned Wall Street veteran who has pioneered investments in biotechnology, paving the way for its explosive growth. *A Philosopher on Wall Street* captures how Fred's wide-ranging life experience led to a successful and continuing sixty-year career that has revolutionized the financial and biotech industries."

—**Peter Salovey,** President of Yale University and
Chris Argyris Professor of Psychology

"As I emerged from a world of surgery and academia into business entrepreneurship, I didn't know what I didn't know. Fred, a giant among giants on Wall Street, took the time to be a guide to me and many others as we navigated this foreign financial universe. He became more than just a trusted consultant who masterfully guided the sale of my first biotechnology company; he became a valued friend and mentor."

—**Arie Belldegrun,** MD FACS, senior managing partner,
co-founder, Vida Ventures

"Fred Frank pioneered the provision of investment banking services tailored specifically for the healthcare industry, including a robust practice with cutting edge biotechnology companies. Fred invariably conducted himself as an old-school fiduciary, with class, integrity, dedication, and intelligence. "

—**David Swensen,** Chief Investment Officer, Yale University

A PHILOSOPHER

ON

WALL STREET

HOW CREATIVE FINANCIER
FRED FRANK FORGED THE FUTURE

DAVID EWING DUNCAN

GREENLEAF
BOOK GROUP PRESS

Published by Greenleaf Book Group Press
Austin, Texas
www.gbgpress.com

Distributed by Greenleaf Book Group

For ordering information or special discounts for bulk purchases, please contact
Greenleaf Book Group at PO Box 91869, Austin, TX 78709, 512.891.6100.

Grateful acknowledgment is made to the following for permission to duplicate
copyrighted material:
Kleiner Perkins, venture capital, and the chairmanship of Genentech, 1976-1995:
oral history transcript / Thomas J. Perkins, BANC MSS 2003/170 c,
© The Regents of the University of California, Oral History Center,
The Bancroft Library, University of California, Berkeley.
"The Ubiquitous Frederick Frank," *Life Sciences Foundation* magazine, Summer 2012.

Design and composition by Greenleaf Book Group and Sheila Parr
Cover design by Greenleaf Book Group and Sheila Parr
Cover photo © Estate of Yousuf Karsh

Publisher's Cataloging-in-Publication data is available.

Print ISBN: 978-1-62634-871-4

eBook ISBN: 978-1-62634-872-1

Part of the Tree Neutral® program, which offsets the number of trees consumed in the
production and printing of this book by taking proactive steps, such as planting trees
in direct proportion to the number of trees used: www.treeneutral.com

TreeNeutral™

Printed in the United States of America on acid-free paper

21 22 23 24 25 26   10 9 8 7 6 5 4 3 2 1

First Edition

"I think Fred Frank was the seminal dealmaker in biotech. He has this amazing way of taking a very complicated problem and finding a very simple, straightforward solution."

—Leroy Hood, MD, PhD

Contents

Foreword by Fred Frank

How truly fortunate I have been. I have lived through the evolution of Wall Street from the cottage industry that it was when I joined it in 1958 to the multitrillion-dollar global financial community that it is today. For more than sixty-two years I have focused on two of the major industries that have interacted with the Street: the business-services and life sciences sectors. During my journey, I have been blessed to know and work with many outstanding individuals who have been instrumental in my good fortune. Many of them are mentioned in this book, and my apologies to any who I have not named in this recounting of the major and most memorable, distinctive, and colorful transactions and events in my long career.

The stories told in these pages remain vivid in my memory because they have certain common characteristics. I have always been interested in transformational technologies and business models, particularly those in which new technology was driving dramatic changes in industries or new industries were emerging because of technology. In the early years of my career, I sought out the emerging growth industries of business services, electronics, photography, healthcare services, and the life sciences. In more recent years, I have focused almost exclusively on life sciences, as biology and chemistry have become inexhaustible sources of the new.

Initially, as a research analyst, my focus was on how the transformational changes coming from new technologies made stocks more valuable, and when such change made for an investable concept for ambitious and risk-oriented investors. In 1971, when I moved from research to investment banking, transformational technology remained my key interest, but I added the skill of making transformational transactions. When I was a research analyst, I often had to wait and incubate my interest in a new business sector or a new company until it was properly investable. In investment banking, watchful waiting is often the key to transformational transactions. "Making the numbers work" is one of the chief duties of bankers. Unfortunately, fundamentals and markets sometimes mean that the numbers cannot "work" the way a client might desire. Often one has to wait for the moment when markets, fundamentals, and "the numbers" all coalesce. Many of the transactions I highlight here required such watchful waiting. This is a major theme in my life and in the life of a vigilant banker.

I hope you enjoy these reminiscences and thoughts from my many years as a banker and a witness to and sometime participant in some of the great deals and technological trends that have occurred since I arrived on Wall Street.

—Fred Frank, January 2021

Preface

A Philosopher on Wall Street recounts the role of the banker as a force of creativity and imagination in financing and fostering long-term innovation, all too rare on Wall Street today, which tends to be obsessed with quarterly earnings, exit strategies, and the bottom line. Fred Frank—in this book we'll call him Fred, as he is almost universally known—has been such a banker. During his sixty-plus years on Wall Street, he has worked his magic in several industries, although he is best known for his acumen in spotting new technologies and companies. He was the first banker in the early 1960s to recognize that the sleepy pharmaceutical industry—then an offshoot of the chemical business—was about to begin its meteoric rise, driven by billion-dollar blockbuster drugs that began to appear toward the end of that decade. Soon after, in the 1970s, Fred helped to nurture the embryonic and innovative biotechnology industry, distinguished in the early years by focusing its research on newfangled therapies based on biology, rather than a reliance on chemical compounds then favored by Big Pharma to develop new drugs.

Over the past five decades, biotechnology has gone from being nonexistent to becoming an industry worth almost $500 billion in 2019. Its rapid growth rate was primed and promoted at its start by Fred and other bankers and investors who grasped the industry's promise and helped create tools like the modern initial public offering (IPO) to finance small biotech and other tech start-ups with great promise but little or no revenues.

Since the first biotechnology companies were hatched in the early 1970s, this industry has produced hundreds of drugs for a myriad of diseases. During this same period, innovative companies and entrepreneurs created a growing range of diagnostic tools to determine and predict disease, new medical devices, genetic sequencing platforms and other bio-industrial tools for delving into and in some cases manipulating molecular structures inside organisms, and more recently, complex bio-computing programs, algorithms, and platforms. Fred was at the center of it all, one of those rare bankers who leveraged billions of dollars to further innovation that at times seemed highly esoteric and risky but in the end proved to be right, succeeding both in terms of business and in producing products that literally changed the world.

Raised in Salt Lake City by a Jewish family that followed in the wake of the Mormon settlement of Utah in the late nineteenth century, Fred studied philosophy at Yale University, a grounding in logic and critical thinking that he said informed his thinking throughout his career. As a private in the US Army in France during the 1950s, Fred managed to parlay deals that landed him in a small grotto near the Place d'Etoile rather than in the barracks, and also behind the wheel of a 1957 Austin-Healey sports car that he purchased for his brother (using his father's money) and took his time shipping back to Utah. At Stanford University, he earned an MBA during the heady early days of high technology rising that would transform what were then orange groves along US 101 into Silicon Valley.

Fred began his career on Wall Street in 1958 during the *Mad Men* era in New York City. He quickly became a key member of the whip-smart cadre of young (almost all male) financiers who were then challenging the stodgy, often risk-averse scions of old-world investment banking. They did this by investing in everything from electronics and computers to drugs and devices, the Internet, and biotechnology. While still in his twenties, Fred rose quickly to become an innovative force on Wall Street, first at Smith, Barney & Co. and then at Lehman Brothers, where he later became the firm's first vice chairman.

A soft-spoken firebrand, Fred, during his sixty-plus-year career, interacted with the likes of former US Commerce Secretary Peter Peterson and legendary investment banker Sandy Robertson, another important early figure who challenged Wall Street's conservatism in raising capital for new technologies. Robertson founded a boutique investment bank in San Francisco, Robertson Stephens, that worked closely with Fred to finance a number of biotech companies that the big banks wouldn't touch by themselves. Now in his eighties, Fred Frank remains an important figure in financing biotech and life science companies on Wall Street and around the world as he works with his wife and longtime business partner Mary Tanner, one of the first women to take on a senior role on Wall Street back in the eighties.

A Philosopher on Wall Street details some of the biggest transactions in the history of biotechnology, starting with the founding in 1973 of Cetus Corporation, one of the first biotechnology companies. This narrative describes the first waves of IPOs for Cetus, Genentech, Amgen, and others, and numerous creative financings that kept the dollars flowing over the painfully long time it still takes to develop a drug. Many of these deals are stories of drama, intrigue, near-death business experiences, and cliffhanger financings involving a fiery and colorful cast of characters—and a business in which millions of lives rest on whether or not a company or a drug succeeds.

Fred Frank oversaw or heavily influenced pivotal deals like the Cetus initial public offering, a launch that at the time shattered all records for money raised in an IPO, and the merger in 1990 of Genentech and F. Hoffmann-La Roche AG. Fred also took public Applied Biosystems, the first DNA sequencing machine manufacturer, and in 1992 worked with famed geneticist Craig Venter and entrepreneur and oncology legend William A. Haseltine on a novel deal that created Human Genome Sciences, a company run by Haseltine alongside a nonprofit sister-institution called The Institute for Genomic Research (TIGR), run by Venter. The new venture was given a huge boost when Fred, working with Haseltine, secured a $125 million collaboration in 1993 between Human Genome Sciences and SmithKline Beecham. At the time, this was the largest biotech-pharma alliance in history. Yet given the strong personalities and the conflicting aims of Haseltine and Venter, the deal, as we shall see in chapter 6, spun apart in 1997. Fred also assembled seminal deals in other industries. For instance, in 1983 he helped save Chrysler with a public equity offering after the company had been bailed out by a US government loan to avoid bankruptcy. Fred also engineered the merger between the polling and communications company A.C. Nielsen and the business-services giant Dun & Bradstreet in 1994. Fred's wife, Mary Tanner, described his priorities in all of these deals:

> Fred has always been most interested in the new. I think it comes from his early training as a research analyst, where he was looking for the big, new, "alpha"—ideas that would generate superior returns compared to the market as a whole—in which to invest. This is why he very early discovered biotech and never deserted it. As an industry, it is forever young and new, since the mysteries of human life do not yield themselves up easily.

A Philosopher on Wall Street is also a cautionary tale—or, rather, two tales—as both banking and biotech, for different reasons, have faced cycles of boom and bust in recent years. For biotech, the challenge has been to fund the precipitous rise in the cost of developing new drugs, particularly in an industry that experiences rises and falls in fortune—and stock prices—with a breathtaking regularity. For banking, the latest crisis came in 2008 when bubbles and high-risk gambits nearly brought down the global economy and numerous industries, including biotech. They did bring down Lehman Brothers that September, a story that Fred knows from the inside. As vice chairman of Lehman, he strongly opposed the questionable trading practices and lending policies that destroyed this fabled financial institution.

Fred also has deep experience and knowledge about the forces large and small that drive markets, from the rise and implications of new technologies for business and society to the sometimes fluid and unpredictable vagaries of human nature that often defy logic, which must be understood, or at least taken into account, if one is going to succeed on Wall Street.

Since Lehman's fall, Fred hasn't slowed down. He and Mary have continued to be passionate about new technologies, investments, and philanthropic projects. Toward the end of these pages Fred shares some of his knowledge and insights about the transformation of Wall Street from a sleepy grouping of small-scale private firms to the global behemoths of today. He also offers up some deep wisdom about a life-science industry that has scaled beyond belief, driven by scientific discoveries.

Author Note: This book was written with the support of the Tanner-Frank Foundation and was written in collaboration with Fred Frank and Mary Tanner.

PROLOGUE

The Quake Heard 'Round the World

OCTOBER 17, 1989

Everything that day was hush-hush as two senior executives from Genentech, a scrappy, thirteen-year-old start-up and biotech legend, traveled to New York from San Francisco to attend a secret meeting at the Waldorf Astoria Hotel. Their mission was to save their company, which only a few people at the time knew was fast running out of cash. Their latest drug, a novel anti-stroke treatment called Activase, had sold poorly, cutting into projected revenues. Costs also had been escalating to run one of the most innovative and expensive R&D shops in the pharmaceutical industry. Another public offering was not an option. The first one, in 1980, was famous for the new stock more than doubling on the first day, making it one of the splashiest debuts at the time in market history. Since then, though, the stock had dropped significantly. If that weren't bad enough, the markets were still reeling from the recent savings-and-loan crisis, and from one of the largest stock market crashes ever. Two years earlier, in October of 1987, the Dow Jones index had plummeted 22.6 percent in just one day. Nor did Genentech want to radically cut expenses just as its R&D pipeline was beginning to produce results.

By coincidence, the meeting at the Waldorf occurred on the same day that millions of fans were gathering at Candlestick Park in San Francisco for game three of the 1989 World Series. In the purely Bay Area affair, the Oakland A's were ahead of the San Francisco Giants two games to none. As the Genentech executives arrived at the hotel in New York, the two teams on the opposite coast were beginning to warm up for a game that was supposed to start at 5:35 p.m. Pacific Time.

Unbeknownst to anyone in either New York or San Francisco, another literally seismic event was unfolding deep in the earth beneath the Santa Cruz Mountains, sixty miles south of San Francisco. As the Genentech men headed toward a private boardroom in the plush Waldorf and fans poured into Candlestick, two massive tectonic plates along the San Andreas Fault near the Loma Prieta peak were mashing and grinding into each other with a continent-size force, building up pressure far more than usual. Within a few hours, this overwhelming stress would go critical.

Caught in a tightening financial vise, the two men from California were in New York to discuss an unlikely solution to Genentech's dilemma. Joining them would be a second pair of executives who soon appeared in the ornate, mahogany-paneled room on the hotel's third floor. Flying in from Basel, Switzerland, they were the number one and number two executives at drug colossus Hoffmann-La Roche, a traditional, even stuffy, corporation that was in many ways the antithesis of the plucky little biotech company from South San Francisco. Not only did Roche and its ilk move carefully and deliberately, taking few risks, they also used the science of chemistry to develop new therapeutic compounds, a focus coming from their origins in the chemical industry in the nineteenth century. In contrast, Genentech's science used cutting-edge discoveries in molecular biology to create its medicines and cures.

When the executives arrived in the Waldorf boardroom, a fifth man was already there, sipping his customary black tea. A compact, athletic banker in a pinstripe suit and oversize aviator glasses, the fifty-six-year-old Fred Frank rose to greet his uneasy guests. The architect of this meeting, Fred was then the senior managing director at Lehman Brothers, where he had a reputation for creating deals almost as imaginative as the businesses created by his many entrepreneurial clients. The purpose of the meeting was to see if a deal could be struck to infuse Genentech with cash from Roche while somehow preserving the biotech pioneer's culture of independence and innovation. Not only were the companies philosophically misaligned, but the man brokering the deal was effectively representing *both* parties—almost always a no-no.

"We had approached Fred with our situation and had asked his help," remembered Kirk Raab, then the president of Genentech and one of the two men from California attending the meeting. "He had worked with a number of big drug companies, and he thought that there could be a fit for us. We were dubious, to say the least. But this was the amazing thing about Fred. He got us to sit down with Roche because both sides trusted him."

Fred Frank had joined his first Wall Street firm, Smith, Barney & Co., in 1958. A quiet man with a playful smile and a steely underpinning, Fred was among the first Wall Street analysts in the 1960s to realize that the previously lethargic and lackluster pharmaceutical industry was about to explode as new discoveries created the first billion-dollar blockbuster drugs. In 1969, Fred had joined Lehman Brothers, where his reputation for creative deals in pharma expanded in the seventies and eighties (and beyond) as Fred also helped finance some of the early deals in the nascent biotechnology industry. This made him the perfect man by October 1989 to broker a deal like the one being quietly discussed that afternoon in the Waldorf Astoria.

"Fred has the most creative brain in the business," said oncologist and former Human Genome Sciences CEO Bill Haseltine, speaking for many of the entrepreneurs, scientists, and investors Fred has worked with over the years. "I always found him the easiest person to work with. He would ask exactly the right question and had the ability to get you to focus on what it took to nail something. And then, when you watched his dealmaking, he had a wonderful ability to make totally novel deals, like the Roche-Genentech deal. Probably the biggest deal in biotech, or in the pharmaceutical industry, with the longest lasting consequence."

On the Genentech side of the table that day in New York sat the company's chief executive officer, Robert A. Swanson. Then forty-two years old and a cofounder of the company with University of California at San Francisco geneticist Herbert W. Boyer, Swanson was a classic entrepreneur: brilliant, driven, and demanding. A former venture capitalist with a balding top and a lively, intense energy that could both engage and flummox, he had steered Genentech from its beginnings in 1976, when he was twenty-nine years old, to become one of the most successful of the companies in the newfangled biotechnology space. Joining Swanson was Raab, the former president and chief operating officer of pharmaceutical giant Abbott Laboratories. Swanson had hired Raab in 1985 to beef up the operations and sales team at Genentech. A large man with a linebacker's physique and a more outgoing demeanor than the wound-up Swanson, the fifty-five-year-old Raab—known as "Captain" Kirk Raab—was once called "the master marketer" by the *Wall Street Journal.*

On the other side of the table that afternoon were two legends of the drug industry. First was Fritz Gerber, the sixty-year-old chairman and CEO of Hoffmann-La Roche, with his flared eyebrows already turning white and eyes that could bore through a person. A lawyer by training, Gerber had led this nearly century-old company since 1978, during its period of rapid expansion into a global colossus. By 1989 it had $5.4 billion in revenues—then considered a staggering amount. Accompanying him was the company's chief financial officer, the fifty-three-year-old Henri B. Meier, a tall, lean-faced Swiss economist formerly with the World Bank who had recently joined Roche after a career that had taken him to South America and the US as well as several postings across Europe.

The Genentech-Roche meeting at the Waldorf came at a crucial moment for biotechnology. Several companies were moving from infancy into young adulthood both scientifically and commercially as their innovative approach to developing drugs was producing results. Genentech had already released a synthetic human insulin product and a treatment for dwarfism called Protropin. Major drugs for cancer and other maladies were moving through their pipeline that would later achieve blockbuster status. To the south, in Thousand Oaks, California, near Los Angeles, another new biotech company, Amgen, was just releasing Epogen. A drug made by inserting human genes into microbes—which in turn generated the red-blood-cell-producing hormone erythropoietin—this drug for anemia and kidney disease would soon become the first biotech industry blockbuster. A slew of other companies were also developing drugs in what was fast becoming a biotech explosion.

In 1989, momentum was building to infuse serious money into this new industry. The markets were still recovering from the crash of '87, but deals were becoming possible again as pharma companies flush with profits from blockbusters such as Prozac for depression and Lipitor to lower cholesterol were hovering. Anxious about where the next blockbusters would come from as their own early-stage shops were struggling, the smartest companies were beginning to look beyond their own labs and traditions for fresh ideas. Into this breach came prescient dealmakers like Fred Frank, who early on understood what would become gospel over the next few years: that the small and nimble biotech companies were good at innovation, while Big Pharma was good at developing, manufacturing, testing, and selling drugs. "It was a simple formula," said Fred, "but it took years for the biotechs and the pharmas to connect up. Both thought they could do it all— the R and the D of R&D. But the reality is that biotechs are good at R, and pharma is good at D."

Raab recalled the Waldorf meeting lasting perhaps a couple of hours. "I remember at the end there was some wine or cocktails and hors d'oeuvres brought in," he said. "It was very casual. There wasn't a presentation. We had asked a consulting firm to prepare a giant book on Genentech—finances, pipelines, personnel, everything. None of the people back at Genentech ever saw this book, because we had to keep this very quiet. We were afraid that if word got out to our employees or to investors, there would be a riot because what we were doing was like talking to the enemy."

After the meeting ended, Raab and Swanson ducked out to debrief over dinner. Raab thinks they ate at a nearby Italian restaurant in Midtown Manhattan. While they dined, Swanson shared his misgivings about a pact with Roche that would cede control of the company's shares. Though no one had yet floated a deal, the men from San Francisco knew that a large dollop of cash would not come without concessions. The question was: What exactly would Genentech have to give up? Later, when Swanson found out that Roche wanted majority ownership of Genentech, the volatile CEO would nearly scuttle the deal. But that wouldn't happen for a few more weeks, when this seminal arrangement in pharma and biotech history entered its endgame phase. That night in New York, after a long afternoon and evening, the two Genentech men were exhausted and ready to go back to their hotel rooms. Raab, a Giants fan, was also anxious to check in on the third game of the World Series.

Saying goodnight to Swanson, Raab returned to his room and turned on the television. "I was expecting the game," he said. "Oakland was beating the Giants by two games, and I expected the worst but I wanted to watch."

What he saw, however, was not the game. For a few tense minutes he seemed to be watching a terrible catastrophe unfolding back home, "the big one" that everyone in San Francisco had feared since the great earthquake of 1906. It had happened just a few minutes earlier as a crowd watched the A's and the Giants warm up in Candlestick Park. That's when the fantastic pressure building up deep in the earth under Loma Prieta finally gave way—at exactly 5:04 p.m. Pacific Time, 8:04 p.m. in New York City.

For nearly 20 seconds, an earthquake measuring 6.9 on the Richter scale at Loma Prieta had shaken the Bay Area: the first major quake in history that occurred live on national television as sportscasters were airing the pregame show.

Raab watched as images of fallen buildings and bridges and burning houses were beamed in from San Francisco. Instantly forgetting about wheeling and dealing, Raab spent a tense couple of hours trying to reach his wife, who was pregnant with twins in Hillsboro, California, south of the city. He couldn't get through because lines were down and circuits jammed. Raab called Swanson and they shared some panicked moments. Finally, they were able to contact a security company that worked for Genentech. The company sent a guard to check on their families and on the condition of the company's campus, which was just across a small inlet of water from Candlestick Park. All were safe.

As the evening wore on, it became clear that despite terrible collapses and several deaths, the Loma Prieta earthquake was not "the big one." Yet, it's hopefully not stretching a metaphor too far to suggest that the Waldorf meeting and the subsequent deal, in its own way, was a bio-tremor of what was coming for an industry that would soon find itself starving for cash—the billions of dollars required to fund a whole new generation of biological drugs. How could an upstart industry make this work?

Already, there was an answer. They would turn to innovative bankers like Fred Frank.

CHAPTER 1

Out of the West

SALT LAKE CITY YEARS, 1932–1948

The banker who brokered the secret Genentech-Roche meeting in 1989 was by then an iconic presence on Wall Street. But Fred Frank was not born into that world. His family had no connection to the great banking dynasties in New York, nor to the upper tiers of American society that tended to produce the sons (not yet daughters) of Wall Street and high commerce.

This was fortunate for the Genentechs of the world in part because Fred came from the West, where out-of-the-box thinking was the norm and technology upstarts, when Fred was a young man, were beginning to pop up in places like Seattle and in the San Francisco Bay Area. Fred's hometown wasn't as far west as California. Yet Salt Lake City shared with the other rising cities of the region a palpable sense of newness, rawness, and anything-goes that had begun when it was first settled in the nineteenth century. By the time Fred was born in 1932, the rising metropolises of Los Angeles, San Francisco, Seattle,

Salt Lake City, and Denver had attracted millions of pioneers from around the globe, people with the gumption to make the journey and the optimism to think that they might be able to recast themselves in a place largely unencumbered by the barriers of more traditional and rule-bound regions of the world. Given this sensibility, it's not surprising that by the 1960s and 1970s, when Fred came of age professionally, a wave of innovation in the West was poised to shake up existing industries and to invent some new ones.

To financiers raised in the eastern United States, used to ordered and sedate financings and public offerings mostly for established companies, the rise of high technology in the West was baffling and poorly understood. But not by Fred Frank. He straddled both worlds, having spent his childhood in Utah and his high school and college years being educated in the East. After Yale, he spent a year in Paris during the Korean War, posted by the US Army to SHAPE (Supreme Headquarters Allied Powers Europe, now called NATO), and then another two years capping off his education with an MBA from Stanford University. Arriving in Palo Alto in the late 1950s, Fred was just in time to start hearing about early tech companies like Hewlett-Packard that were already making a name for themselves in what would later be dubbed "Silicon Valley."

"I grew up in the West when there was this feeling that things were new and just getting started," Fred recalled. "It was much easier for someone to start a business, to strike out on his own, if you were willing to work hard. And there was no one there to say 'no' like you sometimes would get in the East. You learned to think out of the box."

This certainly applied to Arthur Frank, Fred's grandfather. Born in 1873, Arthur immigrated to the US in 1903 at the age of thirty from Grodno, now in western Belarus, which at the time was part of the Lithuanian province of Imperial Russia.[1] "I was a railroad contractor and foreman in Europe before deciding the future lay in America," Arthur told the *Salt Lake Tribune* in April 1953,[2] when he was eighty years old. "I laid the roadbed and track from Grodno to Lodz and Warsaw, and walked every tie as we built the line." Arthur made the sixteen-day crossing from Bremen in Germany to Hoboken, New Jersey, following in the wake of his brother-in-law, Harry Baron, who had come west and settled in Salt Lake City a few years earlier. Arthur took with him his young wife, Bertha, and three small children, settling in Murray, Utah, about eight miles south of Salt Lake City.[3]

The Salt Lake area was a natural place for aspiring young men to settle at the turn of the twentieth century. Founded by the Mormons in 1847, the city was only half Mormon by the 1890s, and had shaken off much of the insularity of the years immediately after its establishment by Brigham Young and his followers. The first wave of non-Mormons, which included a coterie of Jewish traders and merchants, came through this stop on the trail to California during the gold rush of 1849, and a few stayed in Salt Lake City. Twenty years later, in 1869, the Transcontinental Railroad came to town. This launched Salt Lake City as a major regional hub for supplies, shipping, and trade and led to the city becoming the capital of the new state of Utah in 1896.

When Arthur arrived in the early twentieth century, the city of 45,000 had several smart downtown streets with wide avenues and brick storefronts. Horses and buggies far outnumbered the rare horseless carriage. In photographs, men wore hats and waistcoats and women dressed formally in long skirts. "Main Street was quite a place," Arthur remembered in the *Tribune* article, "utility poles in the middle of the street, trolley tracks, and unpaved below 4th Street."

Arthur and Bertha had brought with them from Europe their three small children: Harry, born in 1898; Boris, born in 1900; and Sarah Sally, born in 1902. Fred's father, Simon, was born in Salt Lake City in 1905. Other family members soon followed from Europe, including Arthur's brother Louis Frank. In 1905 Louis opened his own string of general goods stores in Gunnison and Richfield, and later in Salt Lake City.

Upon arrival, Arthur went to work at Harry Baron's clothing store, but it didn't take him long to go into business for himself. Arthur showed a talent for commerce and for making deals that would be passed down to his grandson, Fred. Indeed, a story often told by Arthur's son, Simon—Fred's father—and one he recounted in a 1982 interview in *A Homeland in The West: Utah Jews Remember* by Eileen Hallet Stone, a book about Utah's early Jewish families,[4] sounds like one of Fred's Wall Street stories, with the same can-do moxie and original thinking that Fred would show on the Genentech-Roche merger and many other deals. The tale starts with Arthur going to Harry Baron and offering to buy Baron's store just a year after Arthur arrived from Poland. According to Simon Frank:

> When presented with the proposal to purchase the business, Baron said, "With what?"
>
> "I'll go to the bank and borrow it," said Arthur Frank.
>
> "Well, that's pretty good," said Harry Baron. "I've been here for several years and I can't borrow any money from the bank. How do you think you're going to?"
>
> Dave Macmillan, the president of the bank, took a liking to my dad and loaned him the money to buy the store. In those days, you didn't always have to have collateral. They did that on your character, faith, and whatnot.

"By 1907," said Arthur in the *Tribune*, "I had opened a chain of 12 leading clothing shops called The Leader, [with] stores in such Utah cities as Midvale, Spanish Fork, Brigham, and Bingham." That same year he opened a men's specialty shop in Salt Lake City, "one of the first of its kind in the state," he said. "We sold suits for $5, those narrow-waisted models. A derby hat sold for $1.98. Walkover shoes, a brand selling for about $25 now [in 1953] were $1.98 to $3.50 a pair. Shirts were 95 cents. Vests were just as loud then as now."

Soon after Arthur began to buy up rivals' stores in Salt Lake, with names like The Wonder and The Regent.[5] Not to run them, though. "We bought them out, closed them out, and brought the merchandise into our Union Clothing Store," said Simon, describing a kind of mergers and acquisitions strategy that Fred would later become well known for on Wall Street—although Fred's deals would involve major corporations instead of local clothing stores.

Around 1911, recalled Simon, his father became a diabetic, a dangerous disease before insulin was available as a drug. While he survived his initial bout with the disease, he sold most of the stores and convalesced for a time in California before returning to run just the Arthur Frank stores in Salt Lake City.

At the time, Simon was attending the University of California at Berkeley and was thinking about becoming a lawyer, but that changed with his father's illness. Simon returned home to help with the family business and never returned to Berkeley, something he regretted, according to Fred. Later, Simon finished college at the University of Utah.

Fortunately, insulin arrived in 1922 to treat diabetes, which contributed to Arthur living until 1953, although the disease forced him to slow down his acquisitions and to sell off and consolidate most of the stores. A 1920s account in the *Deseret News* reported:

On Sept. 3, 1921, the Franks consolidated the stores into one outlet at 210 S. Main and remained there for 37 years. Arthur died in 1953. On Oct. 2, 1958, the firm opened a new store at 140 S. Main which doubled the size of the previous location.[6]

Arthur didn't entirely give up on entrepreneurship. In the 1920s, Arthur "had an idea of buying a fleet of Fords that were called jitneys," remembered Simon. "They looked like Model T Fords . . . There were streetcars, of course, in the center of the street. But the drivers of the jitney had an advantage. They could just drive right up to any curb to pick up or drop off a passenger for a nickel fare. It didn't last long, though; something about licensing, and Pop went back into the retail business."

Though Arthur was obviously an astute businessman, Fred said he doesn't remember his grandfather ever talking to him about business. "But we saw him running the store," said Fred, "and it dominated our family's lives. At Christmastime we all pitched in. As a teenager, I stocked the shelves. We saw my grandfather being successful, organizing the store. That had to have rubbed off—although, frankly, I found retail incredibly boring."

Arthur's boys all worked for their father in the stores, although it was Fred's father, Simon, who ended up running them with Arthur and then, after his father's death in 1953, acting as the president of the company. "My father obviously worked for my grandfather," recalled Fred. "All the brothers did. My father was sort of a favorite of the family, though, and the one my grandfather trusted to run the stores."

Fred's brother, Tom Frank, described a letter from Arthur that he found years later describing how Arthur chose his father, Simon, to run the store:

> When my father [Simon] died I found an original paper, which was written by my grandfather [Arthur] to his children, saying it was time for him to step back and this was going to be a family store that everybody had ownership in. And my father [Simon] was to be the president and decision-maker. [Arthur] explained why he wanted that, even though [Simon] was next to the youngest. And [Arthur] did it in such a way that I don't think any of the family was upset with it. From then on [Simon] ran the store.

Simon Frank grew up in Salt Lake City with his older siblings, living within blocks of the vibrant downtown where men in bowlers rode streetcars and thousands of people came and went as they took the railroad to and from the two coasts and points in between. Even as a boy, Simon was highly intelligent and driven to work very hard, attributes his son Fred would inherit. Simon finished grades one through eight in just five years, and attended high school starting at age twelve, in 1917. He remembered this vividly not only because he was very small but also because this was the year that America finally entered World War I, which ended the following year. "When the war was over many soldiers came back, and the government paid for them to go to high school," said Simon. "So here I was about thirteen years old with all of these eighteen- and nineteen-year-olds."

Academically, Simon had no problems. Yet he said it was hard with everyone being so much older than he was. "But I probably picked up some experiences trying to keep up with them," he added. He then began attending the University of California at Berkeley, returning two years later when his father got sick to help out in the Arthur Frank store. "That's the only job I had," he said.

At some point in the late twenties—no one in the family is exactly sure when—Simon met Suzanne Seller, a petite woman with deep-set eyes and a no-nonsense demeanor, at a wedding in Portland, Oregon. Soon after, they were married, in 1928. This was Fred's mother, whom he remembers fondly. He recalled:

> My mother was a wonderful, wonderful woman. She went to finishing school in New York, and I used to accuse her of finishing the school because it didn't exist anymore soon after. Mother was a real classic lady. Everything was very refined; she came from a very refined family. She was one of four daughters. Her father died when she was very young, and fortunately my mother's mother was well off. My mother loved to entertain, particularly for the family and friends. Christmas dinner was always at our house.

Fred was born on May 31, 1932, the second of Simon and Suzanne's three children. His older sister, also named Suzanne, was born in 1930, and his younger brother, Tom, in 1937. "When I was born, we lived in a duplex on South Temple, a red brick building that is still there," said Fred. "Then we moved just a few blocks away to an apartment house, which is still there." The duplex stood across the street from a park where Fred later played football and other sports.

Fred was born three years after the 1929 stock market crash, when much of the US was mired in the Great Depression. This was a rough time in Salt Lake City, as it was everywhere in the US and for most of the world. At its peak, the unemployment rate in Salt Lake City reached 61,500 people, more than a third of the population. In 1932, the annual per capita income had dropped to half what it was in 1929, from $537 annually to just $276. The economic hard times didn't spare the Franks, as Tom recalled:

> From the stories I was told, during the Depression was a very hard time. Luckily, though, the head of Hart Schaffner & Marx clothing stores and manufacturers, the clothing line carried in my family's store, became very good friends with my grandfather and my father. And during the worst years, this man—his name was Mr. Kestenbaum—called up my grandfather when everyone was struggling and business was tough, and he said, "You keep your store totally stocked, as if it were good times. I will send you all the merchandise you need, on consignment. When you sell it, you pay me." And that really kept the store in great shape.

Fred said that the Depression was mostly over by the time he was old enough to remember things. Yet the memory of how so many people lost everything—or nearly did in the case of the Frank family—left an impact. "You can't take anything for granted," said Fred. "I also came away from my family's experiences during those years, which were told to me, realizing that what gets a person through hard times is working hard and sticking to their core values."

The Franks were part of a small Jewish community in Salt Lake City that mostly thrived even if the years of the Depression were difficult. When Fred was growing up, the city's Jews numbered in the hundreds and were divided into reformed and conservative congregations. Fred's family wasn't particularly religious, he recalled, so they joined the reformed temple called B'nai Israel. In 1891, this congregation had built a synagogue that was modeled after the Great Synagogue in Berlin, though much smaller. Still, it was hard to keep the temple filled for services. "The Reformed Jewish community was so small that the temple didn't even open in the summertime," Fred remembered. "The rabbi would say, 'I'm not giving service to only seven people, forget that.'" The B'nai Israel building remains to this day, though it was sold long ago and today is an upscale furniture store.

Fred said that being Jewish in a Mormon city wasn't much of a burden. "There was perhaps less prejudice against Jews in Salt Lake than in other cities at the time," he said, "because in Utah, Jews are considered gentiles, meaning nonbelievers. So there's no difference between Jews and Catholics."

When Fred was about ten years old, Simon moved his family to an area of the city known as Federal Heights and into a large, beautiful home with a yard and later a swimming pool. This suggests that the retail clothing business was improving toward the mid- to late thirties. The house is still there on a quiet, green, tree-lined street that looks like it could be in Westchester County, New York, or any upscale suburb built in the early to mid-twentieth century. Except that if one looks up the street it abruptly ends where a parched, dusty desert ridge begins to climb toward the foothills of the mountains that rise to the east of the city. "On our street, mostly were Mormons," Fred said. "It was my parent's house, and then three houses were Mormons, and then there was the Rosenblatt house, and the Fields, and that was it."

Tom Frank recalled how he and his siblings were raised:

We were brought up fairly formally in many respects, about being at dinner on time and being dressed well. We all had chores to do and made sure they were done right. It could be cleaning the snow off the sidewalks or washing the car. And we got very small allowances, but that was our way to earn it. So he [Simon] gave us a work ethic.

Tom Frank remembered that Fred was an excellent student:

I was not a fantastic student—but Fred was really good in school. A super dedicated learner. I'm a wholly different person. I'm a self-thinker and a self-teacher. But I was having problems in math, in seventh or eighth grade, probably, and Fred would sit down and help me. He would say, "Look, this is the way you do it." Fred was very neat and precise. "You do it this way, this is the way you'll understand it. Your teacher will like the way it looks, and here are the answers." Things like that, he taught me.

Sometime after the Frank family moved into the house in Federal Heights, his parents bought a Steinway grand piano. Fred laughed when he remembered this, because no one in the family, he said, was musical. "My mother didn't play," he said, "my father didn't play, my sister didn't play. My brother decided at one point to play the clarinet or the saxophone, but he didn't continue it." The reason they had the piano was so that Fred's mother could invite to their home pianists and musicians who played with the Utah Symphony Orchestra, which she enthusiastically supported. Some great concert pianists would come to Salt Lake City on tour. Fred recalled their visits to his family's home:

After every performance, they would come for a party at our house. We had all of the great musicians, like Vladimir Horowitz. They'd

come to our house for a dinner party, cocktail party, and afterward
they would play for the guests. My parents were very close to the con-
ductor of the symphony, [Maurice Abravanel,] who was extremely
important in the music world in those days. And they were very close
friends. The Abravanels didn't have a house that could accommodate
a thing like this. They couldn't afford it, so my parents would have a
soiree for them after all these symphonies and performances. I wasn't
interested in these evenings. I was interested in sports. But I think
my memory of them led me in later life to my great love for classical
music, which I retain to this day.

Tom Frank remembered that his father, Simon, pushed his children
to work hard and was particularly eager to push Fred to follow a passion
Simon had developed as he grew older: investing—even though Tom
remembered that at one point Fred was interested in being a teacher.
In Tom's words:

> We were all pushed a little bit. I don't think it was terribly hard. I
> think in his attitude toward Fred, he could be fairly tough at times.
> My father admired Fred, but he pushed him hardest of all. He was
> determined to get Fred into the investment business. My father's side
> business was investing in the markets. He was fascinated by it, and it
> was how he made most of the family money.

During breaks from school, Fred said, he worked to earn
pocket change:

> I worked at the store over Christmas vacations when I was in high
> school, and it was strictly a pay for performance, because I think you
> were commissioned with 6 percent. I was selling. I made good money
> by the standards of the pay for some young kid like myself. I guess I
> was about fourteen when I started. I also worked [in] construction,

and I worked in the parks department one summer. I just picked up rubbish. And I worked several summers and during the school year and weekends at the Standard Optical Shop. That was an interesting experience, because grinding lenses is a very noisy business, or it was in those days. And virtually all the people working there were deaf-mutes. They did everything by sign language.

I started a business one summer because I couldn't get a job, so I started a job by going around to all the houses in our neighborhood and saying, "I'll take care of your car during the summer. I'll wash it once a week, I'll dust it every day, and wax it once a month" for I don't know how much money. And everyone in the neighborhood loved that because it was pretty cheap. I actually got so many orders that I had to hire two people, my neighbors Norman and Steven Rosenblatt. I was the manager.

"Fred has always been a straight-A student," said Tom. "He's always been number one, a very dedicated learner." On the other hand, Tom said, in classic sibling banter, "He doesn't know what end of a screwdriver to use." Fred recounted his dedication to his schoolwork:

I was good at school, Tom wasn't. I was a very serious student. If they gave us homework, I did it. If they gave us homework a week in advance, I'd get it done on day one. I was a real nerd. My brother wasn't, and my sister—they were totally the opposite of me. But that's partly the pressure of being the first son in a Jewish family. And we went to [Hebrew] Sunday school rigorously, and all that kind of stuff.

For those who know Fred as the great speaker he is as an adult, it may come as a surprise that he was a stutterer as a child. He told the story of the accident that caused him to start stuttering:

When I was about eight years old, we used to go to Portland in the summertime to visit my grandmother. I was at that age, eight or nine, when I didn't want to kiss my relatives anymore—that was baby stuff. I had a wonderful aunt in Portland who picked us up, Aunt Jane, and took us to our grandmother's house, and she said, "Well, darling, aren't you going to give me a kiss?" And I said, "Aunt Jane, only if you can beat me in a race." Which of course was not possible.

We staked out the race from the sidewalk up the stairs to the front door. Running up the stairs, I fell down on these cement stairs face-first, and they thought I had knocked my front teeth out. But it was dark out. In the morning we realized I'd knocked them up into my gums. My face was so swollen. Fortunately, my front teeth grew down.

But one consequence of this was that I stuttered, and for a kid that's very traumatic. Because kids really make fun of you when you stutter. I stuttered pretty badly, and my mother was worried about it because she defended me. I actually took some speech therapy to try to get over this, but in school kids are so mean. The teacher would make me read out loud, and of course, all the kids would laugh. And I remember all the time I would come back home crying. But, fortunately, as a little kid, I got over it.

Partly to counter his stuttering problem, which lasted until he was in seventh grade, Fred said, he became enamored with sports:

Sports in Salt Lake were pretty important to me, partly because of my stutter. In sports you don't talk. And I was very fortunate that my Aunt Helen liked to ski. She was very close to Art Johansson, who was the head of the ski school in Brighton, Utah. So I started skiing at the age of five. I was a natural athlete. I also was very good at playing football, basketball, and baseball.

Fred's childhood friend Arthur Fleischer is a longtime lawyer in New York whose family lived in Salt Lake City for several years. The two were in the same class in elementary school and attended Yale at the same time. Fleischer remembered playing sports with Fred:

> We used to play football together, not with all the padding and every-thing. I'm trying to remember if I ran faster than Fred, but he was a much better athlete than I was.

Fred recalled having to make a choice between Hebrew lessons and sports, although for Fred, it wasn't much of a choice:

> We had a very scholarly rabbi at one point by the name of Rabbi Lutz. He decided that since I was one of the best students, I should learn Hebrew. So, I'm taking Hebrew lessons from him after school two or three times a week, and all of a sudden, at a certain point in time, I said to him, "Rabbi Lutz, I have a terrible dilemma. I have to make a choice. I can't take Hebrew lessons, because then I can't be at football practice." And he said, "That's not a dilemma." And I said, "It's true, I'm going to take football practice."

Fred was nine years old when the United States entered the Second World War with the Japanese attack on Pearl Harbor in December 1941. The war, he said, changed everyone's lives in Salt Lake City. "In World War II, Utah became the location for major military bases," he said, "Army, Navy, Air Force, everything, because it was inland, away from the coast. And they built a major military hospital." Fred's childhood friend Arthur Fleischer recalled life during the war from his childhood perspective:

> We didn't feel the pain. In those days, we had rationing and the war news. I used to keep maps of where the various armies were. Not that

I necessarily understood what was going on, but I was thoroughly aware of the fact that there was a war. We had ration cards for food and gasoline. And then when we got to college . . . what were we called, the Silent Generation?

By all accounts, Fred was a curious boy and quite assertive when he wanted something, much like his grandfather was when he left Russia and came to Salt Lake City to found his businesses. Also like his grandfather, by the time Fred was a sophomore in high school, he was becoming restless. This was before television and way before the Internet, when a young man in a distant western city heard about the wider world from the radio and from magazines carrying stories of faraway places and people. Fred was—and still is—an avid reader of magazines, newspapers, and books. One day in the autumn of 1947, when he was fifteen years old, Fred was reading an issue of *Fortune* magazine and came across an article that would change his life. Fred said:

> *Fortune* wasn't like it is today. It was a different kind of magazine, full of great articles about finance and companies and all sorts of other topics. We got *Fortune* in the mail, and I read every issue. My father subscribed and kept all the issues. We had them from the 1920s on up. He never threw them away.
>
> As a kid, I loved going through those old magazines. The September 1932 edition featured an article on the great eastern prep schools. I had never heard of a prep school, and I had never been ten yards east of Salt Lake. I had only gone west. But I asked my parents at dinner: "Can I go away to prep school?" And they said, "What are you talking about?" My dad decided to visit some of them on a business trip, and he came back and said, "These are really pretty fabulous schools. If you want to apply, you can apply, but I doubt if you can get in." Thanks, Dad, right? I was a straight-A student.

So I applied, based on this article, to four or five schools, and the first one I heard from was the Hotchkiss School in Lakeville, Connecticut, which accepted me. The acceptance letter said, "Please let us know within two weeks." I didn't want to wait on the others, so I accepted it.

Fred Frank's childhood ended in August 1948, when he climbed aboard a train heading east for a two-day trip in a sleeper cabin to the school, located deep in the woods of Connecticut's lake country. "My parents sent me on a train by myself to go through New York City to Hotchkiss," said Fred. It was the longest trip he had ever taken, and it began what would become his lifelong obsession with travel. He was a sixteen-year-old alone, leaving the womb of his close-knit family for the unknown, a place he would soon discover was exactly where he wanted to be.

CHAPTER 2

Education of a Conforming Nonconformist

HOTCHKISS, YALE, PARIS, AND STANFORD,
1948–1958

HOTCHKISS: 1948–1950

The teenager departing Salt Lake City's Union Pacific Depot in late summer 1948 was headed into a world that he knew little about. Far from being worried or anxious, however, the short but powerfully built young man felt a surge of exhilaration as he climbed on board the shiny, silver-skinned train that was to convey him to a place as mysterious and novel to him as anywhere on earth, a distant hamlet called Lakeville, Connecticut, where he would attend the Hotchkiss School. "You would think I would have been a bit apprehensive," Fred said, "but all I remember is feeling very excited. It was unusual in those days for a boy my age to travel alone on the train, but I thought nothing of it."

He stopped briefly in New York City, staying with a rabbi the Franks had known in Salt Lake City. Fred then took another train to the station near Hotchkiss. He remembered stepping off that train on a muggy day in the lush, leafy region of northwest Connecticut, so different from Utah. "I had a single suitcase," he said. "I don't remember how I got to the school."

Fred also didn't recall many details of the train trip east. Yet he was passing through a nation in profound transition. The war had ended three years earlier and America was ramping up to become arguably the greatest powerhouse of industry, commerce, technology, and military strength in history. As millions of young American soldiers became civilians, they eagerly plunged into a new world of heavy-metal cars with audacious fins, Benny Goodman big band music, Levittown homes rising in rapidly expanding suburbs, and real wages that would triple between 1940 and 1950. As other wartime allies and the defeated Axis powers struggled to rebuild, the US was abuzz with activity that Fred would have seen firsthand as the great diesel locomotive pulling his train car thundered out of the deserts and mountains of the west and into the ripening, late-summer fields of crops in the Midwest. And onward, as he roared through the great manufacturing centers of Indiana, Ohio, and Pennsylvania. A couple of days later he reached a bustling Grand Central Station, itself a great monument to transportation and a can-do attitude from a previous era.

The vision of a nation on the upsurge, with new ideas and boundless prospects, shaped the young Fred Frank and his generation to believe the world—including and perhaps especially Wall Street—was a place of profound opportunities. "We thought big," said Fred. "We had big ideas, because everything seemed possible."

Hotchkiss was founded in 1891 by Maria Bissell Hotchkiss, the widow of Benjamin B. Hotchkiss, a Lakeville native who invented the Hotchkiss machine gun, a mainstay of the First World War. This connection led to the school being nicknamed "son of a gun." Famous alumni include

Time magazine cofounders Henry Luce and Briton Hadden, future auto kingpin Henry Ford II, and Charles Edison, the son of inventor Thomas Edison and later the governor of New Jersey. Novelist F. Scott Fitzgerald mentioned Hotchkiss in his first book, *This Side of Paradise*. Fred wrote about attending the school:

> I realized from reading the *Fortune* article that I would receive a much more rigorous education there in preparation for university. That turned out to be true. That's why I asked my parents if I could go. Hotchkiss was then an all-boys school. I loved the sports programs, and it seemed to be a place that I would really like and be challenged academically.

Fred arrived as a junior but made friends quickly through sports and with his charming and understated personality, traits that became familiar to people around him later at Yale, in the army, and on Wall Street. He played football and basketball and ran track, which promptly made him popular. "Sports were mandatory," he said. "If you didn't want to do sports, you had to do what's called wood squad. So you went out with the headmaster and cleaned up the woods and that kind of stuff." Fred quickly established himself as a leader. He recalled:

> In the first semester, I don't know how it happened. I was elected vice president of the class. By being an athlete, you get accepted very easily. Otherwise it's kind of hard. We had hazing in those days, so the first week you'd get hazed. You had to crawl through people's legs, and they'd beat your backside and all this horseshit.

Academically, Fred struggled at first. "We took the usual classes," he said, "it was quite traditional." The boys wore navy blue blazers, ties, and slacks and sat in old-fashioned desks with fold-down seats in the front, in which the boy at the next desk forward would sit, and so on up the row. "It was exciting to be there," he recalled, "but I was totally unprepared. During my first semester, my grades were abysmal. I was basically getting Cs and Ds."

Obviously, this was hard on Fred. "He had always been an A student and a star athlete," said Mary Tanner, "from an important family in Salt Lake City." Addressing Fred as she spoke, she added: "You came back from Hotchkiss and your first semester grades were like, terrible."

"Really terrible," agreed Fred. "I was so embarrassed. And, of course, they sent them to parents. I thought: 'Oh my God, what are my parents going to think I've been doing? I'm a straight-A student.' But at least the comments from my head group teacher were positive: 'We're very proud of Frederick, he's doing very well.' I wondered what would have happened if I were doing badly."

Still, as the late summer turned to fall and Fred experienced for the first time a world of leaves turning orange and golden and then falling, he found classes and teachers he liked. He also tended to bond more with his teachers because they were his coaches. Yet his most memorable teacher was not a coach:

My most influential teacher was "Mr. Mac"—Mr. McChesney. He was the English teacher that I had in my first year. He was short, I would say no taller than 5'7" or 5'8". An older man, he wore very round glasses, and he sat in a high chair. His idea of English was to start by teaching you all the Shakespearean plays and sonnets. He was an extraordinary man. He came from a very wealthy family, and he'd sit in the high chair. I remember the first play we read was Macbeth, and he recited it by heart—the whole thing—without ever looking at the book. So that made it very vibrant. He had a very good, deep voice.

Most kids hate Shakespeare, but I loved it. But Shakespeare is complicated if it's not taught well. So we'd have to memorize one sonnet every day, and we'd recite them in class. And then later on he'd give us a subject to write on and you had to write it in two pages. You'd hand it in, he'd correct it and hand it back and say, "OK, now this assignment is to write on the same topic in one page." And the next week you'd write on the same subject in one paragraph. And it's harder to write one paragraph than it is two pages.

I remember I was scared at first. I was an upper-mid, which is a junior, and all the other kids had been there for two years. So they were much better prepared than I was. Then I remember the kid sitting next to me getting his paper back, and it had a big 10 on it. This is 10 out of 100, not 10 out of 10. And it said, "This is just a little bit worse than god-awful." That was my neighbor's paper.

Mr. Mac was an extraordinary teacher because he loved the subject, he made it live, but he was also very rigorous. As were all the teachers, I must say, compared to today. They were in a class by themselves.

Fred remembered being alone during that first Thanksgiving in 1948:

The first year I was quite lonely at Thanksgiving because everyone went home. In those days, there were principally eastern kids going to those eastern prep schools, so they could go home. Only a few of us were left on the campus. When I finally did go home to Salt Lake City at Christmas, the local kids were very curious. They asked: "What's it like, Fred? Do you like it?" I did like it. I told my friends back home that it was really terrific. However, I quickly realized that I had nothing in common with my old buddies anymore. So I was very happy to go back to Hotchkiss, and I was never lonely again. It was a transforming time in my life.

The days at Hotchkiss were heavily programmed with activities, classes, sports, and studying. Lights-out always came too early that first term as Fred worked to catch up to the other boys academically. He was seldom finished with homework by the time the lights snapped off. Fred compensated for this by developing one of the habits he would later become well known for: getting up very early, often before dawn, to start his day. Later, when he was on Wall Street, Fred would rise at 4 a.m. or so, catch up on work, and then walk or jog to work from wherever he was living—usually uptown—to his office downtown. This predilection, he said, began as an expedient when he was sixteen years old at Hotchkiss:

Depending on what grade you were in, the electricity went off at a specific time. In my grade, the juniors, lights went out at 10 o'clock. School started early in the morning and ended at 1, and we had lunch, then sports, then studies. I couldn't get my work done by 10 o'clock at night, and it was rigorous. You couldn't have flashlights— they would check your room. So, I would get up really early in the morning at the first light, and I would go up to the library.

I realized early on that there were a lot of kids who were a lot smarter than I was. But I figured, nobody could work harder than I did, because that's under my control. That's not God-given. I was always convinced that whatever the task was, if I worked hard enough, I could succeed. That's really what drove me.

Inevitably, getting up early, I would run into the headmaster, a very severe guy named George Van Santvoord. We called him Duke. That actually helped me a lot, I think. Not only because I could do my work, but also because I think it helped him realize that I was a really serious kid.

He was a lifetime trustee of Yale, on the board, and this undoubtedly helped me get in. We didn't have SAT tests; those didn't exist. You just had your grades and what you wrote, filling out all the forms. I think what happened is that the headmaster said to Yale: "You'll take that kid, that kid, and that kid." I mean, forty-two of my eighty-four classmates went to Yale.

YALE: 1950–1954

After graduating in 1950 from Hotchkiss, where he had returned to form, eventually getting straight As, Fred was accepted into Yale University in New Haven, some sixty-five miles to the southeast of Lakeville.

At the age of eighteen, Fred found himself in a city of some 160,000 people, framed to the northeast and the northwest by low red basalt ridges locally known as East Rock and West Rock. An aging port and light-manufacturing center, New Haven in 1950 was already fading from its glory years earlier in the century. By 1960, the population would be in a steep decline and would fall to 126,000 by 1980 before the city launched urban renewal efforts that created today's pleasant city of medium-sized skyscrapers and a revitalized deep harbor.

New Haven's downtown, then and now, was dominated by Yale University's neo-Gothic and Georgian Revival architecture and by its green and leafy sidewalks. Arranged like England's Oxford University into "colleges"—square courtyards rimmed by buildings—the structures were mostly made out of light limestone and fashioned to look like castles and medieval manses. Many were decorated with carvings and flourishes, including the occasional gargoyle. Surrounding the campus were streets lined with shops and restaurants frequented by what was then 7,700 male students, including the 1,050 students enrolled in the freshman class of 1950. This compares with recent student populations of around 11,000 men and women.

Fred was assigned to a room that was part of a suite in Lanman-Wright Hall. Built in 1912, this dorm was relatively new compared to the rest of the section of Yale known as the Old Campus, some built in the eighteenth century. Fred shared his suite with three other young men who had their own small rooms and a shared living room. He ate his meals at the Commons, where all freshmen were required to eat, and he played club sports, including basketball and football.

Fred said that Yale was different academically in the 1950s from today. For one thing, he notes, nearly everyone was a white male, with Jews only recently being admitted in any numbers.

> I don't want to overdramatize it, but the quality of the student body is so elevated today. Everyone from my day laughs and says, "I couldn't get into Yale today," as nowadays they accept only 7 percent of applicants. They have 25,000 applicants and take only 1,500 or 1,800. First off, they have women competing now and minorities, which is a very good thing. There's a change in philosophy. When I went to Yale—I don't have the exact number—but about 40 percent were from Andover, Exeter, Hotchkiss, and other prep schools, where people thought they had an entitlement. I don't mean it in a bad way, that's just the way it was.

Fred loved his courses at Yale, but he didn't have a strong idea about what he wanted to do in life. He ended up majoring in philosophy, but that was mostly by default.

> At Yale, I had no idea what I wanted to do when I got out. I said to myself, "I'm going to be here for four years. I'm probably going to work for thirty." (I'm now in my sixty-third year of work, so that wasn't exactly right.) "What is the best thing Yale has to offer me?" I talked to my advisor and to some of the other students. Yale had one of the leading philosophy departments, so I said, "I'll take philosophy." I had no idea what it was, but I took philosophy and American studies, and loved my classes. They were very small. Most people preferred not to take those kinds of classes, but I enjoyed them. They taught me to think conceptually. I liked reading the Greek philosophers and taking the time to just sit back and think about things, including politics and history. I also had to do a lot of writing, which helped me later when I was a researcher on Wall Street. People liked

my research reports, said they were well written. Hotchkiss and Yale gave me that skill.

Shortly after arriving at Yale, Fred ran into his boyhood friend from Salt Lake, Arthur Fleischer, who had moved away from Utah after elementary school. Art remembered bumping into Fred at Yale:

I think it was in the post office. And then we became friends. We used to hang around together, and I became friendly with his roommate, Jay Winokur, who died a few years ago. And I used to play basketball with Fred on the club team.

Fred remembered their encounter slightly differently:

In 1950 when I entered Yale, I was walking across the old campus during what was called "refreshment hour." I was heading to the post office when I heard my name, "Freddy Frank." I look around, I didn't see anybody I knew, right? Then I saw him. It was Art, who was a lot bigger than I remembered. So we became fast friends again.

Fleischer described their friendship:

We took courses together. I remember one winter they gave a course in Marxism, which was regarded as a pretty bold step in those days. It was a very intense course. And it was particularly funny in a way, because when I applied for the bar, they were asking me all these questions. I was in Staten Island, which is a fairly conservative place, and the fellow who was looking at my résumé said: "Are you familiar with any of the writings of Karl Marx?" Now, the fact is, I'd read most of the writings of Karl Marx, so I said, "Yes, I've heard of him." Fortunately, this didn't prevent me from getting the job, although in those days, with Russia, Karl Marx was not the most popular guy around.

In 1951, Fred's parents gave him a brand new car. "My mother and father surprised me for my birthday and gave me a Pontiac," he said. "It was a black convertible with a tan top." That fall, Fred drove the Pontiac to Connecticut, taking with him his brother, Tom, who had been accepted that year as a freshman at Hotchkiss. Fred remembered the trip:

> This was before all the major turnpikes and great highways. We started out on US 40. I don't remember where that ended and we picked up, I think, the Pennsylvania Turnpike, which may have already been built. We drove to New Haven, and I drove Tom to Hotchkiss. That's a long drive, I'll tell you. There are no direct routes from New Haven to Lakeville. It's all these weird roads, even today, because all the roads run north and south in Connecticut. They don't run east and west in that part of the state.

Tom Frank recalled:

> The first year that I went to Hotchkiss, we drove from Salt Lake with a friend, Norman Rosenblatt, who was also going to Yale. He was a very close friend of my family. The three of us drove from Salt Lake to New Haven. I spent two nights in New Haven with Fred, and then he drove me up to Hotchkiss.
>
> On this trip to New Haven, Fred could be fairly conniving at times. He could talk me into anything. Fred and I have a great memory [from this trip]. We were supposed to be heading on US 40 to get back East; it was the main highway then. At one point we saw this crazy little detour thing. We got on it and we thought we were going to the right place, which was supposed to be US 30, but there was this shortcut on some little road. We drove and drove and ended up in the middle of some farmer's field. Fred said, "This is not US 30." It worked out OK, but we still will say sometimes when we're lost or something: "This is not US 30."

We would get to a city, and he'd stop and find the cheapest hotel in the worst part of town, where the bathrooms are four miles away from the bedrooms. And there would be two double beds and Fred would say, "OK, we'll flip to see who sleeps with who and who gets the single bed." Well, Fred fixed it every time, so I was sleeping with Norman while Fred was sleeping alone. And I said, "Wait a minute, this isn't fair." So he said, "OK, we'll do it two out of three," but he still somehow won all the flips.

Tom remembered staying with Fred in his dorm at Yale:

I stayed in Fred's dormitory for a few days. It was a great experience being there. He took me all around Yale. At one point he said, "We're going to go see a Western movie." And I said, "Why are we going to see a Western movie?" He said, "It is very different back here in Connecticut because they never go to Western movies, so they yell and hoot and scream, 'Get him! Shoot him!'" He said it was a real experience, which it was.

During these years, America continued to boom economically. The arts also flourished in what became golden ages of jazz, classical music, theater, film, and books. This was the era of Miles Davis, Leonard Bernstein, Arthur Miller, Alfred Hitchcock, and J.D. Salinger, all of whose works Fred listened to, watched, or read. A flurry of inventions and engineering projects were in the early stages of profoundly changing how Americans and others would live, ranging from the National Interstate and Defense Highways Act, which the Dwight Eisenhower administration had enacted to build the US interstate highway system, to the invention of the first transistors.

In the sciences, great discoveries ranged from a refining of quantum theory by a still very active Albert Einstein and others to the 1952 discovery of the double helix shape of DNA by American biologist James D. Watson and British physicist Francis Crick. The double helix finding, which was announced to the world in a 1953 paper in *Nature* titled simply: "A Structure for Deoxyribose Nucleic Acid"[1] would later make it possible to create a new biotech industry based on genetics and molecular biology, an industry that Fred helped to capitalize starting in the 1970s. Fred doesn't remember anything about the discovery when the paper was published during his junior year at Yale. "I took some science courses," he said, "but to tell you the truth, I had broad interests because I didn't really know what I wanted to do."

Life in the 1950s for a young white male at Yale—even a Jewish one—was predominately one of great possibilities. It was also a time of global unease as the Cold War took hold and the Soviet Union successfully exploded nuclear weapons in tests starting in 1949. Politics in the US descended into anti-Communist hysteria in an era when US Senator Joseph McCarthy held his infamous hearings on Capitol Hill naming supposed Soviet sympathizers. Many of them were nothing of the sort, even if they had flirted with Communism at one point or another. This was also an era when families moving into suburbs and buying cars for the first time would watch programs like *Howdy Doody* and *I Love Lucy* on their newfangled television sets while a few stocked bomb shelters buried in their yards with canned goods and barrels of fresh water in case of a thermonuclear attack. Arthur Fleischer compared the era to today:

> We went through these periods of paranoia, there's no question. I remember when people were building bomb shelters and there was fear of the Russians and so forth. But I think it's a much more precarious geopolitical picture now. Terrorism has also had a pervasive impact on how we live, obviously, in terms of transportation and flying and the buildings. Yet there was a difference, because we felt so incredibly optimistic about everything, despite the bomb.

ARMY: 1954–1956

Fred, now twenty-two years old, graduated from Yale in late spring 1954 and returned to Salt lake City in his Pontiac convertible, as he had in previous summers. This time was different, however, since he would not be returning east in the fall. Nor did he have a clear plan for what he wanted to do next, although he knew what he *didn't* want to do: work in Arthur Frank's department store. Fred's grandfather had passed away the previous fall at age eighty, but Fred's father, Simon, had been running the family store for years.

"Fred and his father had some difficult times over Fred not wanting to come back and work for the store," said Mary Tanner. "He was never very happy with Fred's decision."

"There was too much out there in the world for me to think about," said Fred. "Salt Lake City and the store seemed very small. And by the way, my dad felt that way, too, when he was younger. He might have done something different if his father hadn't gotten sick."

The decision about what Fred would do next was made for him that summer by the United States Selective Service. The draft was initiated in 1950 for the Korean War. When he finished at Yale, he was eligible, and he was drafted, even though the war was over.

That September he was ordered to report to basic training at Fort Ord, near Monterey, California, a posting that soldiers loved, given the nearby beach and the weather on California's Central Coast. Fred's summons came a year after the Korean War was officially declared over in July 1953, but tensions remained high on the Korean peninsula and in several other of the Cold War hot spots around the world.

Fred joined the army as a private E2, although he said he might have gone in as an officer if he'd had better eyesight. However, the disability had a silver lining. He remembered:

The Korean War was underway, so I joined ROTC while at Yale. That was how I got deferred from the army during my college years.

In my junior year, I was thrown out of the ROTC at summer camp, because I failed the eye test. We were being trained as FOs, forward observers, in the artillery. In Korea, the life expectancy of an FO was about two weeks, so it was, perhaps, fortunate that I was thrown out.

Fred joined thousands of troops stationed at Fort Ord at the time. He said that the training was challenging, but not overly so because of Fred's love of athletics. "I was in great shape," he said.

Just six weeks after arriving, he did so well that he was named "Soldier of the Month." "What does that award get you?" he asked, rhetorically, then answered the question:

Well, you get to have lunch with the officers, a weekend pass, your name and picture in the newspaper, and a one-dollar Zippo lighter with your name, rank, and serial number on it. That lighter changed my life. They made a mistake on the inscription. They made me a PFC, a private first class, even though I was an amoeba, a lower form of life two ranks below. I said to the colonel who ran the program, "Sir, this is a great honor, but, unfortunately, they made a mistake on the lighter. I'm not a PFC, I'm only an E2." He called over a captain and said, "Captain, promote this man. Any soldier good enough to be Soldier of the Month deserves to be at least a PFC." The captain said, "I'd be pleased to do that, sir, but ranks are frozen." The colonel was smarter than the captain. He said, "Find out when they froze the ranks and backdate the orders." So I was promoted two ranks after being in the army for only six weeks.

Fred's luck in running through the ranks continued when he finished his training and was assigned to a unit under the command of a colonel whom Fred ended up driving around at Fort Ord.

After basic training I was sent to a special unit that had a colonel, a major, a captain, a master sergeant, and me. The colonel was assigned a staff car but no driver. As the low man on the totem pole, I drove him around. I got to know him well because he had very bad arthritis. Two or three times a week, I would take him to the hospital for treatment. When the colonel heard about my ROTC training, he said, "They made a mistake. You should have been let in the army as a corporal because of your three years in ROTC." He wrote to the Pentagon to change that, but the response was, "Yes, he should have been let in the army as a corporal, but unfortunately it's too late and we cannot change it."

In 1955, Fred left Fort Ord with a new posting even more desirable than Monterey: NATO's Supreme Headquarters Allied Powers Europe (SHAPE). In those days SHAPE was headquartered in Rocquencourt, France, a former commune and farming village situated about twelve miles west of Paris. As a clerk-typist to another US Army colonel at SHAPE, Fred embraced his first experience overseas, which fed his passion for travel and exploration, an inclination that would later make him famously peripatetic, even among his well-traveled peers in global banking.

In France, Fred Frank's penchant for negotiating favorable deals began to emerge with himself as his first client. Though only a lowly private first class, Fred at age twenty-three was able to secure permission to rent a small apartment in downtown Paris in the 17th Arrondissement near the Arc de Triomphe. "It was a single room with a sink," he said. He also convinced his father to buy a 1957 Austin-Healey sports car—which Simon had promised to give to Fred's brother, Tom—by demonstrating that the car was far less expensive to purchase in Europe through the Army Post Exchange system. But as Fred said, "It took me awhile to ship the car back to the States," almost a year, as it turned out. Meanwhile, Fred drove the flashy car with the distinctive triangular front grill and sloping trunk through a Paris that was going through another era when great writers, artists, and musicians drank espressos and absinthe at Les Deux Magots, Café de Flore, and the city's other famous cafes. "I didn't know much about the artists and writers in Paris in the fifties," he said, but he met a number of friends and spent as much time as possible in the museums and walking the streets of the ancient city.

There, he met his first wife, Mary Ann Nahum, a French woman who came to live with him in the States after they married in Paris in 1957. Fred and Mary Ann had two daughters, both born in the United States: Jenny (1958) and Laura (1963).

STANFORD UNIVERSITY, PALO ALTO, CALIFORNIA: 1956–1958

As his stint in the army drew to a close, Fred decided to get serious about what he would do next in life. Taking advantage of the GI Bill, he decided to do what a number of young Ivy League graduates were doing at the time and attend business school. Fred chose Stanford after hearing about it while at Fort Ord and from two San Francisco–based aunts on his mother's side. "A number of people then and now go to business school," said Fred, "when they don't quite know what they want to do. I was one of those people." Part of his thinking may have come from memories of his father investing in the stock market, a passion that Fred had watched his dad engaging in as he grew up.

The San Francisco Bay Area and Palo Alto were different in the 1950s than they are today. San Francisco remained a major focus of the US Navy, a presence that has completely disappeared seventy years later. It also was an important center of heavy industry and shipping, which also has disappeared or shifted to the East Bay. The corridor along US 101, running south of the city, was mostly orange groves and farms, interspersed with the small towns of Burlingame, San Mateo, and Mountain View. The region was beginning what would become a dramatic transformation as people flocked to the peninsula and to new suburban housing developments. Shopping strips, schools, and new roads were popping up, replacing farms and orange groves. Palo Alto, home to Stanford University, doubled in size between 1950 and 1960, from 25,000 to 55,000 people, launching a period of rapid growth that has reached 65,000 people today. The new arrivals, many of them ex-GIs from the war and their families, were part of the rising middle class in America that was making and spending money as the US economy continued to roar along.

"The postwar period began just past the midpoint of Palo Alto's first century," said Ward Winslow, a historian and newspaper editor who wrote *Palo Alto: A Centennial History*.[2] "The transition had a rocky start. Pent-up demand for education and for hard goods and clothing and housing surged, and the nation lagged in satisfying it. Local resources were strained by returnees, veterans enrolling at Stanford, and ex-GIs who'd had a wartime taste of Palo Alto and liked it . . . Demand for electronics products ran high, however, and local industry soared off on a giddy expansion track . . . Growth was the 1950s' watchword in many other senses. During the decade, Palo Alto doubled its population and tripled its area."

The high-tech boom was beginning but had not yet taken off, although the famed Stanford Industrial Park down the road from the university was beginning to forge the entrepreneurial culture that would later become a global engine of innovation and change in not only electronics but also, later, in the life sciences. Local headlines from the mid-1950s tell the story: "GE will establish electronics lab on Stanford land," "Lockheed tells details of Stanford site," "Link Aviation will set up research labs in Palo Alto." Homegrown efforts included Hewlett-Packard and Shockley Semiconductor Laboratory, created by one of the inventors of the transistor, the controversial Robert Shockley. He assembled a band of engineers who would later become major figures in the electronics and computer industries: Gordon E. Moore, C. Sheldon Roberts, Eugene Kleiner, Victor Grinich, Julius Blank, Jean Hoerni, and Robert Noyce.

This concentration of high-tech talent arose out of Stanford's aggressive efforts to create a world-class engineering school and the university's early focus on pushing research into commercial enterprises, a process that was still mostly discouraged in academic institutions that shunned business in favor of pure research. This emphasis was overlaid with the western US mentality of plunging into new frontiers and a fervent belief that human ingenuity could profoundly change the world.

Fred Frank at age twenty-five walked into the middle of this cauldron of rising affluence, transition, and high technology as he attended classes in finance, business administration, and economics. What he remembered most was how hard he worked. "I didn't have a lot of time to do much more than study and go to class," he recalled. After classes, he worked for a company selling encyclopedias. He made cold calls to lists of names culled from the phone book to set up appointments for salesmen to visit people's homes. "It was grueling," he recalled. "I had to say the same three-minute speech every few minutes. People were generally nice, but some were quite abusive about getting interrupted during dinner." He lived in a small house with his wife, paying $100 a month in rent. Fred's father didn't help him financially. It wasn't his father's way, he said. Mary Tanner explained how difficult that time was for Fred:

> Fred was also supporting his wife's family in France. They came from a very wealthy Jewish family. Her father had been some kind of investment banker. He worked for a typical, old-fashioned French bank. They kept fleeing in front of the Nazis, and they finally got to Switzerland, where the Swiss took all their money, but at least saved their lives.

Fred remembered an economics class at Stanford taught by a Mr. Krebs. Just two weeks into school, he assigned the first-year students to prepare a forecast of gross national product for the next few years (now called gross domestic product). For his forecast, Fred assumed there would be a war. "I remember turning in the paper and being so scared that I had screwed up. But I guess Professor Krebs liked it, since I got an A."

Toward the end of his time at Stanford, Fred realized that he needed to decide on a career. "I couldn't put it off any longer," he said. Knowing that he had zero interest in returning to Salt Lake City to work at the family store, something his father still wanted him to do, Fred decided to try finance. Having made this decision, there was only one place to go. For in 1958, all roads in finance led to New York City and to a Wall Street that was still small and genteel compared to today. But as the fifties continued to boom and the early sixties approached, the sleepy street of small firms, three-hour lunches, and gentlemanly deals sealed with a handshake was about to change forever.

CHAPTER 3

Young Turks on Wall Street

EARLY WALL STREET YEARS, 1958–1973

The decade ahead presents a most favorable
gathering of forces for economic progress.

—John F. Kennedy

(quoted by Fred Frank in a Lehman Brothers research report)[1]

In early autumn of 1958, Fred Frank stepped into a world at the
southern tip of Manhattan that no longer exists. Joining the training
program at the investment bank Smith, Barney—he got offers there
and at Merrill Lynch, but liked the research department better at Smith,
Barney—the brash twenty-six-year-old was ushered into a rarified
group of men (there were no women) operating on Wall Street during
one of the greatest bull markets in history. The Dow Jones Industrial
Average had been climbing for most of the thirteen years since the end
of the Second World War and had doubled between 1945 and 1958 to
an index of around 500. Since Fred was born in 1932, when the Dow

was at just 41, it had risen by more than ten times. And it would keep climbing, with some major dips, throughout Fred's life to the present, hitting more than 30,000 early in 2021 when Fred was eighty-eight years old.

Despite the fervor of the markets, major Wall Street firms in the fifties were run by a few dozen partners and total staffs of 100 to 200 people. This compares to hundreds of partners and tens of thousands of employees today. Only a handful of banks had incorporated in 1958, and few had much of a presence overseas. Deals were miniscule compared to now, with financings, mergers, and acquisitions heavily weighted toward established companies and industries, and toward those building on earlier successes like automobiles, steel, retailers, and the frozen-food industry.

Wall Street remained conservative and risk averse. Yet in those heady days when real income in the US had doubled since 1945 and money was pouring into stocks and other investments from a swelling middle class, the firms at the southern tip of Manhattan were also financing wholly new technologies in emerging fields, such as transistor-driven electronics, early computers, and lasers. In 1957, Polaroid went public, and so did Hewlett-Packard, the latter being one of the new high-tech companies that Fred had lived near while at Stanford.

The Soviet Union's launch of Sputnik a year before Fred's arrival on the Street also made it patriotic to support new high technologies, and it opened the federal spigot to fund new ideas and defense-related tech projects. This not only enriched corporate America but also fueled a fresh wave of mergers, acquisitions, and financings that enriched the banks. The old-line firms, however, remained skittish in the late fifties about going too far with newfangled technologies, a reality that would soon chafe young bankers like Fred Frank and a fellow trainee at Smith, Barney, Sanford "Sandy" Robertson, then age twenty-seven. He would later cofound the San Francisco–based investment bank Robertson Stephens.

"There wasn't much entrepreneurial thinking at all," remembered Robertson. "The banks only came in when technology deals were incredibly obvious. There was little or no risk-taking, and they weren't following what was happening in what would later be called Silicon Valley." Robertson gave an example:

> The classic story is that I was once doing a private placement for Spectra-Physics, which had 70 percent of the world's laser market. That's how I met Tom Perkins (later a founding partner in the legendary venture firm Kleiner Perkins Caufield & Byers). I'd helped him merge a company into Spectra-Physics, and he became a director of Spectra. I got the firm, Smith, Barney, to take $100,000 worth of the investment, which is the equivalent of maybe a million today. But they didn't like it.
>
> I went back to a partners' meeting and the guys came up to me and pointed their fingers like a gun and said, "Hey, Buck Rogers, how's our ray gun company doing?" No one took it very seriously. And they turned me down on a deal to do Fairchild Semiconductor.

Robertson recalled that not everyone who came from Wall Street was entrepreneur-averse:

> You know Don Lucas? Don Lucas later was the founding investor of Oracle, and he was the chairman for years. He had hit after hit. But back then he was a junior corporate finance guy at Smith, Barney. They allowed him at night to work on some entrepreneurial things, and he was working on the formation of National Semiconductor. After 5 o'clock, he could work on that.
>
> I helped him make some calls. I called the West Coast about who was using different [micro]chips. They were just single transistors, basically, in those days. He left Smith, Barney very soon thereafter to join Draper [Associates], out on his own. But that was the only

entrepreneurial thing in those days, and I really related to it. Then when I got to California, I discovered where it was in a hurry. But I could never get Smith, Barney very interested in this stuff.

In 1958, biotechnology was unknown as a term and as an industry. Early work was being done, however, on what was then called molecular biology just after the seminal 1953 discovery of the double-helix shape of DNA by James D. Watson and Francis Crick. Some of the basic science around genetics was being developed in places like Cambridge University in the UK, where Watson and Crick made their discovery, and at Harvard University, where Watson founded one of the first departments devoted to genetics and molecular biology. Nothing commercial had yet emerged, with the companies that would later become known as Big Pharma remaining small enterprises compared to the blockbuster companies that would emerge a few years later. "There were fewer shares outstanding in the whole pharmaceutical industry than there were in General Motors alone," recalled Sandy Robertson, "and General Motors had 280 million shares at the time."

Still, prescient researchers and traders were picking up on trends emerging from new mass-market drugs like Valium—one of the first-ever tranquilizers, launched in 1963 by Hoffmann-La Roche—and by discoveries like Jonas Salk's vaccine for polio, released in 1955. These and other developments in the science and in the business of pharmaceuticals were strong indicators that this industry was poised to take off in the coming years. No one, however, anticipated that prescription drug sales would rise from a mere $2.7 billion in 1960 to an estimated $358.7 billion in 2019.[2]

During this era, investment firms like Smith, Barney, Lehman Brothers, and Goldman Sachs were barred by the Glass-Steagall Act of 1933 from engaging in commercial banking activities. So they handled only securities. Many were still run by their founding families or by a close-knit group of longtime senior partners. They made markets and invested using their own capital, an entirely different model from today when publicly traded investment banks spend other people's money (from depositors, investors, shareholders, and others) on investments and deals that can be highly speculative, as we know all too well from the crash of 2008. This disaster, which caused the downfall of Lehman Brothers and severely strained the banking system while plunging the world economy into recession, would probably not have occurred under Glass-Steagall, which was repealed in the late 1990s. This repeal allowed the securities and advice end of Wall Street to connect up with hundreds of billions of dollars in capital on the commercial bank side, a situation that created, at best, a conflict of interest, and at worst, a perverse incentive for banks to steer other people's capital toward their own sometimes risky deals in securities and financial products, from which they reaped huge fees.

From this perspective, the size of deals and the capital at work a half-century ago seems quaint. Sandy Robertson recalled the size of Smith, Barney's funds available for investment in the early sixties, when he and Fred became partners at Smith, Barney:

> The firm's capital at that time was technically only about—I wanted to say 7 million, but it might've been 17 million. Then they had limited partners who would put in money for a couple of days when you did a big underwriting. But the size was really, really small. When I became a partner and Fred became a partner, I think you got a 1 percent share [of the firm] for $100,000. So that's a 10-million-dollar capital of the firm (about $87 million in 2020 dollars).

In the late fifties, banks also made money by dispensing advice to a newly prosperous rising middle class that was hungry to buy stocks. This is why Fred would soon gravitate toward working in Smith, Barney's highly respected research department, which dispensed advice on stocks and industries. It also took advantage of his intellectual bent as a philosophy major from Yale. "I was quite a nerd," he said, "though of course we didn't have that term yet. I enjoyed plunging into the research, and working very hard to understand a stock or a deal from every angle."

TRAINEE AT SMITH, BARNEY

When Fred joined Smith, Barney & Co. at 20 Broad Street, right next door to the New York Stock Exchange, the firm was barely twenty years old. Its roots, however, like many of the venerable houses on the Street, went back to the nineteenth century when Charles D. Barney & Co. was founded in 1873 and Edward B. Smith & Co. in 1892. In 1937 the two firms merged to become Smith, Barney. Over the years, the company changed hands several times, reaching a peak in popularity in the eighties when actor John Houseman uttered the famous catchphrase in Smith, Barney ads: "They make money the old-fashioned way. They *earn* it." (By then, however, the firm was mostly in the retail business and was not held in the same high regard as it had been earlier.) The Smith, Barney name survives today as part of Morgan Stanley.

Fred started as a trainee, one of three young men accepted in 1958. The other two were Sandy Robertson and Burton Malkiel, who later became a famed economist at Princeton University and author of *A Random Walk Down Wall Street* (W.W. Norton & Company, 1973). "For the program, we would work in different departments," said Fred. "It was tough, but it was great training." As Sandy Robertson recalled:

> Fred and I were thrown together in that training program. We were the lowest of the low. There was a third guy with us, Burt Malkiel. The three of us made a pretty interesting group. Burt only stayed with Smith, Barney another year or so and then went off and got his doctorate.

So the three of us hung out together. We went out to lunch at a place where we'd get sandwiches for a dollar, and that kind of stuff. It was a very good time. A couple times a week at 5 o'clock in the afternoon, when things quieted down, one partner would sit down with you and talk to you about what he was doing, what his business was. Maybe even some vice president would do that. So we'd be thrown into these sessions.

By 6:30 p.m., the partner would leave and we'd sit around and talk about what we'd just learned, whether we agreed with the guy or not. There was a guy around at the time by the name of Dick Stanley. He and Malkiel had a bet on the market every day, 10 cents. They'd read the front page of the [*Wall Street*] *Journal* and see who could guess what the market was going to do that day. And neither got ahead of the other by more than 30 cents over the course of the year. I'm sure that's what gave Malkiel his ideas for *A Random Walk Down Wall Street*.

Burt Malkiel recalled his days at Smith, Barney with Fred:

I first met Fred in the late 1950s. He was part of a cohort of young MBA trainees beginning a career in financial markets at Smith, Barney. The training program covered all aspects of the work of a Wall Street bank, and the learning experience was intense. The trainees were extremely talented, but everyone recognized that Fred was the smartest and most competent of the group. Indeed, I have known smart and capable people in business, law, and the academia. And I can truly say that Fred stands out as having an exceptional intellect.

After our training, Fred went into research, first at Smith, Barney and then as head of research at Lehman Brothers. I started my actual work as a junior investment banker at Smith, Barney. But since the bankers shared the same floor with the research department, I had daily contact with security analysts. It was this contact that generated my skepticism about the value of much of Wall Street research in general and active portfolio management in particular. I found most of the research to be lacking in insight and often misleading. Price targets for stocks would be raised after the market recognized success, not in advance. I began to believe investors would be better off just buying and holding an index fund that bought and held all the stocks in the market. This was an idea that informed much of the work I did in the academy and was the thesis of my book, *A Random Walk Down Wall Street.*

As evidence accumulated that indexing was, in fact, effective, I became more convinced over time that the thesis was correct. But I did retain a modicum of doubt, and Fred was responsible for whatever unease I harbored. I had to admit that security analysts existed (and Fred was the prime example) who were capable of producing brilliant, insightful research and who were often able to understand the future even before it was recognized by the market. I followed Fred's work with awe but comforted myself in my own beliefs with the realization that Fred was the remarkable exception, not the rule. And Fred's work could be counted on to make the stock market more efficient as consumers of his work would ensure that their trading would make market prices a better reflection of each company's future prospects and true worth.

Knowing of Fred's uncanny ability to understand the present and foresee future opportunities, it was not surprising to me to learn that investment banking would be the next phase of his remarkable career and that innovation would characterize his work. Fred was one of the first to foresee the promise of biotechnology and to realize the opportunities involved in raising money for investing in and financing early-stage companies such as Genentech. Few investment bankers have secured lasting legacies for innovation, especially for innovations that are clearly socially useful. Fred is unique and far exceeded the high expectations that I and others in our training class believed were possible.

THE FEEL OF THE STREET C. 1960

In Fred's early years, Wall Street retained much of its old-world sensibility and culture. There were a few skyscrapers, but the area hadn't much changed since the eighteenth and nineteenth centuries, with low buildings and narrow, confusing streets that meandered with little rhyme or reason. "Most people worked 9 to 5," said Fred, although he continued the habit he had begun at Hotchkiss of getting up very early and heading into work to get a jump on the day. Even now, Fred gets up ridiculously early by most people's standards, 3 a.m. or 4 a.m. He exercises and then gets ready for work, heading to his office. Typically, he's in bed at night by 10 p.m.

Lunches in the early sixties era were a crucial part of business, particularly for bankers with clients visiting New York. Long-distance phone calls were expensive, and there was no e-mail, fax, or overnight mail. So these lunches were the primary arena for discussion, convened in restaurants like Delmonico's, near the Stock Exchange, or the 21 Club, or in private clubs or firms' private dining rooms. They were often three hours long and included the fabled three martinis, although they were in smaller glasses than those typically served today. ("I was an oddball because I didn't drink," said Fred.) The rooms in these clubs and restaurants were often dark and paneled in heavy wood with wall-size paintings, mirrors, and other touches from the nineteenth and early twentieth centuries. Many people smoked—this was the era when doctors were paid to endorse cigarette brands in advertisements—which left clouds of smoke hanging gauzy in the air in restaurants, boardrooms, and offices.

Mary Tanner remembered why Lehman Brothers had its own dining room:

> One of the purposes of such expensive, high-cost dining rooms for banking firms is that you can do business in private as opposed to in restaurants. Not many firms had [such] dining rooms. It was one of the things that made Lehman Brothers quite distinct.

Banks were still split among ethnicities and religions—Jewish, Catholic, and Protestant—although this segregation by religion was beginning to break down by the late 1950s. As Mary recounted:

> Then there were the Jewish banks, which were true investment banks; there were no Jewish commercial banks. You know, that was Goldman Sachs, Kuhn, Loeb & Co., Lehman Brothers, and Salomon Brothers. Salomon was basically a very small bond house that didn't become a powerhouse until the seventies and eighties. There were others, now long gone. And then there were the brokerage firms and, interestingly, Merrill Lynch, which has an Irish Catholic name because Merrill Lynch and some of the other Irish-sounding names were the only place Irish Catholics could get jobs on Wall Street before and just after the war. They couldn't get jobs in the Jewish houses and they certainly couldn't get jobs in the WASP houses. The other place that was friendly to Catholics in those days was the New York Stock Exchange, where some of the most important specialist firms were run by Irish Catholics.

In those days—an era made famous in the AMC television series *Mad Men*, about advertising executives—rampant sexism was common. Few complained if an executive made a pass at a secretary. Sandy Robertson talks about a secretary who worked with one of the senior analysts at Smith, Barney:

> Well, it was a very male world. Fred ended up working for Bill Grant, who was our chemical and drug analyst, and he had Fred follow the drug industry. Bill had a secretary who was really, really smart and would have been a regular professional. They gave her the cosmetics industry to look at. That was kind of a put-down, in a way. So she followed Revlon and that sort of thing. Fred asked her to work with him.

There was another woman who was a secretary and used to hang out with us. She was very smart, a Phi Beta Kappa from Vanderbilt. She ended up dating the chief investment officer of the Ford Foundation and retired. Today these people would've been treated just like male employees, but in those days they were secretaries or statisticians.

Fred said that sexism on the Street began to budge at least a little bit in the late 1960s, although it remained firmly entrenched. "By the time I left Smith, Barney in 1969, we probably had fifteen women in our research department," he said, "some of them at quite senior levels, though they weren't at the most senior levels of the firm until later, which of course was a ridiculous waste of talent."

Not much happened to change what was really more of a glass fortress than a mere ceiling until feminism came on strong in the mid-1970s and 1980s, and women like Mary Tanner began to assert themselves to gain a toehold in the world of men. In 1984 Mary became the first-ever woman managing director in the elite bastion of corporate finance at Lehman Brothers. More women work in senior roles on Wall Street today, but the struggle continues. Mary recounted her experience:

> I graduated from Harvard in 1973 and really needed a job. I had no idea what I wanted to do, but I knew what I didn't want to do, which was take the typical Seven Sisters exit job into publishing. It was a massive recession. Despite the best education my struggling middle class parents so generously bought for me, really, I had no practical skills. Miraculously, through a friend of my father's, I managed to get a job in the management-training program at the Manufacturers Hanover Trust, a big commercial bank, now long merged into JPMorgan Chase. I think they didn't realize that I was female, because I always signed my letters "M.C. Tanner." When I got there, they were astounded, as if an alien had arrived. They made me be a secretary for nine months.

I finally got to go into the management-training program, became a lending officer, and then eventually left for Wall Street. But it was a hard road even before I got to Wall Street and a harder road once I was on Wall Street at Lehman, where demands for performance were so much higher. The only chance I had was that I was prepared to work harder than anybody else.

WHY WALL STREET?

Fred said that once he had decided on his career of choice, he didn't consider any career other than finance. "It incorporated what I liked about making deals and persuading people and seemed, at the analyst end of things, to require a certain amount of brains." And, of course, there was money to be made as the 1950s and 1960s revved up. Fred's brother, Tom, thinks that Fred liked the prestige of being in an influential firm. "This was important to him, and also helped him get the clout to do what he later did," said Tom.

Fred's choice represented, however, a sea change from how the best and brightest minds of the previous generation had viewed Wall Street. During the 1930s and 1940s, the banking industry was vilified for the excesses and speculations of the Roaring Twenties, the crash in 1929 that plunged the world into the Great Depression, and the stringent regulation that followed soon after President Franklin D. Roosevelt took office in 1933. Well into the 1950s the top graduates coming out of schools like Yale, Harvard, and Stanford went into the automobile, transportation, and electronics industries.

"The smartest kids went to work for General Motors," said Fred. "Even in my era, among my MBA friends, the dumbest guys in the class went into commercial banking, and the smartest guys went into actually making things, or into management consulting." This was changing, however, in the late fifties, as the bull market kept surging and even the once-lowly stockbrokers were making fortunes. "Outcasts a generation before," wrote Charles R. Geisst in his book *Wall Street: A History*, "they had crept into the highest-status group of professionals by the late 1950s."[3]

WALL STREET'S FIRST DRUG ANALYST

Fred finished his nine-month training regimen at Smith, Barney in 1959 and sought out a place on the firm's highly regarded research staff, which was the reason he had come to the firm:

> After you finished your training, they decided what you were going to do, and research was the hardest thing to get into. They didn't take many people, but I was absolutely focused: I'm going to get into the research department. And during the last three months of the training program, if we wanted to go into research, we had to write an industry study or some other research report.
>
> Most trainees picked something that Smith, Barney was really good at. They just kind of took all the information collected by the firm, kind of plagiarized it. I decided to pick an industry that they didn't cover. And I picked the tire and rubber industry. A terribly dull industry, right? But they were very impressed with my work, so they brought me into the research department, and for a time I covered the entire rubber industry.

Fred didn't stay with rubber for long. Within a few months he went to Bill Grant, the head of research, who also covered the chemical and drug industry. He made a proposal that would change the trajectory of his career. (Later, Grant became the president of Smith,

Barney and a frequent guest on PBS television's *Wall Street Week,* which ran from 1970 to 2002.) Meeting in Grant's office, Fred said: "Bill, it makes no sense for the same person to cover the drug and chemical industries. These two industries have little in common. Why don't you cover chemicals, and I'll cover pharmaceuticals?" Grant approved the idea. "He graciously let me do it," Fred said. "I was fortunate." Fred then became Wall Street's first dedicated pharmaceutical industry analyst. Not long after, most of the other firms also added dedicated pharmaceutical analysts.

Sandy Robertson remembered that Grant was very keen on the rising drug industry and that he was a risk-taker with an entrepreneurial flare, which was unusual on the Street back then:

> Bill Grant, who was Fred's boss and a terrific guy, eventually became the number two guy at Smith, Barney. He was president and CEO. He used to pound the table and say, "You have to buy into the pharmaceutical industry. It's a growth industry." It was small then, so this was a little out there for him to say. Grant said, "There's a scarcity value. I don't care which ones you buy, buy a spread of them all, but buy the pharmaceuticals." And he was so right. That, in a sense, was an entrepreneurial thing to say. People didn't understand whether the drugs were going to work and the Food and Drug Administration (FDA) risks, blah, blah, blah. But you couldn't have missed by buying any of them at that time.

In 1962, Fred expanded his portfolio further by making an announcement before 300 partners and clients at that year's annual Smith, Barney research conference that he was no longer covering the pharmaceutical industry. As he expected, the audience was surprised. That's when Fred, who has a flare for the dramatic when giving a talk, explained that he was now going to cover the life-science industry, which included not only drugs but also medical devices, diagnostics, and healthcare services. He was only thirty years old and had been on Wall Street for less than four years, but he was already considered an emerging expert and presence when it came to the life sciences and other related industries.

Fred also became quickly known as a master of cultivating relationships. Another young trainee in 1962 at Smith, Barney, Robert F. Johnston—who later founded Genex, Cytogen, Sepracor, and others—remembered Fred as "the analyst who wrote up the little companies, like Raychem and Millipore, that younger guys like me were interested in." Johnston added, "We didn't care about Dow and DuPont." He also remembered that, back then, Fred already had what Johnston dubs "a golden Rolodex." Johnston and other junior analysts went to Fred to discuss their ideas on companies. "He'd make introductions for us," said Johnston. Smith, Barney quickly realized that Fred was a leader and named him codirector of research in 1962 and then vice president and a director of the firm while he was still in his mid-thirties.

Fred's starting annual salary at Smith, Barney was $4,200 (equivalent to about $37,300 in 2020 dollars), not much to live on in New York even in those days, with a wife and daughter, and another one on the way. This meant Fred had to be frugal about where they lived. "When I first came into New York, we lived in a, well, to say it was a modest apartment would be to exaggerate how nice it was," he said. "It was in a very mundane building at 30 East End Avenue." To make ends meet, Fred took on a second job. "Yeah, obviously I could barely afford to live in New York City, so I had a job at night," he said. "I taught at NYU, a course called Advanced Investment Techniques. And I was one day ahead of my students."

Around 1962, when Mary Ann was expecting their second child and he was about to make partner, Fred decided to get a bigger place. He wanted to move to a more upscale address and found a two-bedroom cooperative apartment on Park Avenue and 89th Street on the Upper

East Side. He found it difficult, however, to get a mortgage, a conundrum that didn't faze the plucky young analyst:

> Being a somewhat positive thinker, I wanted to buy an apartment at 1100 Park Avenue, but I didn't have enough money, even though it wasn't that expensive, around $40,000. It also was a co-op, and at the time New York banks would not lend money for co-ops.
>
> So I went to Citibank to see a senior officer that I was introduced to through a friend of my father. I said to him that I had a great idea for him. He said, "What's that sir?" I said, "Here is an opportunity for you to dominate the market, which has some great collateral benefits for the bank." He said, "Fred, what are you talking about?" I said, "Look, why don't you go and loan money to people who want to buy a co-op, just like you do regular mortgages? Who are the people who live in these co-ops? These are pretty important people within New York City. So if you help them with their financing for their co-ops, you probably get them as customers with the bank." So he did. They made me a loan of $40,000; I think it was almost the whole amount of the purchase price.

During this period Fred remained as physically active as he had been since his boyhood in Salt Lake City. He didn't have time to play football or basketball or the other sports he had played in high school and college, but he did run regularly at a time when almost no one jogged. "I have always been health conscious," he said. "What I did in those days, I ran in the park in the early morning. I started doing that when I joined Smith, Barney." Sandy Robertson confirmed Fred's obsession to stay fit:

> I was in Chicago for a while, and Fred would come through town. He would talk about what he did in the morning. He got up early and jogged around the reservoir, and then came home. And this is when

jogging was really unusual. He was the first person I ever knew who went out jogging.

Fred added:

Yes, no one jogged in those days, and yes, I jogged in Keds. I think this was why, years later, I became interested in Nike, which was a small out-of-the-way company making running shoes. And in 1980, I led their IPO while at Lehman Brothers.

FRED JOINS LEHMAN BROTHERS

In 1969, Fred had been at Smith, Barney for more than a decade. For most of that time he had been head of the research department. He had ridden the bull market of the late 1950s and worked through a Dow Jones Industrial Average that continued to climb in the 1960s, but not as dramatically as in the prior decade. The index during much of this decade also fluctuated wildly between rallies and breathtaking drops. This volatility was driven in part by events in the sixties, a decade that included the assassination of a US president and other top leaders, civil rights and social justice upheavals, a rising tide of government regulations, the arrival of large government programs such as Medicare, the war in Vietnam and the protests, youth rebellion and the advent of the counter culture, and tumult in everything from music and entertainment to education. As a rising star in financial and market research with a knack for making the right calls, Fred was keenly aware of the political, economic, and cultural factors that contributed to the vacillations of the markets, and of the roller-coaster ride it represented for Americans. "There were times in the sixties when it was more useful for a researcher on Wall

Street to read the political pages of the newspaper than the business section," said Fred.

To protect themselves against downturns and capriciousness in markets and businesses, many large American corporations spent the decade snatching up basketfuls of businesses that were often unrelated to their core businesses, creating huge conglomerates like Gulf + Western. Bankers spent a considerable amount of time analyzing conglomerate strategies and facilitating and suggesting deals. "Diversification became the new buzzword on Wall Street," wrote Charles Geisst in *Wall Street: A History*,[4] "and companies actively sought bargains outside their own industries in order to hedge their operations against downturns in the economy . . . Investment bankers made healthy fees by advising on the takeovers."

When Fred turned thirty-six years old, he was one of the top researchers on Wall Street. His opinion was sought out by investors and business executives. He also became a popular speaker known for delivering entertaining talks about trends in the markets and the economy. His style was to make brazen, off-the-wall remarks to get his audience's attention, and then to illuminate pithy issues of the day. He was still on the youthful side as a partner at Smith, Barney, but he had become an important player internally.

Financially, he had long ago stopped needing to teach at New York University to supplement his salary. He had paid off his co-op loan for the Park Avenue apartment and, with his wife, was raising their two young daughters, now ages six and ten. But Fred was feeling gradually more frustrated with Smith, Barney's conservative posture toward new technologies and industries as the firm continued to be skeptical of consumer electronics, microchips, telecommunications, pharma, and what would later be called biotechnology.

Sandy Robertson felt this frustration even more keenly. He had moved out to San Francisco for what was supposed to be a brief stint to open a new Smith, Barney office on the West Coast. "I already knew that something incredible was happening out there," Robertson recalled, having heard about it from Don Lucas and others. "When I got there, it became clear that this was where the future was," he said. "But I couldn't get Smith, Barney interested in the new technologies. That was a big battle. So I decided to start my own firm."

Robertson remembered visiting Fred early one night in 1969 when he was visiting New York for a partners' meeting the next day at Smith, Barney. The two friends often met up when they traveled to each other's cities. They met in Fred's apartment, where Robertson recalled saying hello to Fred's two girls. Fred's wife, Mary Ann, then joined the two men as they headed out to a small restaurant nearby on the Upper East Side. Mary Ann listened as Sandy and Fred chatted about their dissatisfactions at the firm, and the pluses and minuses of staying on. Robertson continued:

> Fred and I had dinner together before the last partners' meeting that we went to. We were both unhappy at the firm because they were so stodgy, and because at least some of the partners weren't pulling their weight. There were only thirty-five partners. So we scribbled on a napkin and figured out that seventeen of them weren't producing any business and were useless. I knew that I was going to start a firm, Fred knew he was going to leave unless things changed within a week or ten days.
>
> So we went to that meeting and made all sorts of demands. I think we were very obnoxious young partners at that meeting. But we had very little to lose, since I knew I could form my own firm, which I did soon after, and Fred could get a job in any of the houses or do whatever he wanted.
>
> It was soon after that he left to join Lehman as a partner and head of research, and then he went from research to banking. I think we left within three or four days of each other. I forget which one was first, but it was almost simultaneous.

Unlike Robertson, however, Fred wanted to stay on Wall Street. "I liked being at the center of things," he said. "I never really thought seriously about going to California or anywhere else besides New York." Robertson had this to say about Fred staying in New York:

> New York is the world's financial center, so that gave him a certain platform. It was the right platform for him. He was a guy who liked doing the high-tech deals, but he liked to anchor this with making money and bringing in the big deals with the big companies. He did this later on with biotechnology, when he was able to push a lot of deals through at Lehman that they might not have done if Fred wasn't bringing in the majors. That was his anchor, and also gave him clout with both the high-tech people and the more traditional players. This was key to the Genentech-Roche deal and many others.

EARLY DAYS AT LEHMAN

In the spring of 1969, Fred arrived at the old Lehman Brothers building at One William Street, not far from Smith, Barney and the New York Stock Exchange. He chose Lehman because it had an underperforming research department that he was given a free hand to reshape, and also because of its reputation for investing in new industries. Over the years, Lehman had underwritten some of the great entrepreneurial efforts of the early and mid-twentieth century, including tech-based companies like RCA, Pan American Airways, and Kerr-McGee (one of the first independent oil exploration companies) in the 1930s; DuMont (the first television manufacturer) in the 1940s; and computer technology pioneer Digital Equipment Corporation in the 1950s.

Fred arrived while Robert "Bobbie" Lehman remained the head of the bank, the last in a steady line of Lehmans. Successive generations of the family had run things since the original three Lehman brothers came from Bavaria to found, in 1850, what was then a retail firm based in Alabama. Later in the nineteenth century, the firm moved into brokering cotton and other commodities. They then moved into securities, which led them to move operations to New York just before the turn of the century. Bobbie had taken over from his father in 1925 and had navigated the firm through the 1929 crash and the Great Depression. A legend on the Street and a major collector of art and thoroughbred horses, Bobbie Lehman was seventy-eight years old when Fred arrived. As Fred recalled:

> Bobbie Lehman seemed to come from another world but was of course incredibly smart. He was ill when I came, so he wasn't always there, but his presence was felt. He had a particular chair in the partners' dining room that no one else ever sat in. I remember after he died no one sat in that chair for something like three or four years, until Pete Peterson arrived (in 1973) to run the firm. One day Peterson sat in Bobbie Lehman's chair, and people were shocked.
>
> I was the first full partner from Wall Street that Lehman ever hired from elsewhere. Yes, the firm had hired other full partners from the outside, but they were all former industrialists or government and military people, such as General Lucius Clay, who commanded the Berlin Airlift. I was not thinking of Lehman as a place to go until I got a call from a Lehman partner named Michael Tarnopol, who was head of institutional sales. He and others at Lehman knew that Lehman research was lagging. Goldman and others were pursuing me at the time, but Lehman seemed really serious about building research. I bought my partnership interest from Bobbie Lehman. Mickey Tarnopol became one of my close friends.

At the time, Lehman Brothers had only thirty-three partners and about 330 employees. "That's compared to 26,000 employees when the firm went bankrupt in 2008," said Fred. The number of employees in 1969 was double what the firm had had ten years earlier, Fred added, and they had leased space across the back alley from their traditional headquarters at One William Street near Wall Street for secretaries and support staff.

The One William Street building at mid-century had all of the old-world grandeur one would expect from a longtime Wall Street firm: lots of polished, dark wood, carvings, leather and overstuffed chairs, chandeliers, and thick carpets. Bobbie Lehman bedecked the walls with a profusion of Goyas, Rembrandts, Renoirs, Matisses, Picassos, and Cézannes, about $100 million worth of art, by one account, from his vast personal collection. On the first floor was located the client services area with comfortable chairs and desks and some teller cages decorated with brass trim. The partners' room on the third floor was outfitted with fresh flowers each day and cigars and liquor, with space for the partners to work and, according to numerous accounts of those days in books and articles, to discuss deals, squabble about salaries and bonuses, and jockey for favor from Bobbie Lehman and other senior partners. The full-service dining room, with its ornate china and silver, was on the tenth floor, and on the eleventh floor was a full-service gym with masseurs. Fred visited the eleventh floor most mornings to work out. Mary Tanner remembered that the gym was a place where older retired partners came to hang out and take steam baths. "We had our own barber," said Fred, "and he charged you according to what he thought you were worth."

Mary remembered that Lehman, still a small place when she joined in 1979, had its share of legendary characters. One of these was Marvin Levy, a longtime banker who had been very successful. Mary, then twenty-eight years old, had just been in the building a few days when she ran into an old gentleman. She shared the story:

> I'm pretty nervous being new (and female) and this guy said, "Come here. Who are you?" So I went and sat down and said, "Hello, I am

Mary Tanner, and I am sorry, sir, but I don't know who you are."
"I am Marvin Levy," he said. So we started talking. He told me
about Bobbie Lehman, that he had a really good eye for recruit-
ing talent. And that when he [Levy] was young he had started as a
runner (literally running back and forth to the Stock Exchange to
place orders and deliver securities). He said that in those days people
really did start as runners and many of them were people of extraordinarily modest means, like him, while others were members of the
[Lehman] family or other famous banking families, and some were
former industrialists, who had joined Lehman as partners after they
had been CEOs.

So, Marvin Levy had become an immensely successful partner on
the trading side of the business. And Marvin owned these beautiful
Rolls-Royces, which he always parked in front of the One William
Street building, or the Stock Exchange when he went there. The
police, who knew him, would say: "Mr. Levy, that's not a parking
space, we'll have to give you a ticket," and Marvin would say, "So
give me a ticket!" And each time, he would get a ticket, which was
probably $5 or something. Imagine parking in front of the Exchange
today with all that security, post-9/11.

FROM RESEARCHER TO BANKER

The first thing that Fred did when he arrived at Lehman in 1969 was to
fire nearly the entire research staff after meeting with them and review-
ing their past reports. "This wasn't pleasant to do," he recalled, "but I
needed the best people, and these weren't the best people. The senior
partners supported me completely, they wanted a top-rate research
team," which Fred put together within months of arriving, drawing in
a number of younger analysts who were eager to work for him.

On August 9, 1969, Bobbie Lehman died. He left no successor either in his family or among the senior partners, which threw the company into a period of confusion at a time when the great post-war bull market was ending and jolts to the world economy were coming, including upward spikes in the price of oil and other commodities, deficits arising from funding the Vietnam War, and the dismantling by President Richard Nixon of the "gold standard exchange" system in 1971. Based on a fixed price of a stable dollar, the gold standard had supported the world's major currencies since the Second World War. Nixon enacted what was called "Nixon's Shock" as the dollar's value eroded in real terms with the heavy toll on the US budget from the Vietnam War costs and a weakening economy. "This was a tough time for the firm," said Fred, "but we continued to do well in research. In fact, with no one really running the place, we were able to do some deals that might otherwise not have been allowed."

During the early 1970s Fred shifted from research into banking at Lehman and began soliciting new clients for underwriting deals. Like he'd always done, Fred continued his relentless search for new business models and new companies that would create new industries, but now applied to banking. This was an extrapolation of his research instinct to find the new, the big, alpha investment opportunities. Top of his list to plunge into was the still small but rapidly expanding business-services sector—a prescient move given the meteoric rise of an industry that today is so ubiquitous that it's hard to imagine a time when it didn't exist. Back then, Fred remembered thinking that business-services companies would become important as companies trended from providing business support services in-house to farming out much of such work to companies that specialized in everything from accounting to human resources and made money by replicating similar services to multiple companies.

One of Fred's business-services clients was the A.C. Nielsen Company, which had been providing market research for companies since the 1920s. "I met Art Nielsen Jr. in 1959," said Fred, "because the head of the Smith, Barney Chicago office lived in the same community and knew Art's father, Art Nielsen Sr., as well as Art Nielsen Jr." In 1969, Fred led the marketing team at Smith, Barney when they issued the company's IPO, a relationship that later led to multiple deals with Nielsen when Fred moved to Lehman. Fred explained the company's importance to the business world:

> Most people thought that Nielsen was only television ratings, but that was a miniscule part of their business. Nielsen was the leading company in terms of consumer product market research. So they would go to Procter & Gamble and analyze the sales of, say, their leading deodorant for January, February, and March. Now, what do you know about actual consumer purchases? Not your sales to the wholesaler or retailer. You had better know this, so you get inventories right, and so on. Nielsen was the only company who could tell you these data.

It was typical of Fred that he had kept up his relationship with Arthur Nielsen Jr. going for thirteen or fourteen years and more, even after leaving Smith, Barney, as he closely watched the progress of the company. In April 1970, Fred wrote a research report for Lehman about the company that set the stage for an additional round of funding that was underwritten by Lehman. The Lehman research report, with its distinctive red stripe on top of the cover page—which included the Lehman logo and a drawing of the One William Street building— concluded that investing in Nielsen was "an attractive, long-term, quality, growth investment." Other points made in the report included:

1. Underlying our optimism is a conviction that the role of marketing research will increase in importance both in the United States and in foreign markets of the more economically advanced countries.

2. The complexity of marketing has increased.

3. Nielsen's management is continually doing research on the timing and feasibility of adding new services or adding established services in new markets.

Fred ended the report by quoting a writer from *Fortune*, his favorite magazine, the one that had led him as a boy to want to leave Salt Lake City and attend Hotchkiss. The writer, Max Ways, wrote an article in 1964 that later became a book titled *Antitrust in an Era of Radical Change.*[5] Fred quoted the book: "What is different now is the pace of change, and the prospect that it will come faster and faster . . . So swift is the acceleration that trying to 'make sense' of change will come to be our basic industry . . ." Fred then connected this sentiment to Nielsen: "A.C. Nielsen, representative of the leading, quality service enterprises, provides an attractive way to avoid the confrontation of competitive developments, yet share in the accelerated pace of change."

Nielsen was one of several deals Fred worked on as a newly minted banker at Lehman. Almost from the moment he began as a banker, he worked on a slew of initial public offerings, financings, and mergers of business-services providers for the likes of IMS International, Manpower, Cintas, the Gartner Group, Businessland, Cegedim, and more. IMS International was the leading provider of pharmaceutical sales and marketing data to the pharmaceutical industry. Manpower was the first company providing temporary help to a broad range of companies in all industries. The Gartner Group provided specialty market data for the technology industry. He also became involved in the emerging industry of clinical research services, supporting companies like Quintiles and Pharmaceutical Product Development; he served on the board of the latter for more than a decade. Later in this period, Fred was involved with Telerate, one of the first Wall Street data firms.

Fred's wide-ranging search for the new and what he calls "high-alpha" companies included industries far afield of healthcare and business services. He was involved early on with Vail Associates Inc., the Colorado ski resort, which was established in 1964 and initially financed in a series of private placements. Fred wrote a detailed research report on Vail in 1973, long before the popularity of skiing had begun to take off, but he saw the potential.

Other industries that were underrecognized both in research and banking in the 1970s were cosmetics and personal care. Men back then didn't cover cosmetics, and most firms were sexist, assigning junior women to work with these companies. Fred elevated Lehman's profile in this industry, recognizing that cosmetics and personal care were going to become one of the major economic dollar spending categories in the US, and that the industry was an important adjunct to the fashion, retail, and healthcare industries. Fred sought out clients in this sector: Revlon, Fabergé, Chesebrough-Ponds, Alberto-Culver, Estée Lauder, Helena Rubenstein, Neutrogena, and others, pursuing investment banking transactions in what was then a dramatically expanding industry from which consumers would pay top dollar for the latest cool brand names and high-quality products.

LEHMAN PIVOTS

By 1973, Lehman needed strong leadership as the US economy continued to flounder in response to the first OPEC oil shock and, later in the 1970s, with the rise of "stagflation"—high inflation with low employment and low production. Lehman experienced a self-inflicted crisis as well when bets made by trading chief Lewis Glucksman in 1973 turned sour.

All of this turmoil led the partners in 1973 to seek out a steady hand to head up the company. This was Pete Peterson, formerly the chairman and chief executive officer of Bell and Howell, known mostly for manufacturing cameras, motion picture equipment, and lenses. Then age 47, Peterson had just finished a stint as the Secretary of Commerce in the Nixon administration.

Peterson turned out to be the man the firm needed. He came in and brought order to the company while also jumping into the fray of investment bank mergers that were then all the rage. In 1975, he acquired Abraham & Co., a retail, high-net-worth brokerage. Two years later, Lehman merged with Kuhn, Loeb & Co., another old-line investment-banking firm then struggling even more than Lehman in the uncertain economy. Lehman Brothers, Kuhn, Loeb Inc. became the country's fourth-largest investment bank after Salomon Brothers, Goldman Sachs & Co., and the First Boston Corporation. This launched a golden era for the former Lehman Brothers, which went from losses to record profits in the years that followed. Mary Tanner, who had just joined Lehman as an associate, remembered the merger:

> I had started at Lehman in August of 1979 as really its second woman ever in corporate finance. The other woman came from a very wealthy family, whose family company was a big client of the firm. I was part of a class of eleven associates, the largest that Lehman had ever hired. I had interviewed at Kuhn, Loeb. It was quite an experience. I went into a small conference room, where the table was covered in green baize, like something out of the nineteenth century, and a bunch of guys grilled me. I left feeling those guys just did not have what I perceived to be the killer instinct. I joined Lehman because it had a reputation of having the smartest people, doing the most difficult deals. There was absolutely no possibility in those days that I could ever become a partner, but I thought that I'd get some experience that almost no women had in those days, and then figure out my life later.
>
> No sooner did I join Lehman than the rumors that Lehman would buy Kuhn, Loeb started, denied by the partners that managed the

associate pool of labor. Sure enough, over Thanksgiving weekend, Lehman did buy Kuhn, Loeb. Now the combined firm had double the number of associates. I was absolutely convinced that I (and others) would get fired. And I really needed a job. To Lehman's credit, they didn't fire any of us, and the combined firm went on to great success over the next several years.

STILL SPECIALIZING IN THE DRUG INDUSTRY

Fred's portfolio in the early and mid-1970s covered numerous industries, but his major focus continued to be pharmaceuticals, an industry that had experienced steady growth as drugs developed in the 1950s were mass-produced in the 1960s. These included Syntex Corporation's birth-control pill, drugs for high blood pressure and heart disease, cortisone, and tranquilizers like Haldol and Valium, which were the most-prescribed drugs in the world during the 1960s and early 1970s, before concerns about addiction and overdependence reduced the numbers of pills prescribed.

Fred's research unit during this period produced highly regarded analyses in reports topped by the distinctive red Lehman Brothers banner and logo. In a June 13, 1972, research brief on drug manufacturer SmithKline & French Co., Fred wrote about the industry as a whole:

> An underlying paradox of the pharmaceutical industry is that a most challenging problem relates to conspicuous success. The derivation of success, defined as a rapid increase in sales and earnings, is a result of new research accomplishments, which, in turn, are not controllable either in time or dimension. Therefore, the greater the success, the more substantial the problem of perpetuating the success. The investor must be alert to the innovation cycle of the individual

drug company in order to capitalize on a potential renewed growth phase (or, on the contrary, to avoid risk).

The "paradox" and the "lack of control in time and dimension" sound like a philosopher's take on this always volatile industry and remain apropos today for both pharma and certainly for the more "uncontrollable" biotechnology industry. Fred concluded this research paper on SmithKline & French by suggesting that this company was about to begin one of those "renewed growth phases."

"We recommend purchase for long-term capital appreciation," he wrote, offering excellent advice for a company that was indeed about to become one of the biggest of Big Pharma. Its sales proceeded to climb from under $2.4 billion in the early 1970s (in 2020 dollars) to nearly $46 billion in 2020 as the company grew into its current iteration, GlaxoSmithKline. This mega-company was created in part by several mergers, including one with the Beecham Group in 1989, in which Fred played a major role.

In the 1960s, the US Congress began increasing the regulation of the pharmaceutical industry to oversee not just a drug's safety but also its efficacy, whether or not it worked as claimed. The FDA also began limiting the financial links allowed between drug companies and physicians as strict standards were developed for clinical research and for the informed consent of subjects enrolling in trials. (These standards were issued in the 1964 Declaration of Helsinki.) To qualify for potentially lucrative patents for novel compounds, policymakers strengthened incentives for drug companies to spend the large sums of money required to develop drugs that would also meet new standards of efficacy and safety.

As the 1970s progressed, the focus of R&D for pharmaceutical companies shifted from anti-infectives to oncology and chronic-use drugs on the eve of what would become the industry's blockbuster era. This officially began in 1976 with the release of SmithKline's ulcer medication Tagamet, which helped launch a steep rise in the industry's growth trajectory and premium investment valuation. Other blockbusters quickly followed, transforming pharma from a mid-level industry to a powerhouse in the 1980s and beyond.

Fred was in the middle of the great pharma surge as he and Lehman became the architects of one mega-deal after another in not only pharma, but in the wider field of the life sciences that Fred was prescient enough to identify at that Smith, Barney meeting way back in 1962.

Along with this explosion in chemistry-based drugs were dramatic discoveries being made in genetics and molecular biology. Scientists were making breakthroughs in techniques like recombinant DNA. Developed by researchers including geneticist Stanley N. Cohen and biochemist Paul Berg, both of Stanford University, and geneticist Herbert W. Boyer of the University of California at San Francisco, this new technology allowed scientists to splice and engineer the DNA of simple organisms, like bacteria, in order to use their cell machinery to excrete designer proteins that, among other things, could be used to create drugs.

Traditional pharmaceutical companies, still driven by chemical solutions to developing drugs, had little interest in these science experiments in academic labs. Nor did most molecular biologists as pure researchers want to have much to do with commerce, although by the early seventies a few intrepid entrepreneur-scientists had begun to develop scrappy start-ups in attempts to exploit the new bioscience that still lacked a name. Independent investors willing to take huge risks also stepped in: venture capitalists like Tom Perkins of Kleiner Perkins and bankers like Sandy Robertson, although his role typically came after the initial venture financing, when his boutique investment bank helped organize public offerings for biotechnology companies that were showing signs of success in the late 1970s and 1980s.

For Fred, the call that got him into biotechnology came in 1974, when an elegant Uruguayan and former pharmaceutical executive named Alejandro Zaffaroni telephoned to say that he had a company in a field he called "molecular biology" in the Bay Area that was ready to go public. This despite the company having no revenues, no product, and only a handful of employees. But Fred knew Zaffaroni well and knew that the shrewd scientist-entrepreneur must be onto something. Certainly, thought Fred, it was worth popping out to California to take a peek.

CHAPTER 4

Bravura Deals and the Birth of Biotechnology

WALL STREET, CAPITAL, AND THE SPECTACULAR RISE OF BIOTECHNOLOGY, 1974–1984

Genentech? That was an offering of passion.
—Fred Frank

Alejandro Zaffaroni, the man who rang up Fred in 1974 about a most improbable IPO, was originally a biochemist. In 1951, he had joined a small start-up drug company in Mexico called Syntex. Soon after, he was running the company and moved operations to Palo Alto, California. There he transformed Syntex into a major player in pharmaceuticals with the introduction of the first birth-control pill. Fred had met Zaffaroni before he left Syntex in 1968 and had followed the Uruguayan's career as he founded the first of a half-dozen important biotech companies that emerged over the next forty years, including

ALZA, DNAX, Symyx, Maxygen, and SurroMed. But the call was not about any of these. Zaffaroni wanted to talk about a little start-up called Cetus in Emeryville, California, across the Bay Bridge from San Francisco. Founded in 1971, this company was working to develop products using a revolutionary new process for rewriting the DNA of bacteria, one that could coax a bioengineered microbe into using its cell machinery to secrete chemicals like drugs.

"I had no idea what he was talking about," said Fred about the call, as reported in Cynthia Robbins-Roth's book *From Alchemy to IPO*.[1] "They were thinking about taking Cetus public, with its eight staff scientists," Fred continued. "I said it was totally absurd, a big mistake for many reasons, but the call got me interested in what they were up to. I learned a lot more about the people and the science and began to see biotech as the future."[2]

Neither Fred nor Zaffaroni could have guessed that seven years later, when Cetus did go public, it would be the largest IPO in history at that time. This was despite that pesky situation of having no profits and no real products yet ready to be sold, a situation that a few years earlier would have been a nonstarter on Wall Street. In the late 1970s and early 1980s, however, something new was emerging in how young companies on the leading edge of new technologies were being funded.

Until the 1960s, early-stage companies—both high- and low-tech—mostly raised money from a few wealthy families like the Rockefellers or the Carnegies, or from small-scale bank loans. This had been the major source of start-up capital since at least the turn of the twentieth century. Now new funding options were changing all of this as venture capital funds, starting in the late 1950s, began to provide funding. This was mostly small amounts in those days, raised from collectives of limited partners and pooled into reservoirs of cash. The model was for a small group of managing investors to take usually small stakes to develop companies commercializing new technologies that were too risky for traditional banks and investors. If successful, these investments would offer rich returns to the pool of partners—and even richer returns to the managing partners—particularly for technologies that, once developed, could be mass produced cheaply (scaled) and sold to thousands or millions of customers.

Pioneering venture capital firms arose during this era that would soon become synonymous with taking huge risks and making sometimes enormous returns. One of the first in Silicon Valley was Draper & Johnson, formed by William Draper and Franklin "Pitch" Johnson in 1962, which later split into Sutter Hill Ventures and Asset Management Company. Others included Venrock Associates, founded in 1969, and Kleiner Perkins Caufield & Byers and Sequoia Capital, both founded in 1972 with offices at what would become "venture capital central" on Sandhill Road, in Menlo Park, California, near Stanford University. "It seemed like the natural next step was to start these funds," said Pitch Johnson many years later. "There were all of these great ideas back then and no real way to fund them."

The capital at work in these funds was quite small by later standards, with total money under management for the whole venture capital industry in 1978 standing at $750 million. (This is equivalent to $2.9 billion in 2019 dollars and compares to $36.5 billion actually spent by US venture funds in 2019.)[3] This was plenty, however, to support a string of companies that soon were posting successful IPOs like Genentech and Cetus in biotech, and Apple in information technology, which in turn ushered in a wave of new venture firms in the 1980s and 1990s with some individual funds rising into the billions of dollars.

The core of this new exuberance was a continuation of the same optimism and sense of destiny that had been powering the United States since the post-war booms of technology and wealth in the United States. By the 1970s Fred and a generation of innovators and entrepreneurs in his age group—the children of World War II—were in their twenties and thirties and knew firsthand what it had meant to grow up during the spectacular rise in lifestyle and real wages experienced in the US since 1945. Fred was on the younger end of a group then in their late thirties, forties, and fifties who had also known the lows of the Great Depression in the 1930s and could contrast this with the heights of the 1960s. In their still short lifetimes, Fred and his peers had seen the emergence of everything from color television, computers, and space flight to a dizzying array of drugs and medical devices that were saving lives. "People experienced real miracles in those days with new therapies," said Leroy Hood, a physician and early pioneer of genetic sequencing technologies, "an expectation that drove people to take chances and to expect the miracles to continue." Hood was associated with a number of important biotechnology companies such as Amgen and the first major genetic sequencing company, Applied Biosystems.

"The most important thing to know about that period and about certain people in America, was their attitude about taking risks," said South African–born Jeremy Levin, former CEO of Teva, the world's largest producer of generic drugs, and now CEO of Ovid Therapeutics Inc. "This was at a time when many people in America were more willing to take risks than elsewhere in the world, an attitude that I found interesting and wanted to know more about." There was also money to be made, pointed out Tom Perkins of Kleiner Perkins. "It's certainly been proven that a handful of venture capitalists can make obscene amounts of money if they back the right biotech ventures," he told Glenn E. Bugos in a 2001 interview for the Regional Oral History Office of the University of California at Berkeley's Bancroft Library.[4]

Optimism prevailed even in the 1970s, despite oil shocks, stagflation, flat public markets, and gloomy talk about America's "malaise," the word used by President Jimmy Carter in a 1979 speech that was so pessimistic it may have been one reason that he failed to get reelected in 1980. Indeed, new technologies continued to offer tantalizing promises of breakthroughs and life-altering changes, while a certain breed of investor remained convinced that picking the right technologies would pay off in major ways. This was certainly the expectation for early biotech start-ups like Cetus, founded using the new science Zaffaroni told Fred about in 1974. "These companies not only seemed to have a new approach to science and fighting disease," said Fred, "they also seemed to offer a new way of developing drugs and creating entirely new industries."

FRED PLUNGES INTO BIOTECHNOLOGY

When Fred took Zaffaroni's call, he was forty-two years old. He had recently been named one of *Fortune* magazine's ten most influential figures on Wall Street, known for dispensing uncannily precise advice and analysis of companies and deals. Mostly he focused on the rapidly rising pharmaceutical industry, which in the mid-1970s was on the verge of launching its early billion-dollar blockbusters. Fred had understood this potential back in the early sixties at Smith, Barney, when he talked his then-boss Bill Grant into being the first Wall Street firm to cover pharma companies separate from the chemical industry. The close connections he then developed with companies like Hoffmann-La Roche and SmithKline & French (later GlaxoSmithKline) positioned him well to be the man on Wall Street that these rising behemoths would come to for what would become a flurry of mergers and acquisitions in the early 1980s, 1990s, and beyond.

Fred's success with these big-money deals also gave him clout with his colleagues at Lehman to indulge in smaller, more speculative financings and deals for small biotech start-ups that his bank normally would have eschewed as being too small and too chancy. "At Lehman Fred was able to spend time tinkering with those early biotech companies because he was hauling in some substantial income from all of his work on the pharmaceutical side," recalled Peter Solomon, a partner and former vice chairman of Lehman who worked with Fred at the firm in the 1970s and 1980s.

Not long after Zaffaroni's call, Fred flew out to Emeryville and met with Cetus. The company was founded by a high-throttle group of scientists: the Nobel Prize–winning physicist-turned-molecular-biologist Donald Glaser, venture capitalist Moshe Alafi, physician Peter J. Farley, and molecular biologist Ronald Cape, who served as CEO. Zaffaroni and one of the coinventors of the birth-control pill, Carl Djerassi, were directors. Stanford researcher Stanley Cohen, co-discoverer of recombinant DNA and a winner of the Nobel Prize, later joined the scientific advisory board.

Fred met the Cetus team in a small warehouse in Emeryville not far from the east side terminus of the Oakland Bay Bridge. Sitting down with Ronald Cape and the others, he heard their excited talk about how their new technology was about to revolutionize numerous industries, not just healthcare. Fred heard about projects being developed by Cetus (and other early biotech companies) in chemicals, agriculture, and industrial dyes. "We were true believers," said Cape. "We were anxious to get the financing we needed and to prove our case." Cape recalled meeting Fred during that first face-to-face. "Fred was a gentleman and listened to us and then basically said we were nuts about the IPO idea," he said. "He said we weren't anywhere close to ready, but that we might be if our science turned out to work."

"I learned a great deal on that trip and afterward," said Fred in an article called "The Ubiquitous Frederick Frank," published in 2012 in the *Life Sciences Foundation* magazine.[5] "I spent a lot of time with Cetus, getting educated. Ron Cape was a good mentor, very patient. In my way of thinking, this was a game-changing opportunity in the life sciences field."

THE SCIENCE BEHIND BIOTECHNOLOGY

The science Fred heard about in Emeryville that day had started in its modern incarnation in 1953 with James D. Watson's and Francis Crick's discovery of DNA's double-helix shape. In the decades that followed, a steady stream of breakthroughs had revealed most of the basics about genes. At the same time, researchers were developing early techniques and tools to delve ever more deeply into the inner workings of DNA and cells.

By the early 1970s, a few key labs were creating the core technology needed to splice genes in and out of bacteria. This led to one of the great breakthroughs in modern biotechnology, when Stanford's Paul Berg in 1971 first spliced DNA from one organism into another. This was followed in 1972 by the successful insertion of foreign rDNA into bacteria by Stanford's Stanley Cohen and University of California at San Francisco's Herb Boyer in a way that allowed the foreign DNA to replicate naturally. This resulted in hybrid cells that could be used like tiny factories to produce specific proteins.

They did this by showing that restriction enzymes could be used as scissors to snip out pieces of DNA from one cell or organism and then to reinsert them into another. This was akin to rewriting the basic software of these cells to churn out on demand enzymes and hormones in large quantities to use as drugs and for various industrial processes. "This was definitely one of the most exciting times of my life," Cohen recalled. "We knew we had something huge, even if there were still details to be worked out."

The Boyer-Cohen discovery led to a famous phone call in 1976 from a twenty-nine-year-old venture capitalist named Robert Swanson to the then 41-year-old Herb Boyer, who agreed to meet Swanson to talk about his work. "Boyer had allocated ten minutes to get rid of this guy," remembered Tom Perkins, who became the first chairman of Genentech. "Swanson charmed him completely." So much so that the ten-minute meeting turned into three hours in a pub not far from the UC San Francisco campus.

It must have been an unusual meeting. This was the mid-1970s when many professors and scientists, like Boyer, wore jeans and leather vests, had long hair, sideburns, and droopy mustaches, and had little patience for people in business. Contrast this with Bob Swanson, who almost always wore either suits or slacks with a sweater or polo shirt—a fashion dichotomy that didn't stop the two men from creating the idea for what became Genentech before they had left the bar. The company, founded in 1976, would go on to develop a raft of hugely successful drugs over the following decades based on the new biological processes. First out was Activase (a tissue plasminogen activator), used to treat stroke in some patients. Next was Humulin, a synthetic insulin that eliminated the need to use pigs as the primary source of insulin, and synthetic human growth hormone, which treated children with severe growth deficiencies.

In later years, Genentech's technology and prowess accelerated the development and release of cancer blockbusters like Avastin, Herceptin, Tarceva, and many others. Today, the company remains a pharmaceutical giant as part of Roche. In 1976, however, none of this was obvious, with the notion of using recombinant DNA to produce drugs still just an idea that few people realized would create an entire industry within just a few years.

Beyond the technical challenges of perfecting recombinant DNA, the notion of using biological innovations for commerce remained suspect among academic scientists. In part this was because biology at the time remained more "pure" than chemistry and physics, which decades earlier had seen their discoveries transformed into products—a purity that had already begun to be breached in 1974 when Stanford University filed a patent on Boyer and Cohen's recombinant DNA process. At the time, most academic biologists believed that their discoveries belonged to the scientific community and were supposed to be written up in journals, not patented, an attitude that was clearly on the cusp of change. This became even more evident when the US Congress began passing legislation aimed at pushing discoveries with the potential to be commercialized out of the lab and into the private sector. Chief among these was the Bayh–Dole Act in 1980, which permitted a university, small business, or nonprofit institution supported by federal funds to pursue ownership of an invention. Bayh–Dole helped to foster more of an entrepreneurial environment around discoveries in academia by strengthening rules around patenting and ownership. This encouraged investors to spend money to develop companies around new findings, which in turn helped fuel the rise of newly formed venture capital firms.

"It was one thing to have discovered this new science," recalled Fred, "but you also needed to rethink the laws and to create a system that allowed patents and other intellectual property so that people would put up the money to develop the technology into products."

The other big issue emerging around commercialization in the 1970s and early 1980s was exactly how to create viable businesses around these new discoveries. Commenting on Cetus and Genentech in the early days, Mary Tanner said, "Both companies' basic business plans were really quite vague at the time. The products they were looking into were not limited to drugs. In the early days, these companies explored using bioengineering to create products ranging from fuels and industrial chemicals, to compounds to enhance the production of cattle and other animals. People couldn't even figure out whether biotechnology should be a hyphenated word or not. You know, was there more emphasis on the bio or the technology?"

UC San Francisco biochemist William Rutter, who later cofounded Chiron, remembered that the early companies often downplayed the use of recombinant DNA for producing human therapeutics. "They were talking about using this technology to make chemicals that would leach metal and synthesize dye stuffs," Rutter said. "It was the most amazing repertoire of stuff. It was only after about five or ten years into it that it became a therapeutic story, because all the other industrial applications had died."

FRED AND PHARMA

Biotechnology remained on the periphery, however, of what Fred was doing day-to-day. He spent most of his time courting top pharma executives in North America, Europe, and Japan, and making himself a valuable and confident advisor to a number of major companies. "Fred was a regular visitor to the boardroom and was always meeting with the senior executives," recalled George Poste, a British virologist who, during the eighties, was moving rapidly up through the ranks of the R&D unit at SmithKline. He became the head of R&D in the 1980s during a particularly productive time for the company.

Pharma's rise, as always, was driven primarily from breakthroughs in chemistry and discoveries of compounds in plants and animals that worked as drugs. Most of these discoveries, however, came from trial and error—from testing large numbers of candidate compounds against diseases, rather than from a deep understanding of the underlying biology of disease. "No one was quite sure why this research worked," said Fred, although it became clear that the raft of new technologies based on biology had the potential to rake in profits when a company found a molecular target associated with a disease, and then discovered a compound that acted on that target.

The hit-or-miss approach also fueled the rise of staggeringly high R&D budgets to encompass all of that trial and error, which in turn led to the invention of highly automated, computer-driven processes like high-throughput screening of compounds against disease cellular models. This allowed companies to test libraries containing millions of chemical compounds to see which ones caused a potentially therapeutic reaction in cells and in animals. "It was a classic shots-on-goal strategy," said Fred, "and for a long time it worked—until it didn't." Expanded R&D budgets also allowed for more work to be done to understand the underlying biology of diseases and how drugs work—so-called "rational drug design." This has helped to focus the hit-or-miss process of high-throughput drug discovery, but in most cases has not eliminated it.

In the 1970s through the 1990s, most of the action around recombinant DNA and biology-driven R&D remained the domain of the new biotech industry. Big Pharma, with its emphasis on chemistry, only joined the bio-quest in the late 1990s. They dipped their toes in first by investing in biotech companies and specific candidate drugs before plunging in and buying up companies starting in the early 2000s. Today the line between chemistry and biology has blurred as companies embrace both, although for many companies the divide remains.

Another trend Fred recognized early was the tendency of pharma companies to develop "me too" drugs. This was partly a reaction to the very high costs of developing novel drugs using trial and error, which could easily chew up billions of dollars and produce nothing that worked or could pass muster at the FDA in terms of safety and efficacy. So companies to this day tend to focus their resources on developing their own versions of others' original research into families of chemicals or biologicals that act on the same or similar mechanisms to treat diseases such as diabetes, depression, and, yes, erectile dysfunction. Over the years companies have offered up, sometimes in rapid progression, their own slightly different versions of successful drugs, including beta-blockers for hypertension and selective serotonin reuptake inhibitors (SSRIs), mainly for depression. For instance, the SSRI known as Prozac (fluoxetine), developed by Eli Lilly, was approved by the FDA in 1987 and was quickly followed by other companies' SSRIs, including Pfizer's Zoloft in 1991 and SmithKline Beecham's Paxil in 1992. "The industry learned that it was much more likely to be successful doing research if companies developed drugs that I call fast followers," said Fred. He explained the term:

> So that means these drugs were best in class, but they were not first in class. That's what those glamour years were all about, copying others' research and improving on it. These included the first blockbuster, Tagamet for ulcers and heartburn. This was followed by Glaxo's

ranitidine, also for ulcers and heartburn, which you know of as Zan-
tac. Glaxo thought that drug would make 300 million dollars, but it
became a three-billion-dollar product. And Prilosec, yet another drug
for ulcers and heartburn, which AstraZeneca brought out soon after,
became a six-billion-dollar product.

Another crucial factor was that therapies and patient care were shifting from acute care—where drug companies and the medical field had
made such dramatic gains with antibiotics, new surgical techniques,
vaccines, and other life-saving breakthroughs—to the treatment of diseases such as diabetes, heart disease, and depression that aren't likely
to be fatal for years. "We went from an industry in the fifties and sixties that provided antibiotics and acute care drugs, which were one-use
and actually fairly miraculous because they were important to use in
distress," said Fred. "Then we went to these chronic care things that
people used and paid for for many years."

George Poste remembered this transition well, and the part that
Fred played in helping to capitalize this growing industry. Poste was
thirty-five years old and a young R&D scientist and executive at
SmithKline & French when he met Fred in 1981. "Fred was a regular
feature at our company and others," said Poste. "Even at my tender age
in the early eighties he let me ask questions. I spent a lot of time just
talking with him. On several occasions I had him come and talk at our
annual R&D retreat to give his perspective on the industry and where
it was going. He was really one of the most experienced bankers in
understanding healthcare, and particularly Big Pharma."

THE NON-PHARMA PHARMA INDUSTRY

Always on the lookout for alpha- and new-industry segments, Fred in the early 1980s began focusing on another emerging industry, the generics pharma industry. At the time, most pharmaceutical products remained "small molecules" that were chemically synthesized and easy to replicate. This meant that when patents for drugs expired and a patent-holder's exclusivity in sales and (usually high) pricing expired with them, it was easy for companies large and small to jump in and start making and selling generic forms at substantially lower prices, often amid stiff competition.

Generics were also given a boost in 1984 when the US Congress passed the Hatch-Waxman Act, which changed pharma forever. Hatch-Waxman was intended to simplify and codify the rights of both innovator pharmaceutical companies and generic manufacturers. The public policy goal was to increase the number of generic drug filings and lower drug prices in the US. Since generics tended to be priced far below the drugs still on patents, Fred at the time warned his Big Pharma clients that their earnings on blockbusters and other drugs would plummet. Fred recalled:

> I had Mary and my team prepare a detailed presentation on the emerging generics market. No major pharma company wanted to hear about it. So, I developed an "elevator pitch call" to CEOs. "Hi, I want to come speak with you about a subject as to which you and your team are either ignorant or prejudiced." I got a lot of interesting reactions. Most CEOs said that if they were ignorant, sure, come by and tell us. However, once the word *generics* came out of my mouth, everyone said, "I'm prejudiced," although many did receive our presentation. The principal objections were that branded, patented products, sold directly to doctors and hospitals, were very different from generics, sold into pharmaceutical distributors. They just didn't understand the change that was coming.

Mary remembered being impressed by Fred's approach:

> It was amazing. We would walk into a major meeting, and Fred
> would deliver this "are you ignorant or prejudiced" to major CEOs
> and their senior teams. I mean, in their faces. And you know, Fred is
> not a confrontational guy, plus when he (rarely) does something like
> this, he does it with aplomb. Nobody but Fred could have gotten
> away with this, but he was held in such respect. We got nowhere in
> terms of either recognition or business. But Fred was right, and the
> first earthquake was the Syntex product Naprosyn (naproxen). After
> losing patent protection, revenues went from well over $1 billion to,
> maybe, 20 percent of that, very quickly. It led to the acquisition of
> Syntex by Roche for $5.3 billion in 1994.

The generics industry did take off, after some scandals, fueled
in part by an increasing number of US states that passed mandatory
generic drug substitution laws. These required that pharmacists sub-
stitute an FDA-approved therapeutically equivalent generic for the
branded, higher-priced version. Once the effect of these regulatory
changes came into force, the revenue effect on branded products losing
patent protection was dramatic, with pricing declines of up to 90 percent within the first year of patent expiry.

Early on, Fred could see this coming. He had identified Teva Pharmaceuticals, an Israeli company, as a company to watch, a company
that Lehman had worked with for years as part of its banking practice
with the Israeli government and several Israeli public and private companies. In 1982, Fred led Teva's IPO listing on NASDAQ, although
the stock was already trading on the Tel Aviv stock exchange.

Mary remembered this NASDAQ offering being a challenging task:

> It was one of the most difficult IPOs I ever did. The company was
> ferocious on valuation, which was tiresome, as the stock was already

trading in Israel, and the view of some on the Teva team was that it was grossly undervalued and we should offer it at a higher price than in Israel, which was not feasible. Up to that point in time, not many Israeli companies had registered on NASDAQ. But we got it done. As I recall, the entire market value of the company was about $189 million. That's about what I guess Teva earns now in just a few days; it has gone on to become a truly remarkable company.

In 1985, Teva's CEO, Eli Hurvitz, approached Fred to help with his vision of turning Teva into a full-service drug company. This wasn't easy because Teva's financial resources were modest. So Fred suggested a different path, hoping to turn Hurvitz's attention to generics, an industry Fred thought Teva was ideally suited for given Israel's recent history with Arab boycotts. During those difficult years, Teva had licensed drugs from foreign originators and deployed its skilled chemists to duplicate them in Israel, paying royalties in Switzerland or elsewhere to the originator to circumvent the boycott and to fairly compensate the originator. Hurvitz agreed, which led to Fred assisting Teva in acquiring US-based Lemmon Co., a mixed generic and branded pharma company.

Fred also helped arrange a joint venture with W.R. Grace, which had a large generics company. The new business was called TAG. Teva bought out Grace in 1991.

Today, Teva is the largest generic drug company in the world and ranks in the top 20 pharmaceutical companies, with both branded and generic businesses.

Teva was not, however, the only Israeli deal run by Lehman during this era. Harvey Krueger, one of Fred's partners, established a team that specifically focused on Israeli companies in Israel and in the US, which propelled Lehman in a relatively short period to becoming the leading mergers-and-acquisitions investment-banking firm for Israeli companies. Fred led the healthcare part of the effort, including a deal with Medinol, a pioneer in developing cardiovascular stents. As Mary recalled:

> Fred assisted Kobi and Judith Richter, owners of Medinol, in an initial transaction in which Boston Scientific invested $60 million in Medinol for a 21 percent ownership interest and acquired the exclusive rights to distribute Medinol products in the US. The relationship between the companies soured because of contested terms in the license agreement, and bitter litigation ensued. Eventually, Fred assisted Medinol in a negotiated settlement, in which Boston Scientific gave Medinol $750 million in cash and surrendered its 21 percent ownership in the company. Fred knew both Medinol and Boston Scientific well, and it was another example of the fact that he was a trusted advisor to both sides, facilitating the settlement.

BEYOND DRUGS: HUMANA GOES AFTER AMERICAN MEDICORP

Another healthcare segment that Fred was keeping his eye on in the 1970s was the rapidly changing landscape around hospitals. Traditionally, hospitals had been owned by municipalities and charitable organizations, with some owned by doctors. Virtually all of them were not-for-profit institutions located in urban, downtown-based facilities. This system, however, was failing to keep up with an onslaught of new technologies in imaging, medical devices, computing, transportation, and more, plus new medical techniques in the operating room and in outpatient facilities. Most traditional hospitals lacked the capital and the managerial depth to respond to these changes. This drove the formation of a series of for-profit companies that began acquiring legacy institutions and building new hospitals in the burgeoning suburbs of the US, particularly in the South and the West.

It was typical that Fred was paying attention to this industry, despite his reputation as a major banker for the drug industry. As Peter Solomon, former vice chairman of Lehman, recalled, Fred at various times worked with industries as far flung as automobiles, energy, airlines, and the media. "At times we wondered: What is Fred going to come up with next?" said Solomon.

What came next for Fred was one of Fred's biggest deals ever, which involved the rapidly growing hospital industry. It was a deal that also led to his meeting his future wife, Mary Tanner.

The deal involved one of those rapidly growing hospital and health services businesses: Kentucky-based Humana. Founded in 1961 with the name Extendicare, by the early 1970s the company that would become Humana was the largest nursing home company in the US. Extendicare sold its nursing home business and renamed itself Humana in 1974. The company was buying up and building new hospitals at a very fast clip in the mid-1970s. (Years later, Humana would spin out its hospital business and become the managed-care and insurance company that it is today.) In 1978, this flurry of growth and acquisitions led the company to set its sights on another large hospital chain based in Philadelphia called American Medicorp, which was struggling with heavy debt and a depressed stock price.

Fred had gotten to know Humana's founder and CEO David Jones and his partner Wendell Cherry and was hired as the banker to handle the acquisition. American Medicorp, however, was unwilling to accept Humana's price and was reluctant to sell. When negotiations broke down, Humana decided to attempt a hostile takeover, a move that Fred advised against knowing that it would be bitterly resisted by American Medicorp's founder and CEO, a former adman named Alan Miller, and would probably fail. Fred told Humana's David Jones and Wendell Cherry to be patient, explaining that Humana's operations were on the rise and American Medicorp's were not. So Humana waited, Fred telling Jones and Cherry, "your time will come."

A year later, American Medicorp's stock price had declined significantly and Fred called Humana and said, "Now is the time." In view of the prior failed discussions with American Medicorp, and the ferocity with which Alan Miller rejected any reason to have negotiations, Humana elected to launch an offer publicly. Once it was announced, American Medicorp announced its intention, also publicly, to reject any offer from Humana. They hired two investment banking firms, Loeb Rhoades and Goldman Sachs, and a law firm to advise them.

As the saga wore on, with Humana chipping away at Medicorp's shareholders, Fred says he woke up one morning—at 4 a.m. as usual to exercise and prepare for the day—to discover that a most unexpected white knight had emerged to make a sweeter counteroffer to Alan Miller's shareholders: TWA, the airline. Fred explained TWA's interest: "They also owned hotels—beds in hotels, beds in hospitals."[6] Although this hardly made the move any less unexpected.

FRED MEETS MARY TANNER

In the midst of the Humana project, a young Harvard graduate named Mary Tanner was dispatched from Lehman's associate pool to work with the team Fred had assembled. Fred's future wife was twenty-eight years old and petite with fiery red hair. She had a no-nonsense manner and impressed people with her verve, energy, and whip-smart intelligence. She recalled her first meeting with Fred:

> One day I am sitting in my office and Steven Fenster, the assignment partner for associates at Lehman, comes in and he said, "Go up to

the tenth-floor conference room, there is a partner there named Fred Frank. He is working on a transaction, and he needs more help." So I go up to the tenth floor, and there's this guy looking very serious with glasses—big thick, dark-green glasses—and he starts explaining about this deal. And I am completely lost, but I play along.

Thankfully, there was a classmate of mine from Harvard, another first-year associate, and he was one of these kids who had done finance undergraduate. So he understood it all, and he helped me to understand.

I didn't know anything about Fred. I hadn't even read the articles that were beginning to emerge in the *New York Times* and other places about the Humana deal. My first thought was that he was very austere. And, as you know, he doesn't speak much. So I was really quite frightened of him. Also, I'd heard in the gossip chain in the firm that this transaction was very controversial and that the partners were very, very worried, and that this wasn't a good assignment to be put on.

Before this I had worked on another tough deal involving Chase Bank and International Harvester, which was going bankrupt. And I go from that to being assigned to this sort of controversial partner, a guy who came from research, which was different from most of the bankers, who thought they were close to God or something.

Mary Tanner was born in 1951 in Norfolk, Virginia. Soon thereafter, her family moved to Bergen County in northern New Jersey so that her father, an engineer, could teach at Columbia University. To support his young family, he soon went into private practice, where he built tunnels and worked part-time for NASA. She recalled:

He used to come home with wonderful stories about the early days of the space program. In the early days of Canaveral, they couldn't figure out gantries, and he was on the team that helped figure out how to get the gantry to fall the right way—away from the thrust of the rocket. And I guess it was from my father that I got this enormous sense that detail is everything, which is what I am known for. You need to have big picture, too, but really it's detail, detail, detail.

"I can verify that," said Fred, listening to this comment with a smile. "Mary is the best person for details. Like she said all the time, she's the nerd. I mean, she's a *real* nerd. Because she dots the i's and crosses all the t's."

"Fred is a big-picture guy, a thinker," said Mary. "He comes up with the concepts, and I execute things."

Mary arrived when women were still rare as executives on Wall Street. "You know, I was among the first generation of women to be able to do men's work," she said, "not God's work, as Lloyd Blankfein of Goldman said." And yet Mary was not the first woman in her family to be in business, she noted:

My great-great-grandmother, Catherine Casey, came over from Ireland, and she founded a couture shop—meaning she was a seamstress who had a lot of fashion and business sense—on Fifth Avenue in the place where Henri Bendel's used to be, and Henri Bendel was her cutter. I am serious. She was a very successful businesswoman. She was married to a very charming, if perhaps roguish, Irishman who was the chief waiter at Delmonico's, which was a really big job in those days. And he had lots of stories about Diamond Jim Brady and other famous customers. And my Great Aunt Mary formed and ran her own small advertising and design firm and somehow managed to survive the Depression.

After Harvard, Mary came to New York, where she took a job in finance almost by accident.

I was introduced to a friend of my father who was controller of one of the big banks—Manufacturers Hanover Trust Company of sainted memory. I was the first woman they had ever hired for the management-training program. So, when I arrived they made me be a secretary for a while, before allowing me to do finance. But I didn't really like commercial banking. So I went to work at a small partnership run by an ex-Lehman partner, Michael Thomas, who was quite a famous guy and an author, and he was an investment banker. When that firm broke up, I wrote letters to all the investment banks asking for job. I write pretty good letters. I signed them all M.C. Tanner, so most of them thought I was a man. I got a bunch of job offers. It was a time when Wall Street was in a transition from the small houses to the mega-firms of the eighties and nineties, and there was this door just cracking open for women.

Even if Mary was ambivalent about working for the controversial partner with the big glasses, Fred immediately became impressed by the young associate. "She was literally one of the best bankers I had ever met," he said. "She needed to learn some things, but her talent was clear from the beginning." He was so impressed that later, when the Humana deal was over and Mary was set to rejoin the associate pool, Fred said no. "She's not going anyplace. She's staying and working in my group."

Mary also benefited by learning from Fred. "One of the main persons who taught me my craft is Fred," she said. "How to think things out, to be thorough and patient. Being patient was hard for me and still is. But it's part of the deal. Fred also used to create these incredibly complicated spreadsheets. Nobody else was doing these at the firm, and he taught me to do that. It's one reason he could be so thorough."

HUMANA GETS MORE COMPLICATED

As the Humana project grew in complexity, Fred dispatched Mary and others to perform extensive due diligence. Mary remembered the magnitude of the project:

> We had to go literally from hospital to hospital to figure out what was happening and to evaluate what was working at these for-profit hospitals. And remember, this was a new industry in terms of public markets, and nobody entirely understood it. For one thing, hospitals have all of these fixed costs before you can let any patients come in, and there was a question of what mix of patients was optimal, and what kind of reimbursements. At the time Medicare was evolving and revenue reporting was a complicated financial spreadsheet because you had to know what mix you had and you had to know about contractual allowances, which was the difference between what you booked for Medicare and what they actually paid you.
>
> You also basically had to go and get mortgages on each property from a local bank or an insurance company for all the 400 hospitals in what would become the combined company. Almost every one of them had a different mortgage on it. And all of those pieces of debt had to be renegotiated before we could close this deal. It was just an enormous amount of stuff we had to do.

Meanwhile, Mary said, the markets were heading downward, which put pressure on Lehman and Humana to hurry up the second step of the deal, the closing. This made Fred, as lead partner, a bit nervous about the time it was taking Mary and the other associates to assess the details.

Mary remembered being anxious, too:

> So one day I go up to breakfast in the legendary Lehman partners' dining room with Fred to talk about this. He couldn't understand

why it was taking so long, so I am just going to have to explain it to him. And I am so nervous. So I walk in and there was this priceless Persian carpet that the Shah of Iran gave to Bobbie Lehman or something like that. I come charging in, and Fred is sitting there. And what do I do? I trip over the carpet. I was so embarrassed.

Eventually Fred put together what was then an unusual arrangement to acquire the stock from American Medicorp shareholders. It was what Mary called a "front-end-loaded and coercive exchange offer." She explained why:

The deal was done in two steps. First, we were going to tender for all of the American Medicorp stock, but we were only going to accept 51 percent of it in exchange for a mix of cash and a preferred stock in the new combined company. And then, when Humana owned 51 percent of the American Medicorp stock, we were going to a merger vote, which Humana would control because of their 51 percent ownership from the first step. The second step would be to give the 49 percent of remaining American Medicorp common shareholders debt in the new combined company. No transaction like this had been done in recent memory, although I am sure the robber barons in the 1920s did stuff like this. The challenge was that the debt would be a huge financial burden on the combined company.

I remember the Lehman Commitment Committee meeting on this deal. You need to understand that the for-profit hospital industry was extremely controversial in those days. One of the older partners on the Commitment Committee said he opposed the deal, as no one should make money off the sick and dying. And Fred said, "Oh, I suppose you don't mind the fact that one of our firm's largest clients is Philip Morris, whose products make the well sick?" That ended that conversation.

And there was a huge amount of litigation surrounding the deal. Antitrust and conflicts of interest (including a suit against Fred, who had done some work years before for American Medicorp). One of the few pluses in the situation was that Fred's old friend from Salt Lake City and Yale, Arthur Fleischer, and his celebrated law firm, Fried, Frank, Harris, Shriver & Jacobson, were representing Humana. And in fact, they won all of the key cases, and the antitrust and merger law decisions from those cases remain important precedents to this day. I can't recall the number of times I had to call Art Fleischer. I got to calling him "Uncle Arthur" because he was a mentor for me on this, the first really big deal of my life on Wall Street. He remains today my go-to lawyer for anything serious.

Meanwhile, we won the first step exchange offer—we got 98 percent of the American Medicorp stock, paid out the cash and preferred stock, and filed the documents for the second step merger. And then there was this problem. Virtually every mortgage and existing debt on all 400 combined hospitals had to be renegotiated.

Everybody at Lehman who had been working for Fred on this deal disappeared. They managed to get appointed to better deals. So here I was, trying to renegotiate all these local, tiny debt deals to permit the second step. Everybody was screaming at me. Interest rates were rising, and Goldman Sachs, representing American Medicorp, along with Loeb Rhoades, had no interest in being cooperative. Understandably, they thought rising interest rates would help their client. I finally got the debt renegotiation done. I called Steve Friedman, a partner at [the law firm] Fried Frank. I told him it was done, and he said, "Mazel tov." I was so embarrassed. I didn't know what that meant, as I was born and raised a Catholic, but I got it later when I called Fred.

So, this done, we had a meeting with Lew Glucksman, who was co-head of Lehman and head of all trading and capital markets. We had to decide what terms to put forth for debt in the second step. As this was a merger second step, we didn't have to actually underwrite these bonds, just set forth fair terms and lay them on the 49 percent American Medicorp shareholders, where Humana, in any case, controlled the shareholder vote. Risk was, if we didn't get it right, there would be lots of lawsuits. So I and two other associates put together a spreadsheet of low-rated bonds trading then in the market—very few, mostly fine old companies that had fallen on bad times, like 20th Century Fox. There wasn't any "high yield" market at the time.

Glucksman was infuriated, saying, "Lousy work. Too little data. You should all be fired." He literally threw us out of his office, physically. I was terrified; I expected to get fired the next day, and I really needed a job, as I came from a very modest family.

Finally, it was done—without anyone getting fired. Mary recalled two of her favorite Wall Street memories from that deal:

Mike Milken was then a senior trader at Drexel Burnham. He used to call me all the time during the Humana deal. He was very polite—very appropriate. He never asked me any questions, just told me what the Street was saying. He was the only person, other than Fred and me, and our client Humana, who understood the real economic outcome of this deal.

The real economic outcome was that Humana's recently built hospitals were losing money but going through their break-even points as hospital patient occupancy was rising. Hospitals are very high-fixed-cost businesses—even if only one patient is in the hospital, all the staff, capital equipment, and so forth have to be there. But once the occupancy is high enough, marginal profitability is high. Milken understood the basic economics story. When it was all over, he called me and said that our front-end-loaded, effectively coercive exchange offer, followed by a back-end merger with debt, was a key innovation in dealmaking. And in fact, this became a signature type of deal for Milken and Drexel in later years.

My second precious memory was of Marvin Levy, the elderly partner, self-made man, of Lehman. One morning after Humana/ American Medicorp had closed, I went up again to the sacred sanc- tum of the Lehman partners' dining room to meet Fred. Marvin was there, and he asked what stocks I liked these days. So I gave him the elevator pitch on Humana/American Medicorp, and why I thought Humana stock would triple in less than two or three years, maybe more. So Marvin said, "Great. Go buy me a hundred thousand."

So, I had no idea how to even enter an order, but I figured it out and bought Marvin $100,000 of Humana stock. About two years later, I again met Marvin in the Lehman dining room and he lambasted me for being a complete idiot, as I had bought him $100,000 of Humana stock, instead of what he had wanted, which was 100,000 shares. It was a complete illustration of my very mod- est middle-class background that it never occurred to me that he wanted 100,000 shares.

Marvin never forgave me for all the money he said I had lost him, because Humana's stock did indeed do incredibly well, and he perpetually reminded Fred that I was a complete idiot. To Marvin's credit, he never said that I was an idiot because I was female, just that I was an absolute idiot. For a man of his generation, it was a very nice thing.

The for-profit hospital industry went on to great investment heights. Several new companies were formed. Fred did business with almost all of them. However, in emerging industries, there is enormous rivalry among the initial companies. "The need to gain investor acceptance always leads to negative comments by compet- itors about their peers," said Fred, "and the problem of conflicts for investment bankers. Who can we represent? Can we only represent one company?"

THREADING A COMPETITIVE NEEDLE: HCA AND HUMANA

Another huge player in the hospital space was Tennessee-based Hospital Corporation of America (HCA). Founded by Thomas Frist, it was run thereafter by his son, Thomas Frist Jr., who asked Fred to help with an acquisition. This was a problem, though, because such a deal might be a conflict of interest with Humana in this highly competitive industry. "Much like Genentech and Cetus," recalled Mary, "the hospital companies were extremely competitive. So you had to choose one or the other." Fred said, "I told [Frist], I think that's great, but I have to get permission from Humana, because this is potentially a conflict."

Before asking Humana's permission, however, Fred needed to know more about the deal to see if it really was a conflict, while at the same time keeping Tom Frist's interest. Fred said there were a crazy couple of days when Frist wanted to come to New York to discuss the deal with Lehman head Pete Peterson and Fred. Frist, however, hadn't yet revealed the specifics of the deal, saying that Fred needed to read some documents in a box then sitting over at Morgan Stanley, one of Lehman's arch-rivals. Originally, Morgan Stanley was going to do the acquisition for HCA but had been fired by Frist. Fred remembered:

> What happened was HCA went to Morgan Stanley to potentially do the deal, and Morgan got real haughty, so Tommy [Frist] told them to do you-know-what. So that's when he called me. And I didn't know what the deal was. He said, "It's highly confidential, and I can't tell you what it is. But I'll have Morgan Stanley send all the boxes and materials to you."

Fred called Morgan Stanley and said, "Dr. Frist asked you to please send the materials over to me." And the guy said, "You can go guess-what yourself. You send someone here to get it from us." But Tom Frist was already on his way to New York for a meeting with Lehman that very morning. "So I said to the people at Lehman Brothers, including Mary and Pete Peterson, who was preparing to meet Tommy in a conference room, 'Look, when these people arrive at 8 o'clock in the morning, do not discuss this subject until I know for sure we can do it.'" Fred was able to put off Frist until that evening, and then went to work trying to sort through the situation. He recounted the chain of events:

> I sent a runner over to Morgan Stanley to get the box with the papers in it. I opened up the first page and then I closed it and said, "Oh my God, this is a potential conflict," because it involved a company that Humana might want to acquire.
>
> I called up Wendell Cherry, who ran Humana with David Jones. I talked to Wendell, and I had to be careful what I said. He said, "Fred, you tell us it's not a problem, so it's not a problem, but you need to clear it with David."
>
> I called up David, who was on a flight from Minneapolis to Chicago. I got David on the phone in the airplane. I say, "David, we've got to get permission for us to do this because it's potentially a conflict, since Humana could be interested in this deal. But frankly, on your balance sheet there is no way you can do this transaction." Which was true. He said, "Well, Fred, I'm not exactly sure what you're talking about but if it's OK with Wendell, that's OK with me."
>
> We met with Tommy that night, and we started on this acquisition project for HCA. We went down to a meeting in Nashville with the board of directors of HCA. There must have been twenty-five people in this room, lawyers, Mary, and so forth. Tommy Frist's secretary comes into the meeting, looks over to me and said, "Mr. Frank, you must come out to take this phone call."
>
> I went out and it's David and Wendell on the phone, and they are furious with me, really ripping. Someone had told them the details of the HCA deal. They said, "How can you do this to us?

You've been our banker." And I said, "Look, I can't even tell you what it is." They said, "Hey, you've got to know what it is; we're calling you at HCA, right?" I never did figure out who leaked this, but we lost Humana's business.

And by the way, we didn't get the deal done for HCA, either. They backed out. We told them how to do the deal, it was great for them, but then they chickened out.

Fred and Mary told the rest of the story together:

FRED: So fast-forward and it's now maybe a month later. It's the Humana annual meeting in Louisville. I said to Mary, "We're going to the annual meeting. We haven't done anything wrong. I think we're still their banker." Mary told me, "I'm not going."

MARY: Well, what you forgot to tell in this story is that all along, I told you that everyone at Humana was going to be furious, and you didn't want to hear it. You didn't want to hear it, because you wanted to do this transaction.

FRED: Probably true.

MARY: And Pete Peterson wanted to do this transaction, and I told you exactly what would happen, and it happened.

FRED: I insisted that we go to Louisville. We're sitting and having breakfast in the hotel, the Hyatt, which was the only big hotel in Louisville at the time. That's where the annual meeting was. So all these Humana guys were there in broad daylight, and they didn't even talk to us. I said to Mary, "We're taking the high road here, and we're sitting in the front row." Mary said, "I'm sitting in the back row." And I said, "No, we're sitting in the front row."

MARY: We went to the meeting, and we eventually resurrected the Humana business. Fred is really good at this kind of thing.

The denouement of this rivalry between HCA and Humana, the first and second leading companies in the for-profit hospital industry, actually came in 1988 when Fred and Mary got married at the Harvard Club in New York City. Shortly before, HCA had decided to go private, and Humana contemplated a white knight/hostile offer for HCA to compete with the going-private HCA deal. Fred and Mary represented Humana, but Arthur Fleischer and the firm Fried, Frank, Harris, Shriver & Jacobson, who had so well represented Humana in its American Medicorp acquisition, this time chose to represent HCA. Mary recalled how the dichotomy crept into her personal life.

> As Fred's oldest and best friend, Arthur Fleischer was best man at our wedding. But he was representing HCA. It was really weird. I left a $5 billion leveraged loan negotiation on behalf of Humana to host my wedding rehearsal dinner. In the end, Humana declined to bid; it was definitely a weird time!

Fred and Mary went on to do significant business in the rapidly emerging and consolidating for-profit hospital industry. Mary also remembers a signal victory for her during this crazy period of weddings and deals. "I got Fred to get rid of those ugly, heavy, dark green glasses," she said with a smile and a roll of the eyes.

IRRATIONAL EXUBERANCE, PART ONE

By the early to mid-1980s biotechnology was shifting from an experiment and a hope to an industry. The defining moment came in dramatic fashion when, on October 14, 1980, the NASDAQ opened and Genentech's stock started to trade as an IPO. The initial offering price for one million shares was $35 per share. Within hours it had soared to $85 a share before floating down to close at a still astonishing $71.25. This doubling of a new technology company's stock in a single day—an unheard-of spike at that time—provided immediate legitimacy to the new science of genetic engineering in the public consciousness, not only as a means of scrambling DNA, but also as a wealth-generating technology.

It also pushed the funding of emerging technologies into a new era for how new ideas were financed. Fred explained:

> With the Genentech IPO we created a new paradigm. This is very important. It was the first time we had a biotech IPO do spectacularly well having been funded by venture capital companies. That's a very important concept and moment, in my opinion. Plus these were companies that were going to take ten to fifteen years for a new product, spending hundreds of millions of dollars with no assurance of success. This was the ultimate in venture capital, but that pre-revenue, pre-profit, pre-product venture capital also included public investors, perhaps for the first time in history.

Fred, however, was not a part of the Genentech offering. He had begun calling on Bob Swanson, the CEO of Genentech, soon after the company was founded. He also had spent time with venture capitalist Tom Perkins, chairman of Genentech's board of directors. Perkins's firm, Kleiner Perkins, had provided early funding for Swanson and Boyer's fledgling company. Perkins had asked Fred to be involved in the IPO, but couched this in a friendly ultimatum. "Fred, you have to make a choice," Fred recalled him saying. "If you want to work with us, you can't work with Cetus. We're too competitive." Fred sensed that the Genentech offering was going to be spectacular, but declined to be involved, with regrets. "I felt I had an obligation to Cetus because I had been working with them for a few years," he said. "I did not accept the Genentech offer, and unfortunately was not involved in their extraordinarily successful IPO."

The IPO was unique for its size and for the rise in the share price on that first day. And yet it made no real sense as a purely business proposition since the company had no revenues and no real products. But as Fred and many others noted at the time, investing in Genentech was driven by more than money. "Genentech was an offering of passion," said Fred. He explained the company's intrinsic appeal:

> When Genentech went public so many people invested because they thought they were going to do good. These investors were people who were reading the lay press about this new world we called molecular biology. Journalists wrote a lot of articles and people read about these magic bullets and silver bullets that were going to cure everything. So, people invested thinking they were doing good. And, you know, they thought they might one day help their families, they might help themselves.

Jeremy Levin, CEO of Ovid Therapeutics and former CEO of pharma giant Teva, agrees.

> What has differentiated the biotech world from that of the pharmaceutical is that the biotech world retains incredible passion to drive medicines, not just from the research side, but also from across the whole spectrum. So one of the things embedded in biotech today is that clearly remarkable focus on passion. It's not just risk, it's passion.

Fred said there was a serious downside to this, however. It created an expectation that turned out to be overblown, an "irrational exuberance."

We created this expectational force for discovering new drugs to cure all these problems: Alzheimer's disease, cancer, whatever it was, because it's the new science. But there was very little appreciation of how complex it was.

In part this came from a kind of technological arrogance, a sense that those who were part of the biotech revolution were creating something new as a kind of unstoppable force that would radically change everything in a way that the "old" world of pharma simply didn't get. British virologist George Poste has jokingly described this superciliousness as a willingness to believe that everything new was great and noble and everything old was irrelevant. He remembered going to a meeting where the new science was being discussed with what he calls "reverential awe and exuberance," and how he responded to it:

> I listened to all these presentations, and rather cynically at the end I said, "Well, I'm really appreciative that I can encounter so many scampering mammals amongst the dinosaurs. But do we really think we're that much smarter than any other generation? It has taken 150 years to generate thirty to forty fully integrated pharmaceutical companies, and now 1,800 new biotech companies think they can make that transition in the next decade? Most of them are destined to be extinct."

Poste was right, of course. It has been extremely rare for newfangled bio-companies to transform themselves into the likes of Merck and Roche. The few that have—Amgen, Genentech, Vertex, and a handful of others—tended to make the jump to the big leagues as much because of luck—Amgen successfully cloning erythropoietin, for instance, which became the blockbuster Epogen just five years after the company's founding—as it was brilliance in science or business.

Fred summed up this idea in a research paper he drafted in the early 1970s about rising tech companies. "Unless the continuity of the old and the new, the linkage of past and future, are brought into the focus of current opinion, it will betray itself into action without the protection of contemplation." He also likened the idea of irrational exuberance as a kind of lottery where everyone—entrepreneurs, investors, even the general public—periodically was sure they were going to win. Certainly, this was the case in the wake of the Genentech IPO.

MORE PHARMA DEALS, WITH A TOUCH OF BIOTECH

As exciting as it was to be around biotechnology in the early 1980s, the real action in terms of mega-deals remained with Big Pharma, which was historically just entering its most explosive period of blockbuster growth. In 1980, only two drug companies were in the Fortune 100—at #78 was Johnson & Johnson, which sold far more than drugs, and Wyeth was at #99. A decade later, in 1990, seven drug companies were among Fortune's top 100 companies.

Fred and Lehman were major players in the river of deals that began flowing in the early eighties, as George Poste remembered:

> I believe Fred was involved directly in SmithKline acquiring Beckman in 1980, and also Allergan in 1981. He was a very regular feature at corporate headquarters in Philadelphia, so I can't recall accurately whether Lehman and Fred were actually involved in those transactions as the primary bankers or just proffering advice, but Fred was very highly visible and trusted by the CEOs of SmithKline, SmithKline Beckman, and SmithKline Beecham.

Fred was also closely following biotech, said Poste, and thinking about how to connect up pharma and biotech, which of course was what happened with the Genentech-Roche deal that Fred engineered later that decade. Poste recalled Fred's insight:

> The 1980s were the heyday in some ways of all aspects of drug discovery, developments in Big Pharma and biotech as well. I think Fred was clearly in the vanguard of understanding the dynamic of the emerging biotech industry and the opportunity to create entirely new financing vehicles, either straight traditional venture capital models or additional creative financing models. So I met him in the context of that.

Poste remembered that Fred was trusted by both sides:

> Fred was enmeshed in both camps: biotech, with all the creative financing vehicles constantly wanting to position those companies in relation to Big Pharma, and at the same time he was an advisor to Big Pharma.

Still, despite all of the heat and passion being generated by Genentech and other biotech companies, pharma remained mostly aloof at this stage from these fledgling efforts that were so far afield from their chemistry-based history. "Most pharma companies didn't think much of biotech," said Poste. "I remember one company executive saying: 'What the hell is happening here, this will all go away.' In most cases with most biotech companies, they were right." Still, contended Poste, there was obviously something important going on with the new bio-based efforts.

> There were those in pharma who had fast ins to what was serious in biotech, and I like to think that SmithKline was one of those. That was a binary dimension. Mainly you either pursued projects internally, which SmithKline did for the most part, or you recognized

the importance of investing externally, including with biotech companies. I think that's what Bristol Myers Squibb did, more than any others.

By the time of the Genentech IPO, Lehman Brothers was among the most important firms doing business in and covering the life sciences. "We had the largest life sciences practice on Wall Street," said Fred, although the Street in those days was much smaller. The community had grown since Fred arrived as a young man in the late 1950s, although the essential elements of that earlier period remained, including investment firms retaining their status as partnerships rather than corporations, and operating by way of informal networks that people like Fred developed among colleagues, rivals, and clients. This was the glue that held the enterprise/ecosystem together. "That is why I spent a great deal of my time," Fred said, "helping out with analysis and advice to people who might or might not end up giving us business. It was how it was done, because when they needed a banker, they would turn to the guy who had been there to help out over the years."

"People really valued advice because there weren't many people with big purview of the world, segments, and industries," added Mary. "Loyalty also mattered."

Mary continued:

Remember that the whole Wall Street community developed around commercial finance, those who trade commercial paper. Commercial paper has existed since the Middle Ages, right? But that's what the investment banks did. They also did bond offerings. Stock offerings, too, but they were not very common in those days because the great boom of entrepreneurial businesses didn't happen until the eighties and nineties.

George Poste added:

Wall Street was a very different beast at that time, because there was something called "patient capital," which no longer exists. That's an oxymoronic term now. I think that the question of value creation, whether for a large company or for a small company, was really still a principle that the banks understood and did their best to support. It wasn't just a strategy to fund a company in order to be better able to flip it. That was the Goldman model for mortgages applied to companies. I think patient capital was definitely an operating principle and an ethos at that time. Of course, with the emerging biotech industry, the numbers of transactions that could occur between Big Pharma and Big Business were relatively small at that point.

IRRATIONAL EXUBERANCE, PART TWO

Even though Fred missed out on Genentech's IPO, he still had his strong connection with Cetus, which had been growing since Alejandro Zaffaroni's call in 1974—even if the company still had no products and no prospect of sales for several years to come. Despite this, not long after Genentech went public, Fred placed a call to Cetus CEO Ronald Cape, who six years earlier had brashly suggested that his company go public. Fred said to Cape, "Now it's time."

"Mary and I led the Cetus public offering along with the investment bank Unterberg, Towbin," said Fred, "with Tommy Unterberg and Andy Malik. It was unbelievable." According to Ronald Cape, there was never any doubt that Fred and Lehman would lead the offering. "Fred was by far the best there was to do this," Cape said, "and he had been with us all along. He also was a very personable man, pleasant to be around and to do business with."

The Cetus offering went live on March 1, 1981, just four and a half months after Genentech, and brought in $122 million to the company's coffers. At the time, this was the largest IPO in history. It rode the over-the-top expectations generated by Genentech and by the biotech sector, and by a new era in America signaled by the election of President Ronald Reagan by a landslide in November 1980. He had defeated Jimmy Carter, the "malaise" president, by insisting, "It's morning in America."

Other biotech deals followed quickly as the early 1980s market revved up, fueled by expanding consumer purchases, looser credit, mergers, and new technologies. In 1981, a total of fourteen biotech companies issued IPOs, including Hybritech, a highly innovative and successful company specializing in monoclonal antibodies and immunoassay technologies that was later sold to Eli Lilly for $480 million. By the end of the 1980s, close to eighty biotech companies were being publicly traded.[7] None, however, reached the heady levels of Cetus, with most offerings bringing in $20 million to $30 million.

Despite the success of Cetus, Lehman Brothers remained reluctant to underwrite most biotech offerings, in part because most of the deals were small by Wall Street standards. The industry was also still nascent and unproven and mired in losses that would continue for years. This left traditional Wall Street bankers asking why anyone would buy these stocks.

It was a fair question. Indeed, just a year after Cetus's breathtaking IPO, the bottom fell out of the biotech market as part of a general downturn in stocks. Investors seemed to wake up to the reality of what they had invested in with such passion the year before. As the *New York Times* wrote in August 1982: "Although more than 100 companies with names like Amgen and Genex have sprung up to explore the commercial possibilities of biotechnology, the only product of gene-splicing to come to market so far has been a European vaccine against diarrhea in piglets."

Then came 1983 and another dramatic general rise in the markets, and in the prospects of biotechs. Incredibly, that year saw twenty-one biotech IPOs issued, including one that Fred worked hard to be a part of but missed out on because his partners were reluctant to plunge into the fray. This was for Amgen, a small start-up in Thousand Oaks, California, near Los Angeles, that would later become the most successful biotech company in history. But in 1983 that was not apparent, even if the company had attracted some stellar talent, including George Rathmann, a chemist and senior executive at Abbott, to be its CEO. Otherwise, Amgen's story was fairly typical of that time: a company founded with venture capitalist money, in this case coming from Silicon Valley pioneers, the venture capitalists Pitch Johnson and Bill Bowes—money that was funding a group of youthful scientists applying new biotech techniques to everything from petrol chemicals to drugs. Also typical at Amgen was how fast the company burned through the $19.4 million that Rathmann raised in 1981. It was supposed to last for four years, but was already running low by early 1983, with no prospects for more money from the original investors or anyone else. Nor were there any real products in sight.

This is where Fred stepped in. He had known Rathmann at Abbott and also knew Amgen's chief financial officer, Gordon Binder, who later succeeded Rathmann as CEO. As Binder looked around for solutions to the mounting crisis, he consulted with Fred, who made a bold suggestion: that Amgen issue an IPO to deal with its precarious cash position.

Binder and Fred took the idea to Rathmann, who was dubious at first. "We're not Genentech. We don't have a product," he argued. Fred replied, "You don't have to. Damon Biotech is going public, and they have less than you have."

Binder presented the IPO idea to the Amgen board and, as expected, it was met with a great deal of skepticism. According to Rathmann, one of the board members said, "What have you guys been smoking? This is terribly unlikely to work." According to an Amgen executive who was at the meeting, Rathmann responded, "Fred Frank thinks we can go public." It was just like an E.F. Hutton commercial. When Fred Frank speaks, everybody listens. Someone at the board meeting quipped, "Fred Frank said that?" And Bill Bowes, chairman of the board, said, "OK."

The IPO was issued on June 17, 1983, although it hardly attracted the response enjoyed by Genentech and Cetus. Priced at $18 a share, the first trade came in at $16.75 a share, which prompted traders at Smith, Barney, who led the offering, to usher Amgen CFO Binder off the trading floor. In part, this lack of interest was caused by a decidedly downward slope in the cycle of exuberance and skepticism that marked the ups and downs of biotech financing. Just a few weeks after the Amgen IPO, the markets closed down altogether to biotech, with *Forbes* opining, "Welcome to the wonderful world of biotechnology companies. Welcome to an investment fairyland where hopes and dreams count more than reality."

Amgen still managed to raise $35 million, funds that allowed them to push through the "fairyland" phase even as their stock fell to under $4 at one point. Then came Amgen's blockbuster Epogen, which boosts the production of red blood cells for anemia and liver diseases, and Neupogen, which stimulates white blood cells to counter common infections and the effects of chemotherapy in cancer. These two drugs were approved by the FDA in 1989 and 1991, respectively. Both became huge blockbusters and helped turn Amgen into a multibillion-dollar colossus, with a stock value that has risen spectacularly since the 1983 IPO.

"I was sorry to miss that one as a banker," said Fred, "although at the time it wasn't obvious that they were going to become the company they became later. And I gave them that advice because there are, sometimes, these windows in the market where a company can jump in like that, while at other times, there is no way. I wanted them to succeed, and the opportunity was there."

LEHMAN COMES AROUND

Eventually, Fred convinced his partners to become one of the more active underwriters for biotechnology, in IPOs and in mergers and acquisitions. An example of the sort of deals Fred engaged in was Applied Biosystems, which Lehman took public in 1983 as one of the first biotech tools companies. This was a category of businesses that, among other things, developed the machines and techniques to commercially sequence DNA and proteins. Using technology developed by Caltech's Leroy "Lee" Hood and Lloyd Smith, Applied Biosystems was founded in 1981 and by 1983 already had a successful product on the market—unlike Genentech, Cetus, and Amgen—a device called the Model 470A Protein Sequencer, which allowed scientists to learn the order of amino acids in a protein.

Lee Hood remembered how Applied Biosystems was established as a separate company, which actually was not the original plan. A biologist and engineer at Caltech, Hood was a pioneer of genetic sequencing technology who at first had tried marketing his inventions to established companies. But none of them were interested. He recalled:

> We ended up going to nineteen different instrument companies trying to sell this. One of them was associated with Caltech, and I visited three times. On the third visit the fellow actually said, "We know what you're selling, we're not interested. Don't come back."

This led to a suggestion by two venture capitalists to start a brand new company, the same two who launched Amgen in 1980, Bill Bowes and Pitch Johnson. Hood recounted the turning point:

> Bill Bowes, who has since become a good friend, called me up and said, "Well, I hear you unsuccessfully shopped this company around. I'll bet I can raise $2 million. Let's go out and get it started as a venture capital company and get it moving."

That caused Hood problems with Caltech, however, which in those days was very much anti–venture capital, as were most academic institutions when it came to biology and biotechnology. Hood remembered the bumpy road that led to the vital new medical tool company:

> Caltech President Marvin Goldberger blew a gasket. He said venture capitalists' money is dirty, contaminated money. Academic institutions can't get involved with them. But after about three or four months, I persuaded him that it was the only game in town. And what happened was, just as we were about to sign these papers and get Applied Biosystems started, I gave a talk to the Caltech trustees. Arnold Beckman, an inventor and founder of Beckman Instruments, was chairman emeritus of the Caltech Board of Trustees. The talk was on the future of biology and these instruments.
>
> Beckman came up afterward and said, "This is exactly what Beckman [Instruments] needs." And I said, "Well, I've been to Beckman several times trying to sell this." He said, "I don't think so," and so we flew up to visit the company the next morning. And you know what those guys that I had talked to before did? They lied. They said to Beckman: "Lee misled us, because he wanted it to be a venture capital company so he could make a lot of money." So the constraint Marvin Goldberger put on me—this was my first company, so I didn't know what it was like—was: "You can have no stock in this company."
>
> That was a difficulty for five or six years before we finally got over it. But I learned two important things. One is if you have a big futuristic idea, you go to the top. You don't deal with the middle-level profit-and-loss guys. And I learned, too, that if you have a big, new idea, don't shop it to an old company, because they'll never give you the resources you need to develop it.
>
> With Applied Biosystems, we hired good people. The entire focus of the company was all on these instruments. They were in the

black in six months because a protein sequencer we had designed was so well engineered; they basically used our designs for it and everything.

It was such an exciting company. And Fred was a part of things early on, as an advisor. Everyone liked and trusted him. And when they went public, they asked Fred to get involved.

The company prospered, reaching $182 million in sales by 1992. The next year, Perkin-Elmer acquired it in a $330 million transaction. Soon after, the Applied Biosystems division of Perkin-Elmer began supplying machines to a raft of genomics start-ups such as Human Genome Sciences, Myriad Genetics, and Millennium Pharmaceuticals. They also became a major supplier for labs working on the $3 billion, government-financed Human Genome Project through the 1990s and beyond—and eventually for the private effort at Celera led by Craig Venter. Fred commented:

> The importance of instruments and tools in the emergence of the biotech industry cannot be underestimated. Science, essentially, is what we can see or measure. Companies like Applied Biosystems, Qiagen—which I took public in 1996—and others. This continues, including the important PCR [Polymerase Chain Reaction] technology invented at Cetus, which allows rapid replication of small protein samples and DNA in large enough amounts to study fruitfully.
>
> More recently, PCR has been an important tool to use in testing people to see if they've been infected by the COVID virus. I sold PCR technology to Roche in 1991, in the context of the Cetus/Chiron merger. It later became a multibillion franchise for Roche Diagnostics.

ANOTHER NON-PHARMA DEAL: "TWAGONS"

Fred has always had extraordinary peripheral vision on investment opportunities. Nowhere was this better illustrated than in the offering for Chrysler that he masterminded in 1983. It was obvious to Fred, as he traveled in taxis in New York, and he saw the roads clogged up with broken-down cars (this was common in the late 1970s and early 1980s), that once the US emerged from the Reagan recession of the early 1980s, that Americans were going to buy new cars again. Lots of new cars. That's what gave Fred a seemingly crazy idea about Chrysler, a company that three years earlier had nearly gone bankrupt and was bailed out by a $1.5 billion loan guarantee from the US Congress, a controversial move that President Jimmy Carter had signed into law in January of 1980.

Chrysler was then being led by its celebrity CEO, Lee Iacocca. Having been fired from Ford, Iacocca came to Chrysler with some of his key colleagues, including Hal Sperlich. Iacocca and Sperlich had collaborated at Ford on one of the most successful cars in history, the Mustang. Iacocca, however, had very little to work with at Chrysler. The only newish model they offered at the time was the aging K Car, but he and Sperlich had moved quickly to remedy this, developing what they called the "garageable van wagon," now known as the minivan. With this backdrop, Fred said, he launched his idea in 1983:

> One day I called the three people at Lehman Brothers who were then leading the firm—Peter Solomon, Roger Altman, and Vincent May. We called them the Troika. I asked them to have breakfast to talk about an idea. They said, "Well, what's your idea?" I said, "Come to breakfast, and you'll find out." So at breakfast, I said, "In my opinion, one of America's 50 largest companies for the first time since World War II was ready to reenter the equity market, and I think this is going to be a symbolic offering." They asked, "Fred, what does that mean? What's a symbolic offering?" I said, "Well, the symbolism is

they've been restored to health, and if they can raise fresh capital, they'll be even healthier, and it'll feed on itself."

They said, "Well, Fred, what drug company are you talking about?"
I said, "I'm not talking about a drug company. I'm talking about Chrysler."

Lehman had represented the banks and institutions that had provided huge amounts of debt to Chrysler before the company was rescued by an act of Congress. So it was an odd situation. Roger Altman, a managing director of Lehman at that time, had been a member of the US government team that made the $1.5 billion rescue loan. Steve Miller, who has since gone on to a remarkable career in restructuring, was at that time chief financial officer of Chrysler. Fred described the details of the deal:

Steve was a brilliant, very detail-oriented CFO. He thought this proposed offering was crazy. Chrysler had just been through hell and back, and the last thing that anyone expected was an offering of shares. Iacocca loved it, but it was a hard sell to banks. They had just been burned by Chrysler with the bailout, and even though the company was doing much better, there was not a lot of love there. Steve wanted to get the banks, which owned preferred stock they received in lieu of their debt, to convert their preferred stock to common stock in this offering, so that the capital structure of Chrysler would become "normal." The shares we would sell would be secondary shares, the old preferred stock converted to common and sold to the public.

Salomon Brothers, Chrysler's lead banker of record, was scared pissless at doing this deal. I wanted to file a $200 million deal, but Salomon wanted to file a $100 million deal, because they were afraid that there would not be enough demand. So we filed a $100 million deal. And as we went through the road show, the demand kept picking up, so we increased it from $100 to $200 million. In the end, we did $400-plus million, and the stock, in the meantime, went from a bit less than $3 to something like $16-plus. So Chrysler did convert the preferred stock, raising a huge amount of money, which helped them get back on their feet and pay their bills, pay back the government loan, get a normal capital structure, and I think, the pensions for their workers, and all the rest.

In all, Chrysler issued 26 million shares of common stock that brought in $432 million.[8] Mary recalled the thrill of working on this deal and credited a bit of her own upward mobility to it:

It was one of the most exciting deals of my life. Very challenging as a finance matter. The documents we eventually filed with the SEC were about two feet thick, reflecting the profound change in Chrysler's capital structure. And then there was the fear that the new Chrysler "garageable van wagon," essentially a concept car, wouldn't make it. I used to call it "Puff the Magic Twagon." In that case Chrysler would be back in the soup.

But Iacocca's and Sperlich's sure understanding of cars, demographics, and the burgeoning growth of the suburbs led to an enormous success, just as they had in a different time with the Mustang. Soccer moms loved the "Twagon." It was two or three years until Ford and GM could catch up.

I think more than any other deal Fred and I did, this one contributed to my being made a partner-principal at Lehman. The older partners were never impressed with Fred's and my Big Pharma deals, or biotech. But remaking one of America's heartland companies was different.

WALL STREET EMBRACES
INNOVATION IN FITS AND STARTS

As the mid-eighties approached, Fred was in his early fifties and Wall Street was now entering a rarified moment in its history when the big firms became a key component to financing a wave of new technologies in computers, biotech, industrial automation, and a number of other new or modernizing fields. Many of these efforts were venture backed, with public offerings or acquisitions as the final stage in a financing pipeline for companies ranging from Apple and Lotus to Cetus and Applied Biosystems, all of whom had developed their novel products during the seventies and early eighties. Wall Street's engagement as the underwriter for significant capital during the eighties was volatile, however, with wild swings that saw periods of heat and speculation and sudden losses of confidence.

There is no better example than the ups and downs of biotech IPOs. For instance, in 1980–81 the number of IPOs soared with the issuance of Genentech and Cetus, leading to the fourteen biotech companies that issued IPOs in 1981, followed by 1982 when only four biotech IPOs were issued. Then came another gush in 1983 when Amgen and Applied Biosystems, among others, issued their offerings. And so the decade went with its wet and dry spells, occurring one right after another.

Wall Street's backing of high-technology offerings, however skittish, was a far cry from years past, when Fred and Sandy Robertson were young bankers at Smith, Barney and the senior partners laughed at their efforts to back emerging companies in everything from computers to "ray guns." In part, this sea change was driven by the passion that Fred and others spoke with to investors and financiers who wanted to support the latest "cool" tech industry, a passion that nonetheless remained disassociated from the real prospects of many companies and efforts. Few industries epitomized this more than biotech. George Poste recalled the dynamic:

With the emergence of the biotech industry, not only did Wall Street see the ability to accelerate innovation, they saw the emergence of this entirely new sector. Probably from 1985 we had quite a proliferation in the biotech industry courtesy of cheap capital and uncritical capital. You could literally come out of any academic lab with any half-assed idea and get funded at that point. The buoyancy of the economy meant that venture capitalists could exit quickly and pass the risk onto others in a way they cannot do today.

Bill Rutter, former CEO of Chiron, remembered some of the factors contributing to the momentum:

> If you look at the talks that I gave in the eighties, the projections that I made—that it would take about five years to get a vaccine done, and stuff like this—well, they were based partly on enthusiasm and partly on what we thought we could do, but without an understanding of the regulatory process and how difficult it would be to make this into a business. The markets, though, went along with this flush of interest and activity.
>
> And Fred and others who controlled capital—Lehman, Morgan Stanley, and the banks out here—gradually became not only captivated, but a small group of folks, honestly, were selecting the winners and losers.

This was Fred's moment, but just as the deals were beginning to flow, the base that had largely supported Fred since 1969, Lehman Brothers, was faltering. The small, close-knit group of partners at One William Street was about to be transformed into something new and very different as the late eighties revved up and the great banks began, in fits and starts, to go from modest-size to globe-girding colossi.

CHAPTER 5

The Banks Get Bigger and the Deals Fly

LEHMAN FALLS THE FIRST TIME, WALL STREET
SEESAWS, AND A GOLDEN AGE OF INNOVATION
AND HIGH TECHNOLOGY ARISES, 1984–1989

*There was a great distinction being a partner at Lehman Brothers.
It gave you pride. You were known as a smart, tough guy who
lived by his intelligence and his integrity. What a passport to
carry. There wasn't a person in the world I couldn't call.*

—Henry Breck, Lehman Brothers Partner, c. 1984[1]

In April 1984, the fifty-one-year-old Fred Frank was on a British Airways flight from London to Copenhagen when a flight attendant approached him. "She said, 'Mr. Frank, you have to get off this plane,'" Fred recalled. "'We have a message that you must return to New York.' She couldn't tell me anything else, which made me a little scared. You don't know if something has happened to your family or what it was. Then I found out that we were having a partners' meeting to decide on the sale of Lehman to American Express.

"This wasn't completely unexpected," Fred said. "Wall Street was going through a very, very difficult period at the time, and the markets were very volatile." Lehman was also going through a dramatic, head-spinning transition from being highly profitable in the fall of 1983 to suffering spectacular losses just a few months later, a turn-around that had as much to do with an intense rivalry among top executives at Lehman as it did with the worsening markets. The situation was so dire that the very existence of the 134-year-old firm was in serious question as Fred hopped on the next available flight from Copenhagen back to New York.

Lehman's distress had begun with a nasty clash the summer of 1983 between Pete Peterson, the patrician CEO of Lehman since 1973, and the scrappy former head of sales and trading Lewis Glucksman, who had been at the firm since 1963. In 1981 Peterson had elevated Glucksman to be president of the firm, running day-to-day operations. Then in May 1983 Peterson had tapped Glucksman to be co-CEO.

Peterson had joined the firm as a partner in June 1973 after his stint as Commerce Secretary to President Richard Nixon. He came from humble roots as the son of a Greek immigrant, but had risen fast in corporate America before Nixon asked him to be part of his cabinet, and had departed the administration before Watergate engulfed it. He had come to Lehman with little experience in banking and few expectations other than exploiting his impressive Rolodex for potential deals, only to be asked by the partners three months after his arrival to run the firm, which had struggled since Bobbie Lehman's death in 1969. Part of the struggle at the time was precipitated by an $8 million loss by the firm's trading department, then headed by Glucksman. The traders had blundered by buying a large cache of bonds that Lehman's traders were unable to sell at a profit. This was a breathtaking loss in those days and had led many partners to demand that Peterson, as one of his first acts as CEO, sack Glucksman.

Peterson demurred, knowing that Glucksman's departure would cause other traders to exit while further sharpening the divide between the traditionally more cerebral and genteel bankers and the rough-and-tumble traders. These two groups on Wall Street had long been wary of each other, but the clout of the traders—whose status had always been below the bankers—had risen in the sixties and seventies as traders for the first time began producing serious profits, even if their business remained volatile and prone to sudden gains and equally abrupt losses.

By 1983, Pete Peterson had guided the firm back into profitability and success from the low point in 1973, increasing its capital tenfold, to more than $250 million. Under Peterson, Lehman Brothers had acquired Abraham & Co. and then had merged with the esteemed but fraught Kuhn, Loeb & Co. in 1976. The combined firms became Lehman Brothers, Kuhn, Loeb Inc., the fourth-largest US investment bank in America. Profits in 1983 were $123 million, up from $117 million the year before, while the average Lehman partner's equity in the firm was $2.3 million. By the standards of that era, it was impressive.

According to Ken Auletta, author of *Greed and Glory on Wall Street: The Fall of the House of Lehman*,[2] a book about the Peterson-Glucksman feud and subsequent sale to American Express, Fred at this time was low-key in terms of firm politics. But he was crucial to the profit machine Peterson had created, being among the banking division's largest revenue producers as he devoted his time not to office machinations but to spinning out deals.

Peterson, who preferred associating with blue bloods and his old pals from Washington, clearly favored the more cultured bankers within Lehman. At one point he told an interviewer that Lehman's "creative entrepreneurial work" was the basis of the firm's success, not trading stocks and bonds. Intellectual dealmakers like Fred agreed with this sentiment, but it rankled the traders, particularly since in the early 1980s Glucksman's trading team had more than recovered from their 1974 loss and were generating more than half of the company's profits. This reality, and the expanding number of traders and other employees, had prompted Peterson to move Lehman from the venerable—but much too small—offices at One William Street to a modern skyscraper at 55 Water Street. Some banking partners grumbled about leaving One William Street but went along as Lehman prospered.

By the spring of 1983 the tensions between the traders and the bankers had reached another fever pitch, with Glucksman's senior trader, 37-year-old Dick Fuld, referring to "those f'ing bankers" to colleagues on the trading floor, according to Ken Auletta. Fuld, a protégé of Lewis Glucksman, would later take the helm of Lehman Brothers when it again became independent in the 1990s, leading it to dizzying heights and then to the spectacular crash in the second and final fall of Lehman in 2008, a disaster that was again driven by fantastic losses by traders. The losses during this second fall, however, were not millions of dollars of partners' money, like in 1974 and 1983, but tens of billions of dollars of other people's money, an amount so staggering that it became a major trigger for the global meltdown in late 2008 and the Great Recession that followed.

According to author and *Financial Times* correspondent Peter Chapman, author of *The Last of the Imperious Rich: Lehman Brothers, 1844–2008*,[3] Pete Peterson in 1983 had elevated Glucksman to be co-CEO in an effort to be diplomatic. In Washington, this was often the preferred method for placating rival groups and competitors. But not on Wall Street, where ambitions could be bare-knuckled and abrupt, particularly when a competitor saw an opening or a weakness. Lew Glucksman saw both emerging in the summer of 1983, sensing that Peterson had lost touch with many in the firm, particularly the traders, and that he was probably going to move on from Lehman in the near future anyway to spend more time with his high-class pals. Peterson also behaved imperiously, speaking in long monologues about his ideas and accomplishments that were peppered with big names like Henry Kissinger and the Rockefellers. This drove a gruff, less eloquent man like Lew Glucksman crazy.

He made his move in the summer of 1983, forcing out Peterson with a combination of threats and a large payout that left Glucksman the sole CEO by October 1. His victory, however, was short-lived as the new commander in chief of Lehman once again courted disaster by first shifting bonuses and compensation away from bankers, who traditionally got the largest bonuses, to traders. Glucksman also snatched a large share of the bonus pool for himself and a few key lieutenants like Fuld. This led to an exodus of prominent bankers, including Eric Gleacher, the king of merger and acquisition deals at Lehman, and Stephen Schwarzman, who later teamed up with Peterson to cofound the Blackstone investment firm.

By the spring of 1984, the departing partners had taken with them some $30 million in capital, 17 percent of the total, precipitating what remaining partners began calling "the capital issue." This issue became more alarming as the markets took a nosedive that spring, driving down the firm's revenues to a mere $7.1 million from October 1983 to February 1984, compared to $87.3 million during the same period a year earlier. Most of this steep decline had come from a fall in income from traders, including a number of disastrous trades by Fuld's department that dwarfed the $8 million Glucksman had lost ten years earlier. By the end of March, Lehman's equity value had fallen by more than $100 million to only $145 million and was still dropping.

Not that Lehman was alone in tumbling fortunes. As an industry, Wall Street houses earned a mere $150 million in the second quarter of 1984 compared to $1.5 billion a year earlier. The difference, as Fred said, was that other banks had larger capitalizations and were able to absorb the decline in revenues, while Lehman could not. This was in part because many of Lehman's rivals had either merged with or been acquired by larger corporations with deep pockets. For instance, Shearson/American Express was sitting on a capitalization of $1 billion and Phibro-Salomon of $1.3 billion. "Glucksman had made a bet again on treasuries like he had before Peterson joined, and it had gone the wrong way again," remembered Mary Tanner, adding that the stunning decline of the firm left everyone reeling. She recalled her thoughts of Glucksman's actions at the time:

> Oh God, what's he doing? Lehman Brothers had gone through the first of its near-death experiences in 1973 because Glucksman had risked the balance sheet on Treasury bonds and interest rates. The firm had nearly collapsed, and the partners had brought in Pete Peterson. Now Glucksman had done it again!

AMERICAN EXPRESS OFFERS LEHMAN A DEAL

As the spring of 1984 wore on, the losses mounted, and the defections continued. Glucksman tried, and failed, to bring in another bank with cash as a partner with a 50 percent stake, which would allow Lehman to stay independent and for him to retain control. Many partners had suggested this option earlier, but the CEO had refused. Now it was too late, with Lehman's fortunes in such a steep decline that there was little interest from other banks for a merger.

In the first week in April, *Fortune* magazine ran a blistering article about how Lewis Glucksman had severely wounded one of the great houses on the Street in just a matter of months. The piece detailed the defections and losses and publicly predicted the further collapse of Lehman, stunning Fred and Mary and other partners yet again.

That weekend, the CEO of Shearson/American Express, Peter Cohen, was at his house in the Hamptons and read the *Fortune* story. Months earlier he had engaged in a brief discussion with Glucksman and with American Express chairman and CEO James Robinson about a possible acquisition or merger of his bank with Lehman, which had gone nowhere. Now the Shearson head sensed the time was right. Robinson agreed. "American Express and Jim Robinson had this desire to become a global financial services company," said Fred, "and now he had a chance to acquire a major investment bank." Cohen contacted Lehman, and a reluctant Glucksman was forced by the firm's board to consider a sale to Shearson.

Like many partners, Fred, who arrived from Copenhagen for the discussions, was horrified by the idea of selling to a mega-bank that would demote Lehman to a mere division of a large corporation. Shearson also was not nearly as prestigious as Lehman. "The deal they wanted was for Lehman to be purchased at two and a half times book value," said Fred, a meager return for a firm that had been worth almost twice as much just a few months earlier. This led Fred and several other partners to discuss with former US Secretary of the Treasury and investor William Simon an attempt to put together a financing to inject money into the firm and save it from the American Express deal. Fred recounted how at one point during this debate he stood up and railed on the situation:

> We were sitting at our big partners' dining table, and I gave this big speech. I said, "Gentlemen, I hate to tell you that we are breaking a covenant with Bobbie Lehman, even though he is dead." I said that I got my partnership interest directly from Bobbie Lehman. I bought his shares at book value. Bobbie could have sold his firm at a huge price, but he wanted to see the continuity of the special character that we had at Lehman Brothers. But the other partners were scared. They strong-armed us to go for the sale.

Mary Tanner, who was at the meeting, added:

> Several of the principals—the nonvoting equity owners of the firm—
> met with Bill Simon, whose private equity firm could have bought
> Lehman or invested in it. But he told us that "the mind of the firm
> was gone."

By April 10, just seven days after Peter Cohen first approached
Lehman, the negotiations were completed, and the board had voted
to approve the sale of Lehman Brothers for $380 million. This put
money in the pockets of the partners—including Fred—but left nearly
everyone in shock. Others were relieved the ordeal was over, even if
they weren't happy with the outcome. "It was like waking up from a
nightmare," partner François de Saint Phalle told Ken Auletta.

A few days later, the new CEO of the combined firms, Peter Cohen
of Shearson, visited the Lehman partners and associates assembled in
the boardroom at 55 Water Street. More partners had exited with the
sale, and of course Glucksman was out, but many had stayed, including
Fred. Mary remembered how she worried about the changes to come,
including the possibility that she and other principals who owned non-
voting equity might be axed as the new firm consolidated:

> We were all terrified because we were sure that many of us would be
> gone, and the system was about to change from this cottage industry
> and mentoring system that had been the Lehman way for so long.
> You started as an associate and worked your way up being assigned
> to partners, and you spent your career there building a reputation.

Cohen later told Ken Auletta his impressions of this meeting.
"They were shell-shocked," said Cohen, recalling that he tried to reas-
sure them. "I want you to know that we have a great organization," he
said to the Lehman partners and associates. "I made $1.2 million last

year, and 17 people at Shearson made more than me." Auletta then
quoted the reaction of Lehman partner Henry Breck to Cohen's comments, "We all rolled our eyes, because after taxes we all made more
than him." Mary describes a meeting the next day with Cohen and just
the associates and other key staff.

> Usually we used the institutional sales conference room for big meet-
> ings like this one, but this meeting was really big, and the room
> wasn't that large. Every associate in the firm was there, and anybody
> else who wanted to come was there. The room was packed like a
> sardine can. It was hot, this was May, and in walked this short guy,
> Peter Cohen.
>
> He had some other people with him and there were always two
> screens up there so the salesmen could see the slide shows. So he put
> up this thing about Shearson. And Cohen starts talking about how at
> Shearson we really understand your business. He started giving some
> examples of the businesses that Shearson did like real estate deals
> and others. He said they had a partnership business that would do
> these so-called "creative transactions." One of the best ones was they
> sold a bunch of barges on the Great Lakes and the Mississippi River,
> although it didn't work out too well because a lot of the barges sank.
>
> All of us were sitting and standing there, with the principals,
> including me, sitting in the front row. We got there early just so we
> could see what was going to happen. So Peter is going on and on, and
> we were looking at him getting more and more involved, and all of a
> sudden this woman faints, passes out cold on the floor. And Cohen
> looks over his shoulder and goes on. Some people who were with
> Cohen picked this woman up bodily and took her out.

Later that day, Mary said that she decided to do something that had
not been allowed in the Lehman days. As a principal, she decided to
have lunch in the partners' dining room. "We associates and principals

were never formally invited to have lunch at the partners' table because we weren't real people. We were sort of . . ."

". . . second class citizens," Fred finished for her.

"But at that point nobody really cared, so I decided, I am going up to lunch. I don't care what they think. I am going up to the partners' table. So I got up to the partners' table, I sat down and . . ."

". . . and you were the only woman there," Fred completed her sentence.

"Yeah, the only woman," she said. "So, I sat down, and no one said anything. I started eating, and I noticed that the seat at the head of this big oval table is empty. That's where Glucksman had sat"—and Peterson and Bobbie Lehman before him. Mary describes what happened next:

> In comes Peter Cohen. He looks around. The table was pretty full that day. He sees the seat at the head of the table, and sits down in it. There was this silence. Total silence—no more clattering of silver or anything. Conversation stopped and everyone looked down the table at Peter. I always liked Peter Cohen. He tried very hard, you know. His whole dream had been to buy a great investment bank, and because of our own partner's stupidity, he got to do it. So then he was always trying to prove, to assure that he was a worthy CEO. Peter was always very kind to me and Fred, and respectful. It was only our idiot Lehman partners who spoiled what could have been a wonderful merger.
>
> That day everyone was quiet, and one of our wonderful waiters—most of them had worked for Lehman for twenty, thirty, forty years, and—one of them had worked for fifty years, since the time he had been a boy—one of them comes up to Peter and asks, "What would you like for lunch, sir?" We were all just transfixed because Peter is sitting in Bobbie Lehman's legendary seat. And Peter goes, "Well, what are we having?" At that point somebody—I can't remember who it was—said, "Oh, we always have caviar to start," because Peter

had made some reference in the morning speech to expense savings and running the firm better and all.

And, of course, all of us knew that no one had ever even seen caviar in this dining room. So we look at Peter, and he said, "All right, I will have some of that." This server goes back into the kitchen. We didn't even know if he had caviar, and he comes out with this enormous tin of Beluga caviar, the thing must have cost 1,000 bucks, even in those days. Peter opens it up, takes a spoon and eats it. And we were all just dumbfounded, because he must have thought that's how things were done at Lehman.

"It was the most phenomenal thing I ever saw," added Fred.

MARY BECOMES A MANAGING DIRECTOR

Not long after the Lehman acquisition, the thirty-three-year-old Mary Tanner was elevated to managing director at the new firm, one of only a handful of women managing directors on Wall Street in the early 1980s. "Wall Street was still totally a men's club," she said. "It was beginning to change just a little bit. But it wasn't easy. I still got the 'aren't you a secretary?' thing, but less so. I was ferociously independent and determined that I was going to have a big career, so I put up with it.

"I liked competing with the guys," she added. "You had to be four times as good, which actually meant you had to deal with some people who weren't all that smart. It was a strange time."

Mary remembered that feminism was a big deal in that era, with women trying to compete with men by dressing in power suits with shoulder pads and de-emphasizing their femininity—a look epitomized in the 1988 film *Working Girl*, starring Melanie Griffith as a secretary aspiring to be a woman executive. "I didn't much go in for that," she said. "I wasn't big into feminism, Gloria Steinem, Betty Friedan, and all that. I just wanted to do something important."

As an example of how unusual it was for a woman to make partner or managing director on the Street, the producers of *Working Girl* visited Mary to get pointers. They brought along Sigourney Weaver, who played Griffith's female executive boss, to chat with Mary. She remembered:

> I'm sitting in my office one day and somebody in PR called me up and said: "On Friday Sigourney Weaver's coming here because she wants to talk to some women about the real experience on Wall Street, so you have to see her."
>
> I said, look, I've got a meeting, and so on, but they insisted. So Sigourney comes into my office on Friday with a whole entourage of people, and it was one of the most mystifying experiences I think I've ever had.
>
> Somebody had given her a jargon sheet of words she should slip into the conversation. She had absolutely no understanding of what we did. But I didn't want to look bad, since the firm seemed to think this was a really important thing, so I did the best I could. And she sashayed out. I remember when the movie came out, it took me a long time to go see it, hoping it wasn't as bad as that interview was. Part of it was OK, but most of it was just a surface thing about what things were really like. It missed what was motivating me, at least, which was to do things that were impactful for businesses, for people.

THE ROARING EIGHTIES

In 1980, Americans shook off the shocks and economic stagnation of the late 1970s and embraced a new optimism that included a headlong rush to build new businesses and make money. This ethos was captured in the 1987 Oliver Stone film *Wall Street*, where Michael Douglas played the ruthless trader Gordon Gekko, who gleefully declared that "greed is good," which became a kind of battle cry among the brash, unapologetic capitalists of the 1980s. Part of the economic revival that emerged as the decade wore on—and fueled a rise in profits and soaring stocks, as well as a genuine increase in the standard of living for many Americans—was powered by the wave of technology launched in the late seventies that swelled upward in the eighties. It included the introduction of personal computers, telecommunications, fuel-efficient and safer automobiles, and more. A massive increase in American defense spending aimed at overwhelming a faltering Soviet Union helped, too. In biotech, the groundswell of companies like Genentech, Cetus, Chiron, and Amgen burned through vast amounts of cash for R&D, but by the end of the decade were introducing the first major products coming out of this new industry, including synthetic insulin and human growth hormone, and in 1989, Epogen, Amgen's mammoth blockbuster that used a synthetic version of the protein erythropoietin to boost red blood cells in people with anemia and other diseases.

Once again Wall Street became bullish over the new tech, launching a steep rise in the Dow and other indicators after the dip in 1983, a rise that was also fired up by a loosening of regulations in real estate, margin rules on borrowing money to buy stock, and what risks banks were allowed to take. The epitome of this freewheeling decade was the emergence of so-called "junk bonds": a high-risk, high-return security that a previous generation of leading bankers would never have touched. These included bonds that were rated as being below "investment grade" (BB or lower) because of a high risk of default. "This became a big business," said Fred.

During this decade investment banks continued to briskly expand in terms of capital, revenues, profits, and employees, leaving behind forever the vestiges of the old world epitomized by Lehman Brothers in the days of Bobbie Lehman and One William Street. As money flowed like never before, some younger bankers created a culture that veered at times into excess, which was indeed captured in films like *Wall Street*, and more recently in Martin Scorsese's *The Wolf of Wall Street*.

Biotech companies grew and proliferated as Hybritech, Genzyme, IDEC, and other companies that launched in the late 1970s and early 1980s raised serious venture money and developed new products based on the latest discoveries in genetics and molecular biology. The IPO roller coaster established by the Genentech and Cetus offerings early in the decade also continued as did the volatility of biotech, with hot IPO markets emerging in 1983, 1986, and 1991–92, with dead periods in between. The first major acquisition of a small biotech by Big Pharma happened in March of 1986 when Bristol-Myers bought Seattle-based Genetic Systems, a company that was developing therapies based on monoclonal antibodies, immune cells that are all identical and designed to bind to a specific molecule or substance, for $294 million. That same year Eli Lilly and Company acquired Hybritech, another monoclonal antibody company based in San Diego, for approximately $300 million.

Fred was in the thick of many of the major biotech and pharma deals of this era, including another company founded by Alejandro Zaffaroni called Dynapol. Mary remembered the company and their role in what was a typical example of their work during these years.

MARY: Dr. Zaffaroni at one point founded a company called Dynapol, and Fred and I worked on it. It was a wonderful idea. The idea was that, as we know, many food additives are carcinogenic. Red dye, yellow dye, you remember all those.

FRED: Sure, yeah. Red dye number two, especially.

MARY: Dr. Zaffaroni found a polymer to which you could hook these additives without any diminution in the performance of these chemicals in food. But because it was bound with polymer you would just excrete it. So it completely got rid of any kind of carcinogenic deposits in the liver, the kidney, or any other place. He funded this company, we worked on it, and we took it around to raise more funding.

FRED: I was on the board.

MARY: Right. We took it around to all our food and chemical clients. And it wasn't actually very high technology, but it was low risk because the polymer was known; it was generally regarded as safe. The chemical bonding on the polymer was not complex. There were not a lot of issues [surrounding it], compared to hybrid monoclonal antibody molecules.

So we took it to the people at General Foods. These are the people that brought you Kool-Aid and Jell-O. All the food companies then had these products like Jell-O that cost about a penny a pack and Jell-O was then selling for about 17 cents a box, something like that. They didn't want to hear about the Dynapol product. They didn't want to spend one shekel on something like that, although eventually there was a licensing agreement. And further ones with Seven-Up and Coca-Cola. Eventually, the company was sold to DeKalb AgResearch, and then to Monsanto. But the technology was eventually abandoned because food companies would not take it up in a commercially meaningful way.

It was a great, if poignant, lesson for me in technology adoption. The technology was cheap, easy to execute, and clearly meaningful in terms of health. But sometimes that is not enough. Today, given the emphasis on organic food, healthy food, perhaps the outcome would have been different.

BIOGEN

Another deal during this period that helped Biogen survive a difficult time for their balance sheet was in 1985, when the company decided to sell off a Swiss subsidiary called Biogen SA. A new CEO, Jim Vincent, had just joined Biogen, which was losing more than $100 million per year, largely because of a worldwide research budget that exceeded $40 million per year, and worldwide operations that drained additional cash. Royalties from legacy products were also falling, and the company was near insolvency. Fred explained how he and Lehman dealt with Jim Vincent, who insisted that Fred work with First Boston on the deal:

> Jim Vincent was the ex-president of Abbott who got fired. It was a bad market. He called me up because at that time they had a Swiss subsidiary called Biogen SA. He said, "Fred I want to sell it." I said, "OK." He called me back maybe a week later and said, "I decided that I want you to do it jointly with First Boston Corporation." I said, "No, you don't understand Jim. I am going to do all the work. They are not going do anything, they don't know what they are doing in this field, and I am going to give them half the fee."
>
> "No, no I have talked with the CEO," he said. He assured me that they were going to put a real great team on this. "They have these fabulous contacts in Europe," he said, and so forth. So I said, "OK, I will only do it on the following terms. First, Boston tells me which pharmaceutical companies—US or Europe, doesn't matter—that they have really good contacts with and can access for this project. But everybody else is mine." So that's very fair; it's generous, right? Because there will be some of those companies I would like to talk to.
>
> So they came back with a list of about seven pharma companies that they wanted to contact. We started the process. It was like three days after we started, and they told Jim, "None of our clients, none of

our companies, are interested." I said, "How do they know that?" He said, "Well, they called them up and asked them. They said they are not interested." In this kind of situation, you don't call somebody up. You go and see them and explain to them why they should be interested. So I said, "OK, since their clients aren't interested, they don't care if I call their clients, right?" So to make a long story short, the company who bought it was Glaxo, which was on their list of those companies that weren't interested, right? So they get half the fee, and I do all the work, per my prediction.

"That transaction cut Biogen's burn rate on cash by more than half," added Mary, "and allowed the company to go on and become the awesome enterprise it is today."

FRED AND MARY GET MARRIED

Not long after she made managing director, Fred and Mary's business collaboration began shifting to what became a romantic partnership. Fred's first wife had returned to France, and they divorced in 1982. "She was missing France, and I think life with my traveling and all the rest was hard on her," said Fred about his first wife, Mary Ann. Mary Tanner added that Fred's first wife also had a hard time fitting into the Frank family back in Utah, which was still a close-knit group that made Fred's French wife feel uncomfortable. "Fred's mother was quite a woman," said Mary. "I was a little scared of her at first. She loved Fred with that fierce Jewish mother thing, and any other woman had better measure up. I was never sure I would."

By the time they started dating, Fred and Mary were already a formidable business team. Former Genentech CEO Kirk Raab remembered:

Well, there was Fred, and then there was Fred and Mary—they were two different people. Mary had some curious power over him—and Fred over her.

"I wasn't interested in Fred at first," said Mary. "I was a little afraid of him, and he seemed a little bit strange, with those glasses and the way he was so quiet." Mary counted it a small victory that she got Fred to give up his giant aviator glasses for more stylish specs. "She convinced me they were ugly," said Fred, "and she was right."

Fred and Mary kept their romance quiet at work since Fred was Mary's senior on many projects and the idea of coworkers dating was beginning to be frowned upon in many US corporations. When they decided to marry, however, Fred took the news straight to the top at American Express. Fred remembered:

I didn't know the policy about marriage. We were part of American Express, so I called CEO Jim Robinson, and I said: "Jim, I don't know what the company's policy is about having married couples who work in the same firm, but if one of them has to resign, one of us will resign."

He said, "Fred, I don't know what the policy is either, but whatever it was it just changed."

Fred Frank and Mary Tanner were married on October 10, 1988, in a ceremony at the Harvard Club in Manhattan. Mary recalled a skit that a friend put on during the rehearsal dinner:

Rodger Krouse had been one of our prized associates at Lehman, but he left to found his own firm, Sun Capital, which is now enormously successful. At our rehearsal dinner, he pretended he was Frederick Frank Jr., who wouldn't exist for another five or six years, but Rodger anticipated that we would have this son. He acted out a conference call about Frederick's Jr.'s birthday between Fred and Mary and Frederick Jr. It's hilarious: "Yeah, Dad, yeah, Dad. Dad, can you get off the phone for a minute? 'Cause I've got to talk to Mom. Mom, I need money. And I want you to send me money because I don't want to talk to Dad. If I talk to Dad, he's going to do another one of those earn-out deals about my future compensation." That was absolutely a classic.

One issue around Fred and Mary getting married was, of course, that Mary was an Irish Catholic and Fred was Jewish. "I wasn't going to convert," recalled Mary. "I told Fred straight out, I'm not doing that," although she told him they did need to think about this, especially if they had children, which they planned to do. Mary remembered saying to Fred:

> We can't just drift through this one. Kids can't drift through that kind of uncertainty. I said, "We're going to go join a temple." So we found Temple Emanu-El in New York, I guess the largest Reform congregation in the world, which was very welcoming because 50 percent of the congregation is in an interfaith marriage. In fact, not our current rabbi, but the one who welcomed us, Rabbi Sobel, was so grateful to meet me, because obviously there's always a concern on intermarriage, that you lose the children. And he thought it was amazing that I was willing to go through joining the temple. I felt that raising Fred's only son in the Jewish faith was the one unique gift only I could give him.

Mary shared the story of later enrolling Frederick Jr., born in 1993, in Sunday school at this temple.

> At one point, we put Frederick in Sunday school, at Temple Emanu-El, which is run by a group of women from the congregation. When I went to enroll him in this school, I put on my best daytime

Chanel and went down to see this lady. That was a good instinct, because she was decked out from head to foot. Only mine was less impressive than hers, which was even better. She said, "Well, tell me, dear, about your family." I'd rehearsed this. I said, "I married into this fantastic Jewish family that's part of the history of the western part of the United States," and I went through that a little bit.

Then I started talking about Mrs. Frank, how much I loved her, and what a great family it was. How we would always go out there for Christmas, and she would give Christmas lunch. The word Christmas came out of my mouth, floated across the room, and went splat against the windows. But I was trying so hard to be whatever I thought she wanted me to be that I didn't notice.

She went on, very carefully, "Oh, tell me about Christmas." I'm usually extraordinarily attuned verbally, and I don't know what happened to me that day. I said, "Oh, it's such an important time in the Frank household. The family decorates everything, the children all come home." And she said, "Decorate?" And I said, "Yes, well they have a Hanukkah bush." And she said, "Oh, a Hanukkah bush." I said, "Yes, it's a very large Hanukkah bush. Usually about eight feet, Douglas Fir, and it always smells so wonderful." And I could see this woman's face—you know how people's faces cloud over—she was totally offended by this. But Frederick got in.

Not surprisingly, Fred and Mary's wedding that October became entwined with the major deal they were working on at the time: the battle between the Hospital Corporation of America (HCA) and Humana, where HCA was trying to buy itself back from its shareholders and go private, and Humana was fighting them, threatening to overbid HCA and buy the company themselves. She described the situation:

So here I am in the middle of a $5 billion loan negotiation with this deal, and I rush away to go to my rehearsal dinner on a Friday.

Fred was nowhere in sight, and it was pouring rain, and he was out at Roche in New Jersey. And here we are, many cases of wine and several hours into the evening with no one having had anything to eat because Fred hadn't shown up. People are saying to me, "Calm down, calm down, he will show up." Finally he calls and says, "Well, I'm just not going to get there, so feed everybody." And I was like "boo-hoo" [pretends to sob], but it was okay. The deal is always what's important.

Oh, and by the way, our best man—and everybody else who was in our wedding party or close to us—was on one or the other side of this deal, which was so funny. Humana eventually backed away from the deal. The rumor was, from HCA, that Fred and Mary were distracted because they were getting married, so Humana backed down—hostilities were actually suspended. And by the way we never went on our honeymoon—we did have that Sunday off because of a major failed deal.

Fred continued telling this story:

That was because Humana CEO David Jones said: "The good news is, we're going to be at your wedding. The bad news is you can't go on your honeymoon." I said: "What do you mean we can't go on our honeymoon?" He says: "We have a project for you, you're not going on your honeymoon." But the deal failed shortly after because the impact on Humana's stock price would have been too great.

Fred and Mary also had to contend with Fred's parents in Salt Lake City. They had never entirely bonded with Fred's first wife, and Mary was determined to get along with them.

I'll tell you, the first time we went there, to Salt Lake, we fly in, and everyone kind of knew I'd be the newbie. Needless to say, this was quite stressful. We arrive in Salt Lake and I'd thought a lot about what I was going to wear, you know. Then, they had a pool. In those days almost nobody had an in-ground pool, mechanical cover, gorgeous garden around it, beautiful spot. And his father was like, "You have to use our pool. I understand you used to swim, even at Harvard." Sure enough, I go out with his father and go swimming in this beautiful pool.

I get out, wringing wet, and there was no such thing in the Frank house as a hair dryer, because his mother went to the beauty parlor once a week. So I'm sitting there with wringing wet hair, when the entire family arrives. It was totally traumatic. That was the first night.

The second night, Fred's mother decided she was going to give a party for the family and some friends. This is great. This is like, the viewing. Right. So I decided, I love to entertain. And his mother gave me even more instinct for it. I decided I'd help her set the table. Out comes the gold ware, the Irish damask, and the rest, and I'm thinking, "Oh my God. I am too poor. I don't belong in this family." It was a tense night. But I loved her greatly.

I schemed and plotted to try to get her back to New York for years. She loved New York, but her husband Simon Frank never wanted to come. They did come back for the wedding. The whole family came, which was really great, because it would've been bad for both Fred and me if not. But his father was good about that kind of stuff if it was a family event.

Mary soon became part of the Frank family's routines of traveling and spending holidays together. "The big weekend we used to go see them was Presidents' Day weekend in the California desert, in La Quinta," she said. "They used to go down there for the winter and come back in late April."

"Because they were all golfers," added Fred. Mary explained that the significance of these holiday weekends was lost on her at first:

This was a source of enormous family tension, because nobody else in the family ever got invited to La Quinta. And particularly, no one else in the family got invited to La Quinta on Presidents' Day weekend, because I didn't understand until I'd been there for one or two years that everyone in La Quinta was a Wall Street hitter, now retired, or a corporate hitter, now retired, and they invited their children so they could show off their successful children. So we would have this endless party from the time we arrived.

Mary remembered the Franks' cars:

I'm a New Yorker. I would take a taxi to the shower if I could. But they would insist on picking me up at the airport. They always drove Cadillacs. They became stooped as they got older, and inside there were these two short, little, elderly people. It looked like a ghost car, as their heads didn't rise above the tops of the seats.

I'd get in the car, and Mr. Frank would be so anxious to talk to me. First, he would look in the mirror, because I was sitting in the back seat, and then he would turn around to talk to me in this giant car. I used to think I was going to die on the way to their house as this giant Cadillac wandered over the road while Mr. Frank tried to find out how much money his son Fred made. Because Fred certainly wasn't going to tell him.

NEW HOME

In 1988, after their marriage, Fred and Mary decided they needed a new place to live rather than his co-op on Park Avenue. "I wanted a town house," said Fred, "a different sort of living, vertical rather than horizontal, and very private." Fred decided that there were only two ways to do this, either buy a house in perfect move-in condition, or buy a wreck and rebuild it. After a long search, they bought a wreck, but an unusual one, 38-plus feet wide and six floors, plus a full basement, a roof level, and back gardens.

The house was originally built in 1916–17 in the Georgian Revival style by the Winthrop family, who for generations were top political and business leaders in New England and New York. It was later sold to New York Senator Kenneth Simpson, a noted Republican. After he died in 1954, the house became rundown and was eventually purchased by an artist named Patrick Mueller, who gutted the house entirely, intending to recreate the first two floors as an art gallery. Mueller, however, abandoned the project. By the late eighties the house lay gutted and empty with holes in the roof, and the grand marble staircase between the first and second parlor floors lay on the floor, in ruin. Fred and Mary told a story about their first visit to the property. Fred recalled:

> There were no floorboards, no walls; the only thing working was the charming, old-fashioned Otis elevator, which we took to the fifth floor. We then climbed the last flight of narrow stairs to six. The caretaker was a hippie with a wife and baby—but also with a parrot. This was not just a parakeet sort of bird, it was a three- or four-foot-tall macaw that greeted us on arrival with a loud "F— you; f— you."
>
> Meanwhile, the wife was playing Joan Baez songs on her guitar, and the baby's diaper definitely needed help. Mary left the house in near hysteria, saying there was absolutely no way we were going to buy this wreck. How would we get rid of the hippies and the macaw? I told her not to worry—no hippies, no macaw—the property had been on the market for four years, and it was going to be a really good deal.

Mary added:

A curious thing happened while we were restoring the house. The Berlin Wall fell in 1991. We received almost two feet of mail from Russia, addressed to Alexander Kerensky [a leader in the 1917 Russian revolution]. Our new property was the last address many Kerensky family and friends had before the Soviet Union closed down their world. I packed it up and sent it to Alexander Kerensky Jr.

As always, Fred's investment judgment on this wreck was perfect. Town houses had been underappreciated and undervalued properties for years. And few were available, almost none of the size and width of our wreck. About nine months later, town house values began to rise sharply, because people figured out that first, you could mortgage them at much more favorable rates and percentages of value than fancy co-ops, which often required full cash purchase. Second, you didn't have restrictions on renovation, such as times that workmen might enter, when they had to leave, having the co-op supervisor paid to keep the service elevators open, etc.

Fred's investment acumen also evidenced itself in what we would do about the interiors. It was an unusual time in many regards. The US dollar was very strong—the rate was 10 francs to the dollar, probably about 2:1 to the euro today. It was also one of the very few times in memorable history when French eighteenth century furniture and objects were out of style and in our view undervalued. So Fred said, "We are going to acquire the best French eighteenth century furniture and objects collection, now."

It was also a convenient time for us to do that. Both of us were doing extensive investment banking work in Europe, with Sanofi, Rhône-Poulenc, and Synthélabo in France, and Hoechst, Boehringer Mannheim, Bayer, and BASF in Germany, and others. So we were always in Europe and managed to coordinate our schedules to spend weekends in Paris or Belgium, hunting antiques of quality and provenance.

The lucky thing was that, after all this trolling around, we came into a network of family dealers. These were small businesses, usually run by women of distinguished families who were divorced, had majored in art history, couldn't find business employment except for antiques, and really knew what they were doing. Their sources were largely family and friends, who were château rich and cash poor. Once they knew that we were committed Francophiles and what the French call genuine amateurs, meaning a class of collectors who knew the difference between the mediocre and the great, we entered a special world. They would call us and say, "We have something special for you," and we knew it would be so.

Finally, we finished our dream house in 1993, just in time for the birth of our only child, Frederick, in May 1993.

Mary recalled a story told by their son's nanny about the new house:

Our nanny once said to me, "Mrs. Frank, I love entering this house, as it is like a museum. But what I especially like is when I see your little son Frederick's Tonka trucks on or underneath the eighteenth century chests. Frederick thinks the antiques look better that way. He knows his soccer balls, baseballs, and Frisbees are strictly prohibited on either the first and second floors, given all the priceless antiques, but he insists that the antiques look better with his Tonka truck collection on them. What should I do?"

I told her to leave the Tonka trucks, because however late I returned from the office, the sight of the Tonkas on my eighteenth century chests made me happier than she could imagine.

BUY, CONSOLIDATE, BUY AND
THE CONTINGENT VALUE RIGHT

During the late 1980s, forces were driving a coming era of consolidation in the pharmaceutical industry. "The first driver," Fred said, "was the underlying paradox of the pharmaceutical industry: Conspicuous success and a rapid increase in sales and earnings from product accomplishments are not controllable either in time or dimension. Therefore, the greater the success, the more substantial the problem of perpetuating the success, meaning new products." Plus the pharmaceutical industry until this time had been composed of a large number of companies that did not have global scale. Some were very strong in the US, or the EU, or Japan, but few had complete global reach. They usually operated in geographies where they were weak through licensee and distribution arrangements.

These factors all contributed to a period of consolidation that began in the 1980s as the industry responded to the industrial realities of what was becoming a global market and the greater stakes in research and development for new products, including new biotechnology drugs.

For instance, in early 1988—just after the disastrous October stock market crash of late 1987—Fred worked with Kodak, a company traditionally not known for its pharmaceutical acumen, to acquire Sterling Drug. Kodak had begun a pharmaceutical research effort and sought to expand that effort by acquiring a US company with a commercial and research base in pharmaceuticals. The transaction began as a hostile tender offer by Roche for Sterling, with Kodak becoming the white knight, acquiring Sterling—a company founded in Wheeling, West Virginia, in 1901 that mostly sold over-the-counter meds—for $5.1 billion, with Fred and Mary representing Kodak.

Mary commented:

It was an amazing transaction, especially coming in January right after the disastrous stock market crash the prior October. Roche didn't think it was a hostile offer. However, they just put the offer out there, publicly, before any discussions with management. So, what did they expect?

As the pipeline at Kodak/Sterling disappointed in the ensuing years, Fred and Mary assisted the company in a series of worldwide research and marketing joint ventures in 1991 with Sanofi. The pharmaceutical joint ventures between Sanofi and Sterling/Kodak did not produce the new products expected on their creation, and in 1994, Fred and Mary represented Sanofi in acquiring the pharmaceutical interests of Sterling Drug/Kodak for $1.68 billion.

In 1989, the pace of industry consolidation accelerated. Fred and Mary participated in one of the largest pharmaceutical mergers that year when Bristol-Meyers acquired Squibb. Fred and Lehman represented Bristol-Myers. Bristol was seeking new products, and the prize at Squibb was Capoten, a blockbuster drug used to treat high blood pressure and certain heart conditions. The Bristol-Meyers/Squibb transaction, effected in common stock for $12 billion, with a combined market value at that time of $27 billion, created the second-largest pharmaceutical company at that time. "And the transaction was highly successful for all parties, including shareholders," said Mary.

EWING KAUFFMAN SELLS MARION LABS, BUYS A PITCHER

In 1989, Fred engineered the merger of Marion Laboratories and Merrell Dow Pharmaceuticals, a subsidiary of Dow Chemical Company. Dow wanted to spin out Merrell Dow, and combine it with another pharma company—which they were searching for—but retain control of the new combined entity. Dow would not have been capable of a traditional cash purchase, because the valuations of pharmaceutical companies were so much higher than that of even a major chemical company like Dow. Marion Laboratories, in Kansas City, was the ideal target. The fusion of these two pharmaceutical companies made sense to both businesses because Marion Laboratories, which obtained its products through licensing and acquisitions, had a very effective sales and marketing force, while Merrell Dow offered up a strong R&D capacity that Marion lacked. Merrell had developed successful drugs such as Seldane to treat allergies and Lorelco to reduce lipids.

At the time, Marion Laboratories was a super performer on Wall Street. They had the highest sales and profit per employee of any company traded on the New York Stock Exchange. This made the company highly desirable but expensive. To make the price more palatable to both sides and achieve the objectives of a continuing publicly traded, combined company stock, Fred pioneered a novel transaction structure that allowed Marion and the combined company, Marion Merrell Dow, to remain public, but controlled by Dow owning a majority of the new company's stock.

The structure included Dow contributing its pharmaceutical business, Merrell Dow, to the new company for the new company's stock, a cash purchase of a portion of Marion's publicly traded stock, and a financial instrument called contingent value rights (CVRs) for the transaction that many others later imitated in biotechnology deals. CVR securities act to insure sellers in acquisition against losses if the buyer's stock underperforms after closing, or reward legacy shareholders if certain milestones are achieved. In the Marion/Merrell deal, the first to use CVRs, the CVRs issued entitled those who held these securities to a cash payment if the stock of the new company traded below a certain threshold by a certain predetermined set of dates. Fred also concocted the CVR's opposite, called a contingent payment rate (CPR), which protects buyers and links payments for a transaction to certain predetermined milestone achievements in an acquisition's science or business in subsequent deals.

As Fred explained, CVRs and CPRs are designed to close gaps in valuation and performance to make parties comfortable with acquisitions that depended on either future performance or the realization of promised scientific accomplishments—issues that could make one side or the other skittish without some sort of protection built in. "Marion's shareholders wanted to know that CEO and founder Ewing Kauffman's company, which had been so successful and profitable, would be properly valued over time," Fred said.

Ewing Kauffman was a former pharmaceutical salesman who had founded the company in 1950 out of his basement in Kansas City with a mere $4,000 in capital. His first product was calcium supplements made out of crushed oyster shells in his home. By the late 1960s Marion Labs was a huge success, and Kauffman was wealthy and influential enough in his hometown to found and pay for a new major league baseball team in Kansas City. In 1967, the Kansas City Athletics stunned the city by moving to Oakland, and Kauffman, as a major civic leader in the city, decided to push to locate an expansion team in his hometown. He called the team the Royals, which quickly became a powerhouse team in the American League after its first season in 1969.

Fred, who served as Kauffman's banker and advisor for years, recalled what happened:

He [Kauffman] knew nothing about baseball back when the Royals started up, but he acted as a concerned citizen because the previous team in Kansas City had moved to Oakland. He said, "This is too important for Kansas City." So he paid for the team. Or 50 percent, something like that, and he eventually bought everyone out. He ran the baseball team like he ran the company. There was no baloney with that. If practice was scheduled at a certain time, you were there at a certain time. Your uniform would be clean, and you would be looking proper. And Kauffman's wife, Muriel, became Kansas City

Royal Blue. Muriel would wear a Royals blue silk team jacket and blue stretch pants, even to society benefits and board meetings.

When Mary and I were married, we invited Ewing and Muriel to our wedding, because they were good friends. Ewing was actually quite ill so he couldn't come, but Muriel came. For our wedding present they gave us a silver platter engraved with all the Kansas City Royals team members' names. They also gave me a baseball, which player George Brett signed—and George Brett signed very few things. And, they gave me a Kansas City Royals jacket, which I've now given to my son.

Fred remembered one day in the early 1980s when Kauffman contacted him to sell some Marion Laboratories stock, which he had never done before. Fred told the story:

> I got a call and a secretary said, "Mr. Kauffman would like to see you, so on your way to the West Coast, please stop off in Kansas City." I said to myself, "He doesn't ask these questions for no reason," so I scheduled to go out there a couple of days later. The meeting was with [Kauffman] and two others. Mr. K said, "Fred, did you know that I've never sold a share of stock in Marion Laboratories? But it's Muriel's birthday, and you know, she has everything—a Rolls-Royce, a big house—but I've thought of a great present for her. And as a consequence, I'm going to have to sell some stock. I want your counsel on how to execute this, because I've never sold any stock."
>
> So I said, "Ewing, that's pretty interesting, but what are you going to buy Muriel for her birthday present that's so important that you have to sell stock?" He said, "I'm going to buy her a right-hander."

In the final deal between Marion and Merrell, Dow contributed Merrell Dow to the new company for stock and paid $2.2 billion for 39 percent of Marion's shares through a tender offer for a portion of the shares held by the public, with an option to buy Kauffman's stock and the issuance of CVRs to Marion shareholders. In the combined entity, Dow ended up owning 67 percent of the new company, and through the CVRs issued to the Marion shareholders, guaranteed a level of stock price performance by the new company for a period of time. The deal created the fifth-largest pharmaceutical company in the world at that time. When the CVRs opened trading on the American Stock Exchange (which was the main market for derivative securities and listed options then), it was the largest registered derivative ever listed, with an opening trading value of approximately $900 million.

Mary Tanner recalled the cultural atmosphere of the deal:

> Everyone at Marion Laboratories was incredibly loyal to the company, the Royals, and to Ewing Kauffman. He was a self-made man, having come from the wrong side of the tracks in Kansas City. He would not let anyone refer to "employees"—everyone, highest to lowest, was an associate. Today that sort of thing is common, but in those days it was unheard of.
>
> Everyone in the company owned stock. And I mean owned stock, not just options. The receptionist, who had been with Marion for twenty-plus years, was a multimillionaire. The transaction inspired fear up and down the ranks of the company, but everyone's sense was, "If Mr. K wants to do it, we will."

Mary also recalled Ewing Kauffman's wife:

> Muriel Kauffman was a real character, who inspired both fear and great respect. She was a lawyer, quite accomplished. She never tired of telling Ewing that she had made a million dollars before he did.

The Kauffmans were childless. Ewing left his fortune to a family foundation, which remains an important force in American philanthropy to this day. "In those days, there were many family-controlled pharmaceutical companies (Marion, G.D. Searle & Co., E.R. Squibb & Sons, others)," said Mary. "They are almost all gone now. But Fred was particularly good with this type of company, because they trusted him."

While subsequent tax and accounting rules later made this particular type of Marion/Merrell Dow structure less attractive to major companies attempting to spin out and merge divisions but remain in control of their pharmaceutical businesses, the CVR and CPR have remained durable, useful securities in financial practice.

A FRENCH NATIONAL CHAMPION IN PLAY AND STRUGGLES AT SHEARSON LEHMAN

Fred and Mary went on to use the Marion/Merrell Dow CVR structure again the next year, in 1989, in a transaction with the largest French chemical and pharmaceutical business at the time, Rhône-Poulenc, a company that was then 100 percent owned by the French government. Rhône-Poulenc spun out its worldwide pharmaceutical business, received stock in Rorer, a US public pharmaceutical company, and issued CVRs to the Rorer shareholders to assure future stock price performance of the combined company. Rhône-Poulenc had the same motivation as Dow Chemical, to retain control of an enlarged pharmaceutical business. It chose US-based Rorer as one of the most highly sought-after targets for acquisition, because it was a substantial US business with an affordable acquisition price—as long as its shareholders felt protected from downturns after the deal went through. Rhône-Poulenc ended up with 68 percent control of the publicly traded Rhône-Poulenc Rorer. This transaction made Rhône-Poulenc Rorer a major worldwide pharmaceutical company.

The Rhône-Poulenc Rorer transaction was unfolding at a time when Shearson Lehman/American Express was under enormous financial pressure, owing to the "junk bond" crisis in 1989. Junk bonds that had risen precipitously during the eighties crashed, and the Dow Jones Industrial Average fell by 6 percent in one day, on Friday, October 13, 1989, helping to trigger the recession of the early 1990s. Shearson Lehman also had recently failed in a high-stakes bid for RJR Nabisco at a time when trading conditions in general were tanking. Mary remembered this period vividly in the context of the Rhône-Poulenc Rorer deal:

> I had worked with Rhône-Poulenc for years. I was so delighted to get the engagement on a Rorer acquisition, including using our innovative deal structure that we had successfully executed with Marion Merrill Dow just shortly before, which had gotten very good press. But it was a very bad time for Lehman—financial crisis, the RJR Nabisco failure, bad press on our firm—and I was representing a French national champion, one of the oldest companies in France. A bunch of banks lobbied the French government to have Lehman fired. Some also used the old misogynist comment, "How could a woman lead this effort by a French national champion?"
>
> At the same time we were doing this deal, Shearson Lehman was reacting to fragile markets and stresses on the firm by reducing headcount. So I found myself during this time commuting to France every Sunday night where I'd take a fast shower at the Air France lounge, head into town, work on the transaction, and then the next night take the last flight home to fire my people at Shearson Lehman. Then I would get back on the last night flight to Paris. It was a very stressful period. But we succeeded in doing the Rhône-Poulenc Rorer deal.
>
> What was amusing in all this horror was that Rhône-Poulenc was totally worried that Roche would come in and top their bid. What Rhône-Poulenc didn't know was that Fred was negotiating

with Roche on the Roche-Genentech deal. The security on the Genentech deal was so tight that no one but Fred and I knew that Rhône-Poulenc had nothing to worry about from Roche. But I told Rhône-Poulenc there was nothing to worry about from Roche, just based on my personal assurances, no information. And I will always be grateful to the Rhône-Poulenc senior management team for their confidence in me at that time.

The transaction ended up with a "face price" of $1.7 billion, which belied the value the worldwide pharmaceutical business Rhône-Poulenc had contributed into the new public company.

All of this frenzied activity, however, was but a prelude to the pharma-biotech deal that would begin to take shape in the summer of 1989 as the leaders of America's leading biotech company, Genentech, began to realize that they were in serious trouble and needed help.

The man they would turn to was Fred Frank.

The Arthur Frank family, circa 1947 (Courtesy of the Utah Historical Society)

Arthur Frank, Fred's grandfather, circa 1950
(Courtesy of the Utah Historical Society)

Simon Frank, Fred's father, circa 1927
(Family photo)

Fred and his siblings: Suzanne, Fred, and Tom,
circa 1938 (Family photo)

Fred in eighth grade, with his footballs
(Family photo)

Arthur Frank store, circa 1932 (Courtesy of Utah Historical Society)

HOTCHKISS

Above: Fred's Hotchkiss class of 1950 (Courtesy of The Hotchkiss School)

Right: John McChesney: Legendary English teacher at Hotchkiss, circa 1950 (Courtesy of The Hotchkiss School)

Bottom right: Dedication of the Hotchkiss Science Center. Fred with his son, Frederick, who later attended Hotchkiss, graduating in 2012 (Family photo and courtesy of The Hotchkiss School)

Bottom left: Dedication of the Frank House for the headmaster, 1995. Fred and Mary with John ("Rusty") Chandler, then headmaster, and his wife, Tina (Courtesy of The Hotchkiss School)

Below: George Van Santvoord, Hotchkiss Headmaster, 1926 to 1955, known as "The Duke," circa 1950 (Courtesy of The Hotchkiss School)

54/50 DINNER • JUNE 2, 2004

Class of 1954 at their 50th reunion, during which the class presented Yale with a gift of $120 million, then the largest class gift in history (Courtesy of Yale University)

Left: David S. Swensen, Yale Chief Investment Officer; Mary Tanner; Fred Frank; and Frederick Frank at investiture of the Fred Frank and Mary Tanner Chair Professorship at Yale University, 2012

Peter Salovey, President of Yale, and Fred at the 65th reunion of the class of 1954, as Fred prepares his speech for awarding the class gift of $165 million (Courtesy of Yale University)

Fred and his son, Frederick, at Frederick's Yale graduation in May 2016. Fred is wearing the academic robes of Davenport College, of which he is a Fellow. Frederick, also a Davenport member, is carrying the Davenport flag.

Above: Fred in his office, circa 1980s, from "The Ubiquitous Fred Frank," an article in *Life Sciences Foundation* magazine, 2012 (Courtesy of the Science History Institute)

Left: The legacy headquarters of Lehman Brothers at One William Street, circa 1970s (Reproduced via Wikimedia Commons: Wikipedia Takes Manhattan)

Fred and Mary in Fred's office at Lehman, 1991 (Personal photo)

Top left: Fred introducing Hillary Clinton to keynote the Lehman Annual Healthcare Conference in 1993 during Mrs. Clinton's health care initiative (Personal photo)

Top right: Fred and Shimon Peres at the Albert Einstein Awards in 2004 (Personal photo)

Left: Inscribed photo from Francis Crick and James D. Watson, circa 2003. Fred served on a board of directors with Watson and had a long association. (Personal photo)

Bottom left: Fred awarded the Science History Institute Richard J. Bolte Award for leadership in the growth and development of the chemical and molecular sciences, 2019 (Courtesy of the Science History Institute)

Bottom right: Fred awarded the Irvington Institute for Immunological Research Award in 1998. Fred with fellow award winners Carroll Petrie and Charles Janeway, MD

Arthur Fleischer Jr. Fred's childhood and Yale friend and business colleague, senior partner of Fried, Frank, Harris, Shriver & Jacobson

Burt Malkiel, PhD: fellow trainee with Fred at Smith, Barney in 1958, author of *A Random Walk Down Wall Street*, professor of economics at Princeton University

George Poste, PhD, D.V.M., Regents Professor at Arizona State University, serial entrepreneur and major executive research scientist. From 1992 to 1999, he was chief science and technology officer and president, R&D, of SmithKline Beecham.

Sandy Robertson, a fellow trainee with Fred at Smith Barney in 1958. Founder, Robertson Stephens & Co. and Francisco Partners Management, LP

Leroy (Lee) Edward Hood, PhD, systems biologist and entrepreneur; co-founder, Institute for Systems Biology; closely associated with the founding of Applied Biosystems and numerous other companies

William A. Haseltine, PhD. Former professor at Harvard Medical School and known for his groundbreaking work in HIV/AIDS and cancer

Jeremy M. Levin, DPhil., MB, and BChir. CEO of Ovid Therapeutics, former CEO of Teva, and senior positions at major pharmaceutical companies, including Novartis and Bristol-Myers

Randy Scott, PhD. Geneticist, serial entrepreneur, founder, and former CEO of Genomic Health and Invitae Corporation

CHAPTER 6

Biotech's Wild Ride

"FRED'S DEAL" (GENENTECH-ROCHE I & II) AND THE HEADY YEARS OF PROMISE, 1989–2001

> *Only those willing to risk going too far can*
> *possibly find out how far one can go.*
>
> —T.S. Eliot

When the fifty-six-year-old Fred Frank completed the Marion Merrell Dow and Rhône-Poulenc deals, he had worked on Wall Street for thirty years. During those three tumultuous decades, the Street that Fred had known when he was a young man had become mostly a memory. Most firms, including his, were no longer physically in or near New York's old financial district clustered around the street called Wall. The venerable system of partnerships with a few hundred employees had given way to corporations that employed thousands, while the previously dominant focus on the US market had morphed into operations spanning the globe. By 1989, investment banks were raising and spending levels of capital—and producing profits—never before imagined. This provided the billions of dollars needed to create and grow new technologies and burgeoning business empires on a massive scale.

Politically, the Cold War was ending as the US was poised to become the world's sole superpower with the collapse of the Soviet Union in 1990. George H.W. Bush had replaced an ailing Ronald Reagan as president but would serve only a single term, as a new generation was about to be led by Bill Clinton and others who came of age after the Second World War.

The new biology that had fueled the creation of Genentech, Cetus, and other newfangled companies was running through the prodigious cash those companies had raised during the biotech IPO and funding binges of the eighties. They were finding that they needed even more money as the new science turned out to be more complicated than originally thought. The long and expensive process of getting drugs tested and approved was also becoming more complicated, as regulations proliferated. Still, the exuberance for biotechnology and the promise of genetics and molecular biology continued unabated, jumping from the lab and the boardroom to the US Capitol, where politicians jumped on board to support the Human Genome Project, an expensive Big Science program that set out to sequence every base pair in a representative genome of *Homo sapiens*. Some likened it to the Apollo Project that put men on the moon twenty years earlier.

The transformation of biology coincided with the still nascent but already quickly expanding revolution in disruptive information technologies that were poised to bring us, by the nineties, newfangled personal computers, mobile phones, a greatly expanded Internet, and a slew of dot-coms. In 1989 these technologies were about to reshape the lives of billions of people while smashing old market norms in terms of deal sizes, market caps, and risk. Stock prices would also soar to spectacular heights in the nineties before crashing just after the turn of the new millennium. Several technologies that had begun manifesting as early as the late 1950s—and had attracted the notice of prescient investors like Fred Frank and Sandy Robertson—were now about to enter the steep part of the hockey-stick-shaped line touted by economists as part of the pattern of growth for new technologies that at first expand slowly, then faster, then so fast as to be a blur.

ROCHE-GENENTECH DEAL, PART ONE

As it turned out, much of Fred Frank's life up to this point was actually an overture to a transaction that started to take shape in early autumn 1989—the Roche-Genentech merger that began with the secret meeting in New York on the day of the Loma Prieta earthquake in California, a project that would later be known to many as "Fred's deal." More than just a business deal, however, Roche's acquisition of Genentech represented an attempt to fuse two distinct industries and cultures: one young and impetuous, fighting disease utilizing cutting-edge biology; the other one conservative, risk-averse, and steeped in a long tradition of developing drugs using chemistry.

The deal began to take shape soon after the Marion Merrell Dow merger was concluded in the summer of 1989, when Genentech chairman of the board Tom Perkins, CEO Bob Swanson, and president Kirk Raab concluded that their company, the darling of the rising biotechnology industry and a symbol of western US technological prowess, was fast running out of money. In the article published in 2012 in the *Life Sciences Foundation* magazine titled "The Ubiquitous Frederick Frank," Fred described the company's dire situation: **

** In this section about the Genentech-Roche deal, many of the quotes from Fred come from "The Ubiquitous Frederick Frank," the 2012 article in the *Life Sciences Foundation* magazine. When quotes from Fred are not attributed to the *LSF* article, they come from Fred in conversation with the author. Fred has told certain stories multiple times with remarkable consistency.

In 1989, Genentech was the leading biotechnology company in the world, but it was in a predicament. The company had employed recombinant DNA techniques to develop three major pharmaceutical products—human insulin, human growth hormone, and TPA (a protein that dissolves blood clots)—but the success was doubled-edged.

The general expectation on Wall Street was that such a company would increase revenues and earnings at a rate greater than twenty percent each year. Genentech's leadership knew that earnings rate would not be sustained if the company continued to support its promising research and development programs.

The company had a strong pipeline of drug candidates but taking full advantage of it would require huge R&D expenditures. The spending would place a drag on earnings. In addition, sales of Genentech's TPA, marketed under the brand name Activase for the treatment of heart attacks, had not generated the substantial revenues and profits that had been expected. A high price per dose and an equivocal result in a clinical comparison of efficacy (in terms of mortality reduction) with the less expensive standard of care had attenuated the drug's market penetration.[1]

In the summer of 1989, the company's stock was sliding and appeared as if it might drop into single digits. Two years earlier, it had traded in the fifties. It was hovering at $21 per share.

Kirk Raab recalled:

We were primarily worried about both not doing something and doing something, that either one might hurt the company. Doing something would have been letting our drug development people go. We couldn't cut back on the sales force because they were getting the cash flow. We were worrying toward the end of July (1989). I think we had about $150 million in the bank, something like that. It may have been $200 million. But we had a really aggressive R&D program. It was something like 40 percent of our spending. It was wonderful. But it was a giant dilemma. And we were afraid because the stock was down so much that we were at risk of takeover by Big Pharma.

Few of the exuberant investors who ran up Genentech's stock price nine years earlier could have anticipated this. As Fred and Mary and many others have said, the new science and technologies represented by Genentech were originally supposed to greatly accelerate the pace of drug development and to produce rafts of new products and stratospheric revenues and profits within a short period of time. Instead, although Genentech had brought to market three new drugs since its founding in 1976 and more seemed to be on the way, the journey had been fraught with more scientific and business hurdles than anticipated. Human biology, it was turning out, was far more complex than many realized when DNA and other molecular processes were being first characterized in the fifties, sixties, and seventies. Likewise, the process of funding pipelines and clinical trials and of understanding the often-bewildering vagaries of regulation and reimbursement was proving to be as expensive and difficult for biotech as it was for pharma.

Genentech, more than most, was doing reasonably well navigating all of this. Most other companies had no drugs at all on the market and were years away from FDA approvals, with some on a pathway to failure. Still, even for a relative success like Genentech, the reality was becoming clear that more money and longer timelines were required to stay afloat and to pay for what was turning out to be a new science that had a huge R&D price tag.

As the company's stock continued to drop late that summer, Perkins, Swanson, and Raab came to the painful conclusion that the only way to save the company and to protect shareholder value was to sell it. To preserve Genentech's potential, however, they needed to find a buyer willing to infuse up to billions of dollars in exchange for a majority ownership while agreeing to keep the company intact, including its promising R&D pipeline and the edgy scientific culture that had been key to its R&D success. This seemed highly unlikely, since most large companies that acquire smaller or struggling businesses want to absorb their purchase, recast it in their own image, or sell off or squeeze its patents, royalties, and other assets for maximum profit.

In the fall of 1989, the Genentech board agreed to pursue an acquisition strategy that would not only be tricky but also needed to remain hush-hush. "If word got out that we were selling the company, there would have been riots," said Raab, talking about the likely reaction of both employees and shareholders.

So Perkins, Swanson, and Raab turned to Fred Frank. Despite missing out on the Genentech IPO in 1980 because of his loyalty to Cetus, Fred had stayed in contact with Bob Swanson and frequently spoken with Tom Perkins. In the late eighties Genentech had engaged Fred and Lehman to sell its 25 percent share in Genencor, a joint venture originally of Genentech and Corning that produced industrial enzymes. But Fred's most important advocate at Genentech was Kirk Raab, who knew Fred from his days as a senior executive at Abbott. Raab described his impression of Fred:

> Fred and I had a good relationship. Not that we had yet done any banking together, but he had done work for Abbott that I wasn't really involved in, and so I got to know him as president of Abbott. I really liked and respected Fred.

Raab described Fred at the time:

> Fred was incredibly informal. Never used a limousine, just rented a car, stayed at the Westin Hotel near the airport in San Francisco, and wasn't into fancy restaurants. I don't think Fred ever drank. Of course, he was jogging before the word jogging was ever used.

Raab said that it was at Fred's preferred hotel near the airport, which is near Genentech's headquarters in South San Francisco, that he first broached the company's delicate situation with Fred:

I was having dinner with Fred at the Westin Hotel. I talked to him about our dilemma, and he said, "There's gotta be a deal you can make with Big Pharma. Either sell the company to a company that gets what Genentech is doing or we'll figure out something else."

Bob Swanson was less enthusiastic about Fred, having dealt with him in 1986 during furtive discussions with Amgen CEO George Rathmann, who had proposed a merger between the two companies. Nothing came of it, nor was Fred closely involved except as an advisor to Amgen. Yet Swanson was soured by the experience, according to Raab. "Swanson resented Fred," he said, referring to the Amgen talks. "But I knew that Fred was the best."

Fred also had impressed Tom Perkins. "He was very important in making the Roche deal happen," said Perkins in a 2001 interview with Glenn Bugos for the Program in the History of the Biological Sciences and Biotechnology at the Bancroft Library at the University of California at Berkeley.[2] Perkins recalled how Fred lived up to his reputation in the transaction:

On the acquisition, Raab and Swanson spearheaded the effort. I remember a meeting in New York where we talked to Fred Frank. I think that was my first involvement with Fred Frank, though I subsequently used him on other deals. I have a very high opinion of Fred Frank. He was a well-known investment banker with a good track record in pharmaceuticals. Kirk Raab was the primary promoter of using Fred Frank. Swanson went along with it . . . Frank did an excellent job for Genentech. The Roche thing was complicated and record-breaking and precedent-setting . . .

I was so impressed with him that subsequently, on another big deal where I was doing it all—merging Tandem Computers into Compaq Computers—I used Fred. Even though it was a computer industry deal, not a biotech deal. He hadn't done all that much in computers. Again, he did a great job. I was delighted with their work.

When Fred agreed to work on the Genentech deal, he began quietly vetting potential buyers that September. Vice president of sales and marketing Jim Gower, the only other person at the company besides Perkins, Swanson, and Raab who was let in on the secret, assisted Fred.

"I quietly made a few calls," recalled Fred, "knowing this would not be easy." He focused mainly on pharma companies, since they had the know-how to develop and sell drugs, and in the rising blockbuster era they had cash to spare, even if culturally they tended to be worlds apart from biotechs like Genentech.

One initial candidate was Merck. "I had some phone conversations with them," said Fred, but Merck management didn't like Genentech's insistence that they remain operationally independent. Raab said that Merck would eventually want to turn Genentech into "Merck West." "They didn't think that was a good idea," said Fred in the *Life Sciences Foundation* article,[3] "they could pay to build Merck West cheaper than they could buy Genentech."

Fred next tried DuPont. According to the *Life Sciences Foundation* magazine:

> Frank then made a trip to Wilmington, Delaware, to explore the possibility of combining DuPont's pharmaceutical business with Genentech's. The idea made sense, he believed, because "DuPont, having acquired a mid-sized pharmaceutical company, still had no idea what they were doing in pharmaceuticals, not a clue." In theory, Genentech could sail into a safe harbor, DuPont would benefit from Genentech's innovative capacity and R&D expertise, and there

would be little incentive for the big firm to smother the small one by drafting it into the service of larger corporate projects. It would make more sense to let Genentech put DuPont's pharmaceutical research to its own ends.[4]

Fred later recalled the brief conversation with DuPont's investment bankers:

I went to Wilmington to talk to DuPont and met them at the DuPont Hotel. They had hired these famous investment bankers, Bruce Wasserstein and Joseph Parella of the firm Wasserstein & Parella. Everybody knew them as "Wasserella." They said: "Fred, we've recommended that DuPont not do this deal." I said, "Well, why did you have me come here?"

Miffed, Fred left this meeting and made a call to Basel, Switzerland. "So from the DuPont Hotel, I called Roche," he said.

The *Life Sciences Foundation* interview continues:

[Fred Frank] proposed pushing Roche's US business in Nutley, New Jersey, into Genentech. Roche expressed interest; negotiations commenced. Frank met with Roche officials in Zurich rather than Basel, in order to keep the negotiations secret. Although officially retained by Genentech, he effectively represented both parties.[5]

Tom Perkins expanded on this extraordinary situation in the Glenn Bugos interview:

I don't know if anybody has pointed out to you that Fred represented both companies in that deal. Roche had enough confidence in and respect for Fred Frank that they did not use an investment banker. Maybe at the last minute they got an opinion from somebody. But, basically, he represented both companies. That's pretty astonishing. Very few investment bankers have that kind of support from their clients. That was very impressive.[6]

Perkins went on to describe how Fred worked with him:

As we got deeper into the deal and approached the recommendation to the Genentech board of directors, I did have telephone conversations with Frank. And Fred Frank, being as good as he is and realizing I was chairman, made it his business to keep me informed. He would be calling me, "This is just a quick update, Tom. Here's what's happening. This is what's being done. Swanson is doing this. Raab is doing that. I think you ought to know that I think they're a little out of line here or there, or whatever." Asking me to help if needed. We had two or three conversations a week in the early days. And then daily. And then hourly toward the end.[7]

Fred had known the two primary negotiators for Roche for years. They were CEO and chairman Fritz Gerber, and chief financial officer Henri Meier. At the time Gerber was sixty years old and a legend in the pharma industry. A lawyer by training, Gerber had led this nearly century-old company since 1978, guiding it through a period of rapid expansion into one of the largest pharmaceutical companies in the world, with $5.38 billion in revenues in 1989. Henri Meier, age 53, was a tall, lean-faced, Swiss economist formerly with the World Bank. He had recently joined Roche after a career that had taken him to South America and the US as well as Europe. Another key player for Roche was 56-year-old Jürgen Drews, a former internist and the company's head of R&D.

Fred's first challenge with the Roche group was to convince them to keep Genentech intact and not to meld its scientists and executives into Roche. "I explained that Genentech had a very special culture, which was different from theirs," he explained, according to the LSF article, suggesting that attempts to make Genentech operate like Roche would kill its uniqueness and its potential. "At Genentech, you came to work anytime, day or night," continued Fred. "At Roche, you came to work from nine to five, and you wore jackets and ties. I warned them not to upset the culture because that was what made the company distinctive and innovative."[8]

Gerber and Meier agreed. "They had the vision," Raab told the Life Sciences Foundation, "to let Genentech be Genentech." Raab continued:

> They both, Meier and Gerber, knew that our only worth was if their people didn't screw us up. And certainly, Fred played a role in helping them understand why they should do the deal in a way that prevented Roche [from] being able to screw us up. It was in the deal, actually. Nobody from Roche could visit us unless Gerber and I agreed.[9]

Perkins recalled being relieved that the Roche executives got what they were asking for:

> I remember meeting with them in New York—I didn't go to Switzerland for this deal—talking for a couple hours in private with them. They were impressive people. I liked them and felt comfortable with them. Particularly Fritz.[10]

The deal that emerged was unique in many ways, starting with the agreement by Roche to pay a cash sum that would end up being $2.1 billion for 60 percent of Genentech's stock, while having no direct say in managing the company. Roche also only got two seats on Genentech's board of directors. "This was something we wanted," said Perkins, "something that Fred Frank sold to them as being good for them. They shouldn't let the employee stockholders and the world in general think that Genentech was just their errand boy, their lackey.

That it would be good for all parties if that's the way the deal was done. It was done that way and it worked."[11]

"They couldn't tell us to do anything," said Raab, "other than stop us from selling our 40 percent minority interest to another pharmaceutical company. That, and we couldn't go out and make a giant acquisition and dilute it. But fundamentally, as far as running the company, what we did, they had no rights to our profits."

The Life Sciences Foundation describes some other features of the deal as it emerged:

> In the matchmaker role, Frank had to find a way to harmonize the interests of two corporate entities in very different sets of circumstances . . . As always, price was an issue. Genentech needed protection while it developed products. How much would it cost Roche to provide it? Initially, Frank attempted to replicate a structure that he had crafted for the Marion Merrell Dow deal. In that transaction, Fred had pioneered the use of contingent value rights (CVRs), instruments that have since proven to be particularly well-suited to biotech finance. In the Genentech-Roche case, Frank envisioned CVRs persuading Genentech shareholders that the company's development pipeline and scientific capabilities would be properly appraised.[12]

Because of the need for secrecy, Roche didn't conduct the usual due diligence. Typically, in a deal like this a small army of researchers and financial experts descend on the acquisition target and pore through records and books, inspect labs and facilities, and interview key personnel. Instead, Fred and Genentech engaged a technical writer to interview company scientists and others, which contributed to a thick book about the company that Fred's team at Lehman oversaw the creation of and handed over to Roche. "That was pretty extraordinary," said Fred. "It took a lot of courage and foresight on Roche's part."

This was all a prelude to the first face-to-face meeting between

Genentech and Roche in New York on that fateful day, October 17, 1989, when the deal became serious—and the earth shook during the World Series game in San Francisco. This meeting was held at the Waldorf Astoria hotel with five men present: Swanson and Raab, who were there from California, and Gerber and Meier, who had flown in from Switzerland. The fifth man was Fred Frank, drinking his customary black tea and wearing his oversize aviator glasses. Kirk Raab recalled:

> It was just talking. There was a lot of questioning from both parties. But Fred was the orchestrator. He was the conductor. We didn't know how it was all going to fall together, but we'd been assured. Fred had said, "They want you to be independent, they want you to have stock options. They don't want to change Genentech." So it was very amiable, and we fundamentally agreed, "Let's go to work."

The men then had drinks, except for Fred: "Like a glass of wine," said Raab. "We didn't stay long. Everyone wanted to separate and talk."

It was that evening that Swanson and Raab, after dinner in a nearby Italian restaurant, returned to their hotel rooms and saw to their shock that an earthquake had occurred in San Francisco. Raab described how he turned on the television to watch the World Series. What he saw was not the game, however, but reports about the 6.9-magnitude earthquake that had rocked San Francisco just a few minutes earlier.

Tom Perkins was in California when the quake struck, preparing to fly to New York to attend a Genentech board meeting about the Roche deal. He recalled in the Oral History interview with Glenn Bugos:

> That earthquake in October 1989 was a pretty big one. I was on the middle of the Golden Gate Bridge when it hit. I'll never forget that. It scared me. That bridge is awesome. It shook. Being an engineer, as it was happening I was sitting there thinking, "How many degrees of freedom does this bridge have?" It's going up and down. It's going

sideways. It's twisting. Cables are moving. I got to twelve degrees of freedom before I realized that I may lose my freedom when this thing falls down. I might die.

The next morning, Dave Packard [cofounder of Hewlett Packard and a director of Genentech] and I were supposed to fly out with Dave Tappan [a Genentech director and CEO of Fluor] in the Fluor jet to go to a Genentech board meeting in New York. It was all part of this Roche thing, so it was a very important meeting. Reports were that bridges were down; it was horrible. But I knew Dave Packard, and he would damn well leave, and that I better get to the San Jose airport.

I had been able to ascertain that Genentech hadn't been badly damaged. I asked Dave, "How's Hewlett-Packard?" He said, "Gee, I don't know. My telephone was out." And I asked about the Monterey Aquarium, which, of course, he had built. He said, "I don't know." Here he is flying out to a Genentech board meeting without knowing what happened to Hewlett-Packard or to his aquarium. I was so impressed by his dedication. So I talked to the pilot and asked if there was any way he could call somebody at Hewlett-Packard and at Monterey and find out. The pilot did and came back and told Dave that everything seemed to be fine. Packard said, "Well, that's good. Thank you."[13]

Back in New York, Raab and Swanson shared some panicked moments until a security company that worked for Genentech was able to check on their families and on the Genentech campus and confirm that all were safe.

The next step in the Roche deal was for Raab and Swanson to go to Europe to hash out details, mainly around the price per share that Roche would pay for Genentech stock. Roche was being coy about what it was prepared to offer, which was frustrating the Genentech team. "We could never get a price out of them," said Raab. He continued:

Fred and I talked, and I said, "We've got to get the number." Then Fred worked on them. He would work on the back of an envelope. He'd always look at ways of doing something in a way that would bring you together. I don't want to call him a mediator, but that's part of it. But he also was so creative, and he had the ability to say, never using the word: "Assholes, this is great for both of you. Stop negotiating, I've had it." And he did that with Roche.

But that happened later. First, Raab recalled, Fred suggested that Raab go to London to meet with Armin Kessler, Roche's chief operating officer:

Fred set up the meeting. It was in London, and Armin Kessler and I met in a hotel room. I had a presentation, and it was me convincing him that the company was more valuable than they were making it.

Raab and Kessler didn't resolve the impasse on pricing in London, however, so a few days later Raab and Swanson traveled to Zurich to further hash things out with Gerber and Meier. Raab remembered:

I think it was on December 2nd or 3rd that we went to Zurich, just Bob and I. Fred didn't come to this meeting. But he was very much behind the scenes. We stayed at this Swiss hotel that had a golf course above the lake. It was very old-fashioned, very elegant and understated. We went and had this meeting, and now we're talking price. Bob said, "We have to do this right. We have to get the price. Fred isn't being hard-ass enough. We've got to go over there and tell them it's $42 [a share]." So we're there, Bob and me, Henri Meier, Fritz Gerber, and now Armin Kessler, a South African and longtime pharmaceutical guy. He was a business guy, and he had the business side approach.

We were in a fairly small room, and Bob was being really obnoxious. I was trying to calm him down. You could see that Fritz Gerber was a pretty important person in Switzerland. He was on the Merck board, in fact, and others. I had been president of Abbott, so I had a little more credentials than Bob, which made Bob a little nervous. He was being pushy about the price, and things were a little tense. Armin Kessler takes out a big Cuban cigar and lights it up, and Bob said, "Nobody smokes a cigar in my presence."

There was silence. I thought, "Oh God, it's going to be over, for a goddamn cigar." I said, "We're going to take a break. Bob, come with me." It was freezing out, and there was about a foot of snow. I said, "We're going to walk out there." He said, "Let me get my coat," and I said, "No, we're going to walk out there without our coats." And so I went out there, and I said, "Bob, either I go back, or you go back, but we're not both going in, because I'm not going in that room with you again. You just fucked up. I'm going back in to get this thing back on track. If you don't trust me and you want to do it, there's nothing I can do. You're the CEO. But, you're going to blow the deal."

We walked on the golf course, feet all wet. We had fancy Gucci shoes on, but it woke him up and made me tough. He walked back inside. He didn't say anything to me, and he went up to his room or whatever.

I went back in and said, "It's got to be $30, otherwise, we might as well stop talking. I'm not kidding, because Bob, as you know, is at $42. The distance is so great, and you haven't moved at all. You're talking about moving $28 to $30, and if you want Genentech, that doesn't have anything to do with anything." I was talking as if I were Fred Frank. I learned a lot from Fred. Like how to comport myself better.

I got them to $30 by the end of that meeting. And I told them, "I apologize for Bob." They said, "Don't worry about that." What Bob really did was to ensure that I became CEO. That was one of the big things he did that day. I think they would've wanted it anyway, but that certainly ensured it.

Raab added a personal note:

That was a hell of a time for me. We were in the middle of this intense deal, and things were going back and forth. And on the 29th of November, my twins were born. On the 11th of December my father died. Later, when my ex-wife and I were getting divorced, she actually mentioned this meeting in London during the proceedings. And I said, "The money you're getting is because I went to Zurich that day."

The price at $30 a share, though, was still far too low for Swanson even as Roche was still talking $28 to $30. That's when Fred suggested a price of $36 a share, which Swanson still didn't like, although he eventually gave in. "Perkins and Fred of course had a big role in convincing Bob about the price," said Raab.

The deal also nearly fell apart over another demand from Swanson—that he become a board member of Roche as part of the deal. Tom Perkins told Glenn Bugos about Roche's reaction to Swanson's stipulation:

Swanson was adamant that he wanted to go on the Roche board. That was just a nonstarter. They were not going to agree to that. Meetings took place in German, a language he didn't even speak. It was a deal point, and he wasn't going to cave on that. Kirk and I had our hands full in talking him out of that one, but we did. It was Bob Swanson wanting—a natural thing, I guess. But Roche wouldn't even consider it. I remember discussing this with Fred Frank, and he said, "I presented it to them because I was obliged to, but oh boy, this is not going to happen, and we have to get Bob off of this kick." Which we did.[14]

As the deal heated up, so did the pressure from Roche to make Kirk Raab CEO of Genentech. Tom Perkins told Glenn Bugos that at this point the change became inevitable:

Yes. That seemed to have been understood early on. This was something that was going to happen with or without Roche, in my view. Roche was just the event to make it happen. If we hadn't done the Roche deal, Kirk still would have become the CEO, but it would have been a more difficult, long, drawn-out thing to accomplish. Bob was so schizophrenic about it. On the one hand, he made a fortune, wanted to travel and enjoy his family, take some time off, which is certainly the right thing to do. On the other hand, he didn't want to give up the perks and glory of being CEO . . .

In a sense, the Genentech board used the Roche transaction as the trigger to make that happen. I probably presented it to Bob as a deal point demanded by Roche, which it was. But it may have been put in Roche's head along the way. It had to happen. Raab had a good track record at Abbott.

Raab remembered Fred's role in his transition to CEO.

Tom Perkins helped, although he eventually turned on Bob completely. And in this Fred was very helpful. He was always very calm. I mean he's the calmest guy I've ever known. His mind was always, "Get the deal done." And I never felt Fred did it because he wanted to make a lot of money. He did make a lot of money and should've. But his motivation was to do the deal.

When the deal terms had been worked out and approved by the Genentech board, Fred took the arrangement to Meier and Gerber at the Dolder Grand hotel in Zurich—and then ran into another snag. Fred recounted the meeting:

After the Genentech board agreed to the deal we had put together, I went to Zurich and met with Roche and they said, "We can't do this deal the way it is set up." I was thinking, "You've got to be kidding."

But they clearly wanted a deal, so I rewrote the terms on the spot, right there in the meeting. And it was actually a better deal, but I had to go back to the Genentech board.

As the Life Sciences Foundation reported:

At the eleventh hour, Meier announced that Roche couldn't go through with it, as Fred had explained the fine points of the CVR. Fred was dismayed. "Here I am, thinking I had an agreement with both parties. My client thinks that Roche agreed to this deal, and now I have no deal. At lunch that day, I created what became the Genentech-Roche deal." He jettisoned the CVRs and created a new structure that Roche was prepared to accept, one that has since been widely studied and discussed. The new arrangement would result in a larger cash payment to Genentech.

On Frank's advice, Genentech and Roche agreed to the following: Roche would buy $494 million worth of new stock from Genentech at the then market price of $21 a share. The company [Roche] would simultaneously offer to buy half of the [Genentech] shares outstanding at a 67 percent premium—$36 per share. Roche would pay $2.1 billion in all and own 60 percent of Genentech. The remaining shares would be exchanged for a new form of redeemable common stock with an embedded option: Roche could acquire additional pieces of the company, or all of it, at any time during the next five years, for a fixed price which would escalate every quarter ending at $60 per share in 1995.[15]

Fred explained his process:

People ask me how I came up with these terms like this on the spot. I say: "Roche had mixed goals. They didn't want to buy Genentech outright, as they knew its unique culture needed to be preserved by independence, and remaining public was a key indicator of that. But also they didn't want to not be able to acquire the remaining interest, virtually automatically. So the embedded option seemed to me, instinctively, the way to go.

Both parties were relieved and credited Fred with saving the deal. Perkins told Glenn Bugos:

> Both Roche and Genentech had confidence that Fred Frank had gotten a very good deal for both parties. We were not unhappy or disappointed at this strike price.[16]

Fred described another key moment in the negotiations. Roche's Henri Meier was in a conference room at the New York office of the Wachtell, Lipton, Rosen & Katz law firm, where they were finalizing details. Fred remembered that he looked at this "room full of lawyers" and decided to do an end run around them:

> I pulled Henri aside and told everyone we were going to meet outside the room, just the two of us, no lawyers, no one. So Henri followed me out of the room and we went over issues like how many board members Roche should have on the Genentech board. He had wanted one, and I said, "No, you should have two, a businessman and a scientist." There were a lot of issues like that, and we just ticked through them and went back into the room and told the lawyers that we had agreed on the following list of issues, that they were decided, and we wanted them written up in the agreement just as we had decided them. The lawyers didn't like that, of course.

Incredibly, said Perkins in the Bugos interview, the two sides had managed to keep the negotiations and the deal a secret until the end:

These things are so hard to keep secret, but you have to keep them secret because of all sorts of securities laws. As soon as the circle starts to broaden, the probability of leaks expands exponentially. Probably to the fifth power of the number of people involved. Prior to engaging with Roche, we had scanned the horizon and picked them as being the best possible and the only acquirer to be considered. I think that we were right about that. History has shown that that was the right decision.

We were very careful that this not become an auction. When we announced the deal, we wanted it to be so comprehensive and complete that it would discourage anybody else. Which it did. We were concerned about a hostile takeover, sort of the rape of the technology, and something that wouldn't be to the benefit of the shareholders or employees.[17]

The deal was finally announced in February 1990. Raab remembered the day that he and Swanson told the employees of Genentech:

We had to get all the employees together. So we had a big empty warehouse in South San Francisco. And it hadn't leaked. But one guy came up to me from the maintenance department, and he said, "You know, are we getting acquired? Something big is happening." And I said, "Really, why do you say that?" And he said, "Because I heard from the fire marshal that you asked for a permit to have 2,000 people in the warehouse."

So there were all these people in the room, and Bob actually made the announcement. He couldn't bring himself to announce that I was the CEO, though. Genentech cofounder Herb Boyer did that. But when Bob announced the deal, there was a mass: "Oh, no." It was pretty bad.

Fritz Gerber came to the announcement, but he did not speak to the employees. There was a big discussion over that, and we decided on a really good message. He had a press conference. I think Henri Meier was there, too.

Raab described the reaction of the shareholders:

Shareholders were upset, too, at first. Everybody in the Bay Area was a shareholder, and all the employees were, too. The employees had been pissed that they couldn't come to shareholder meetings because there was not enough room. We had masses of people coming to the shareholder meeting about the deal, because any-body with any sense realized that the stock was at $36 and the day before it was at $26, or whatever it was. And they all got a bunch of money. They got half their money at $36 a share. So it didn't take long.

But nobody really believed the governance thing—a lot of people didn't. But after a few years, Roche was never mentioned anymore. Until the second deal in 1995.

Fred tells an amusing story about this shareholders' meeting:

A young lady stood up and said: "I got on the Genentech train in New York and expected it to take me to California. Instead, you're letting me off in Cleveland." I wanted to tell her that this was the sure way to realize that dream.[18]

In the end, employees and shareholders were mostly pleased with the aftermath of the deal, when Roche not only abided by the agree-ment to leave Genentech alone but also saw the company's stock price rise. "The stock went up and up and up," said Raab, "and we were able to carry on with the cash we got from Roche and a strong stock." He continued:

The stock tracked up. And Fred forecast it—over the five years, what would happen to our stock. Because of this number they would've had to pay for the company. And the years went by, we got closer and closer to the date and our stock crept up. He had down to the cent what the increase was in which quarter. And the stock tracked almost exactly to what that increase was. It was awesome.

As the Life Sciences Foundation reported:

The merger stabilized Genentech's stock without compromising the firm's autonomy or destroying its unique culture. It enabled the company to maintain its research programs and introduce a string of important new biopharmaceutical products to the medical marketplace in the 1990s. The industry enjoyed an extended period of (mostly) fair weather on Wall Street from the mid-1990s until 2008. Genentech's highly visible success through these years helped to maintain the favorable climate.

"Fred's deal," as it came to be known, allowed the company to continue its research-focused forward progress. It became an exemplar for configuring relations between biotechnology and pharmaceutical companies in mergers and acquisitions.[19]

Geneticist and physician Lee Hood expressed a sentiment felt by many about "Fred's deal." "Genentech might well have faded away, absolutely, without this deal brokered by Fred," Hood said. "Roche gave them the security to be able to invent the future." Tom Perkins agreed. "Fred Frank found a way to do it," he said in the Bugos interview. "I don't think we could have done it better."[20]

With Fred's structure in place, the price of Genentech's stock over the next five years closely tracked the linear rise of Roche's option price (while most public biotech stocks fluctuated more or less wildly during the period). The deal had stabilized Genentech, just as it was intended to do. Genentech also had preserved its operational autonomy, and it had cash to spend aggressively on R&D, which it did.

In the years following the 1990 agreement, Genentech went on to introduce a remarkable series of innovative blockbuster biological products for treating conditions such as stroke, cystic fibrosis, asthma, and various forms of cancer.[21] The 1990 deal had allowed Genentech to thrive. That same year, the company launched the first commercial life sciences experiment in space when it sponsored research aboard the space shuttle Discovery. It also received FDA approval to expand the marketing of Activase to include the treatment of acute massive pulmonary embolism (blood clots in the lungs).

The Life Sciences Foundation article takes up the story, which is summarized below; the quotes are also from the article.

In 1995, near the end of the option period, with the stock trading at $57 per share, Frank went to Genentech and said, "My assumption is that when this option expires, Roche isn't going to exercise it." He reasoned that the terminal option price did not reflect the actual achievements of the company, which despite successes had substantially lagged behind original projections.

Fred advised Genentech to renegotiate and extend the arrangement. As an enticement, he suggested offering rights to market Genentech products outside the United States. "You're not going to be able to market outside the United States and Canada as effectively as they are," he told the leaders of Genentech. "They have a huge marketing organization."

Roche accepted, and the option was given four more years of life. Both parties agreed that options and obligations would terminate with finality in 1999, with no further extension. In this second iteration, Frank inserted a put option for shareholders. "Henri Meier was very much against this," Fred said, referring to Roche's CFO, "but the CEO, Fritz Gerber, was willing to do it." Roche's purchase-option price would escalate over the four years to a maximum of $82.50 per share in 1999. If Roche had not exercised its option by that time, Genentech shareholders could then sell their shares to Roche for $60 each. "Given Genentech's success and pipeline at that time," said Fred, "no one ever thought the put option would be exercised, but it was a good protection for shareholders."

Fred believed that this structure would encourage Roche to complete the acquisition at the new option price of $82.50 per share. Calling in all shares at $82.50 would be Roche's last chance to fully control the company, as the 1999 agreement prevented any extension of another option. Fred believed that Gerber and his colleagues would do it.

As the 1999 option deadline approached, Wall Street got the idea that Roche would not exercise it. This notion came from Genentech's huge success in developing and releasing the raft of new products, and the fact that Roche already held 60 percent of the company. "It was sort of strange," said Fred, "the stock was above the embedded option price, but investors seemed sure Roche would not exercise."

The price of Genentech stock continued to rise, reaching $96 just before Roche surprised Wall Street by exercising its option. They purchased the remainder of the company for $3.7 billion, at $82.50 per share. "Roche then did a remarkable and prescient thing," recalled Fred years later. "It then took 22 million shares of Genentech and put them up for sale in a public offering at $97 each." On July 20, 1999, Genentech's stock resumed trading on the New York Stock Exchange under the ticker symbol DNA.

Kirk Raab remembered how Fred's deal provided for the company's continued success:

> Roche went on to do brilliant things. They relisted the stock. Genentech remained Genentech. Art Levinson was the CEO, and it continued to be a wonderful research and development and domestic marketing machine. Fred's deal, protracted as it was, became the

model of an ideal merger and acquisition involving biotechnology and pharmaceutical companies.

In 2009, Roche finally made a decision to acquire the remaining 44 percent of Genentech it did not own. The enormous success of the Genentech cancer pipeline, which Roche marketed outside the US after the 1995 option renewal deal, had led the businesses to be so intertwined that Roche eventually wanted a seamless face for the company. Genentech as an independently operating entity also was competing for some of the same in-licensing deals, which didn't make sense to Roche executives. The takeover, however, was bitterly contested for more than eight months as the two sides sparred over the valuation of the company and the culture.

After some negotiations with management were not fruitful, Roche launched a public hostile offer for Genentech at $89 per share on July 21, 2008. The bid was not well received by either Genentech's board or its shareholders. Then on September 15, 2008, came Lehman Brothers' bankruptcy and its fallout as markets tumbled and worldwide recession loomed. This led Roche to lower its offer to $86.50, eliciting a predictably negative reaction. Finally, Roche raised the offer to $93 per share and then $95 per share to counter Genentech's proposed $112—the $95 figure was then accepted. The final agreement also included ways to preserve the entrepreneurial culture of Genentech, which continued for several years thereafter.

Fred's role in the Roche-Genentech arrangement over the years was acknowledged in the annual CEO meeting in 1997 at the Ritz-Carlton in Laguna Niguel, a resort in Orange County, California, where biotech CEOs still gather each year (in nonpandemic years) as a guest of Brook Byers, a legendary venture capitalist with Kleiner Perkins Caufield & Byers. Each year, Byers would poll attendees and give out the "Oscars of Biotech" awards by category for Top Company, Best New FDA-Approved Product, Best Financing, and Best M&A Deal. At the

Sunday night formal banquet that October, Byers announced that Fred had won Best M&A Deal of the Year and also was recognized as the top biotech dealmaker for the past decade. The setting was outdoors around the luxurious Ritz-Carlton resort pool, which prompted Byers to joke in his remarks that Fred's acumen made Byers wonder if Fred, seated on the other side of the large pool, might walk on water to accept the award. Fred got up to applause for the award, smiled and started walking directly toward Byers to accept the engraved crystal award. But instead of walking around the pool, he stepped right into it. "It was crazy," remembered Fred, "I had on a silk suit and tie and just walked right into the water and started to move toward Brook. People were shocked. I was shocked."

"It was the most amazing thing," said Mary. "He just stepped out over the pool and to this day, some people who were there swear that he got halfway across the pool before he sank." Fred waded to the other side, climbed out of the pool, and walked to the podium where Byers led the 250 CEOs, spouses, and guests in thunderous applause and hollering. Fred delivered a short acceptance speech, dripping wet, as though nothing unusual had happened, and returned to his dining table seat.

Byers has reflected often that over the many years he and so many there that night had worked with Fred, "we always knew him to be the most disciplined, serious minded, exquisitely dressed, formal yet friendly investment banker we knew. His energy and determination inspired us all. That 'walk on water' gesture showed us another side of Fred that we came to understand was there all along, a subtle sense of humor and playfulness. In that gesture, Fred became a legend in more than just business."

A BLIZZARD OF DEALS

For Fred, the Roche-Genentech deal signaled an even busier time than the eighties, which had been plenty busy. The deals that came fast and furious included, in 1991, the sale of Cetus to another rising star of biotechnology, Chiron, for $660 million. Founded in 1981 by three UCSF biochemists, William Rutter, Edward Penhoet, and Pablo Valenzuela, Chiron became best known for using biotechnology to combat infectious diseases, developing products such as a Hepatitis C test and a vaccine for Hepatitis B. Chiron acquired Cetus after Cetus failed to get approval from the FDA for Interleukin-2, an immune system modifier that was being tested in clinical trials for renal cancer. Significant side effects led the FDA to deny approval and to ask for additional information, news that sunk the company, which had devoted most of its resources to developing the drug and needed an approval to get additional funding. A year after buying Cetus, Chiron was able to get the Interleukin-2 drug approved, and it remains a staple of therapeutic use today.

At the time of the sale, Cetus cofounder and CEO Ronald Cape, whom Fred had first called on back in 1974, talked to the *New York Times*:

> "If I were to tell you that I stand here exhilarated, you'd know I wouldn't be telling the truth," a somewhat somber Ronald E. Cape . . . said at a news conference . . . But he added: "We couldn't have found a better partner. We couldn't have found a better home."

Curiously, Chiron did not opt to buy a technology owned by Cetus called Polymerase Chain Reaction (PCR), a chemical process invented by Cetus chemist Kary Mullis, PhD, in 1983. PCR allows bio-researchers to replicate molecules like DNA in the large quantities needed to run experiments and tests. Previously, scientists had to scrape together naturally occurring DNA molecules that were always in very short supply—and expensive. The PCR discovery was important enough to garner Mullis a Nobel Prize in 1993, but oddly, was not important enough for Chiron to purchase the rights to it as part of the Cetus deal in 1991. Fred remembered it being Chiron's loss:

> Well, it's funny how things happen. We were representing Cetus, which I had taken public, in the merger with Chiron. Chiron was run by two really terrific scientists and a really terrific businessman. And what did they tell me? They said, "Fred, you keep telling us about the value of this thing called PCR. Trust me, it doesn't have any value. We're not going to buy it." So Cetus kept it. It was not part of the merger, and I sold it to Roche for $375 million. It was $300 million upfront and $75 million earned out.

Chiron's assessment was understandable at the time, as the technology was very new and needed robust development. But it was wrong, as PCR eventually brought in more than $25 billion a year in global revenues and made billions of dollars for Roche before the exclusive patent ended in 2005. But Chiron was not the only financial loser in the PCR saga. Inventor Kary Mullis, whose work was owned by Cetus, said that the only money he ever made directly from PCR was a $10,000 bonus the company paid him in 1983. "I did win the Nobel," he said, "but I got none of the billions made on PCR."

Fred remembered receiving a unique expression of gratitude for his role in this and previous Cetus transactions:

> The usual tradition on Wall Street on completing a financing or merger/acquisition assignment is to memorialize the transaction via a Lucite cube. This time, Ron Cape, the CEO at Cetus that I had worked so long with, gave me a very special and unusual gift. He arranged to have me photographed by one of the world's most

famous photographers, Yousuf Karsh. He was "the" photographer for famous people, i.e., Winston Churchill, Albert Einstein, President Kennedy, Martin Luther King, Mandela, and the list goes on. Ron knew Karsh because they were both Canadians.[*]

In April of 1992, Fred worked on another seminal deal involving the Wellcome Trust, the world's largest medical charity, which floated shares in its operating company, Wellcome Plc, with the intention of using the proceeds for medical research. Wellcome Plc was particularly known at the time for its drug AZT, one of the first to treat AIDS, and Actifed, an antihistamine. The global offering raised about $4.14 billion. In the US, Wellcome floated 73.5 million shares at a price of $15.25 per share, for $1.12 billion. Fred, who had a long-standing relationship with Wellcome, brought Lehman into the US portion of the global offering. He continued work with the new company and served as a behind-the-scenes advisor to Wellcome when Glaxo bought the company in 1995.

In 1994, Fred helped Neutrogena sell itself to Johnson & Johnson for $982 million. Fred remembered making the match:

> Neutrogena retained me to sell the company. I thought the perfect home for this iconic brand would be Johnson & Johnson. So I called Ralph Larsen, chairman and chief executive officer of Johnson & Johnson, and explained that I had an exceptional acquisition opportunity for them. Naturally, he asked what it was. I explained that I could not discuss it on the phone. He said, "OK, come down and let's have lunch." So at lunch at Johnson & Johnson, I explained that I was representing Neutrogena. He said, "Really? We have been salivating about that company for several years." I said, "Yes, and I am prepared to let Johnson & Johnson preempt the process. If you don't

[*]   One of the Karsh photographs appears on the cover of this book.

offer an acceptable price, the process will go to an auction." He said, "Fred, I want you to work exclusively with Pete Larson, head of our worldwide consumer sector." So Peter and I had one meeting, two telephone calls, and the deal was agreed to.

I went to present the deal to the board of Neutrogena in Los Angeles and explained that Johnson & Johnson was prepared to pay cash or cash and stock or all stock. I recommended an all-stock deal, saying, at the time, in my opinion, Johnson & Johnson was undervalued, and it would be a tax-free deal. A fierce discussion ensued. Most of the board [members] were in favor of an all-stock deal. But the company accountant convinced the CEO, Lloyd Cotsen, that stock was too risky! So it was an all-cash transaction.

I excused myself to call Johnson & Johnson to congratulate them and explain that the board determined to make it an all-cash transaction. Then I said we could issue the joint press release, which had been written. There was a moment of silence. Then, Pete Larson said, "Fred I have a problem." After my heart skipped a beat, I said, "What's the problem? We have agreed on your proposal." He said, "Look at the second paragraph of the press release, where it said we, Johnson & Johnson, have agreed to acquire Neutrogena in an all-cash transaction for X per share." I said, "OK, what's the problem?" He responded that only Pete and I knew the number.

I laughed (probably a sigh of relief) and said, "You mean, I can put in any number I want." And he said, "Absolutely." So we issued the joint press release. Everyone was very happy.

In hindsight it was probably one of the best acquisitions that Johnson & Johnson ever made. And in all fairness to them, they really made a global success of a very distinguished product brand. Still, the shareholders and all constituents would have been far better rewarded had they elected a tax-free, all-stock transaction.

In yet another game-changing deal, Synthélabo, a privately owned French pharmaceutical company, was acquired by Sanofi in 1999. It was a complex transaction, with the two core shareholders of each company, Elf Aquitaine and L'Oréal, contributing their stakes to the new combined company for an ownership of 35.1 percent and 19.4 percent, respectively. Public shareholders exchanged their shares at a ratio of 13 Sanofi shares to 10 for Synthélabo.

The combined market value was approximately $29.5 billion. The new company was the sixth-largest in Europe and the second-largest in France. "Individually, Sanofi and Synthélabo were both below world scale," said Fred. "So when the merger in which I represented Synthélabo (whom I had been calling on for many years) was completed, it set the base for building a competitive European drug company."

THE NINETIES HEATS UP: OF GOLD RUSH AND BUBBLES

As the late eighties revved up and the early nineties turned into the roaring nineties in terms of high-tech deals and money flowing, another wave of Big Biotech companies were emerging with names like Millennium, Vertex, Human Genome Sciences, and Celera. This came about as a fresh round of investor and market exuberance commenced over new scientific breakthroughs that promised to treat or even cure diseases ranging from diabetes and heart disease to cancer. Part of this excitement was generated when the United States Congress in 1990 funded the $3 billion, 15-year Human Genome Project (HGP), an audacious effort to sequence the entire human genome. The HGP energized the molecular biology community in general and also funded and engaged scientists around the world to plunge even more deeply into the science fueling the biotech industry.

As the bio-excitement rose, money came pouring in from everywhere: from Big Pharma, flush with blockbuster cash, and from a US government that would pay for not only the Human Genome Project, but also, in 1998, for a five-year plan to double the budget of the National Institutes of Health (NIH). During this same time, the public markets were in a runaway boom from 1993 to 2000 that created trillions in new wealth (partly on paper), driven mostly by new information technologies like computers and dot-coms, although life science advancements were important to the boom, too.

This cyclonic high-tech boom was mostly driven by investment capital in both the venture community and among mutual fund investors, but also by the banks—big ones like Lehman in New York, and several smaller boutique banks in California and elsewhere, such as Robertson, Stephens & Company. Founded in the seventies, these smaller banks were playing a key role in engaging the "Bigs" on Wall Street, and in co-brokering deals to finance high-tech companies ranging from Apple to biotechs. As the nineties revved up, the small banks grew larger and eventually became large banks themselves, or were acquired by mega-banks such as JPMorgan and Goldman Sachs. (Robertson Stephens was sold to Bank of America in 1997 and then was sold again to BankBoston in 1998, where it remained until being shut down in 2002 after the stock market crash the year before. The name survives today as Robertson Stephens Wealth Management.)

A moderate Democratic president took office in 1993 to complete the gradual dismantling of the system created at the height of the Great Depression to reign in banking excesses that led to the crash of 1929. In 1933 Congress had passed the Glass-Steagall Act, which, among other things, had forbidden investment banks from using depositors' money held in commercial banks. In 1998 the US Congress, prompted by the Clinton administration, struck down this provision and Depression-era regulations. As a result, for the first time in sixty-five years, investment banks now had unfettered access to the vast capital of commercial deposits to invest in securities, both solid and speculative—a banking "reform" that added significantly to the already expanding tech bubble that by 1998 was building toward a spectacular bust in 2000–01.

THE GENOMIC REVOLUTION REALLY RAMPS UP

During the nineties, the idea of using DNA to better understand human biology—and how genetic differences among people contribute to some getting diseases and to others staying healthy—became all the rage. Gene-based companies that used sequences of DNA to develop new drugs had been around since the seventies, when companies like Genentech and Cetus were founded and started to use techniques like using recombinant DNA to manipulate bacteria or animal cells (Chinese hamster ovarian cells) to excrete drugs like Herceptin and Epogen. In the late eighties and nineties, as the technologies of sequencing both animal and human genes accelerated, and more sequences from a wide range of organisms became available, a number of new start-ups began to develop genomic platforms that promised to deliver new gene-based drugs that the companies claimed would revolutionize medicine. Fred summarized what was happening:

> So, we had a genomic revolution, with all of so-called genomics companies having these incredible valuations in the mid-nineties. They all went public about the same time because, you know, these offerings based on new technologies feed on themselves. Take Millennium—after its IPO, the market cap became something like $11 billion. Human Genome Science came out with a market cap of $8 billion or so.
>
> Less than two years later, every one of those stocks declined more than 90 percent. I don't have the figures in front of me, but let's say

we're talking about valuations of companies that collectively equals $30 billion. So, $30 billion from these companies goes to less than $3 billion. That's a lot of money.

So why did so much money move into biotech during this era? There are two fundamental reasons. Number one, because the lay press started talking about this new world, making very extravagant claims that these companies were creating magic bullets and silver bullets which were going to cure everything from diabetes to Alzheimer's to cancer.

The other reason is that people didn't understand that biotech was different than other high-tech and dot-com companies. For one, biotech is highly regulated. Let's take Intel or eBay or any of the high-tech companies. It comes up with a creative idea, you still see this all the time today in the Internet. You can introduce your idea, and you try it. And it works pretty fast or it doesn't, because this is not in a highly regulated industry. In biotech, everything is highly regulated. You can have an idea for a new product, and you have to test it and run it through clinical trials and the approval process. That's a ten-year process, ten to twelve years. It's a long time, and it is extremely expensive with the probability of success less than 10 percent. So it's difficult to support this industry using the classic venture capital model of private money that wants a faster return. I used to have to tell people, let's just understand what you're getting into. This is also why biotech turned to the public markets to raise money in what essentially became public venture capital.

Fred and Mary also talked about how biotech companies changed in their focus during the nineties. "In my view, biotech moved from being a science-determined definition to a vague business model," said Mary. "That's an important point," Fred agreed. "How did that happen? If you go back to the early companies, they were all started and then run by scientists. If we move forward, they became operated like pharma companies, a world dominated by marketing people. Because they came to be Wall Street–centric rather than science-centric."

Jeremy Levin, a serial entrepreneur who was CEO of the generic drug company Teva Pharmaceutical Industries, and is now CEO of Ovid Therapeutics, recalled Fred's advice for anyone looking into running or investing in genomics companies:

> Fred was involved at a moment that at the time was all about creating biotech platforms—not drugs, but platforms. This included Genentech and other gene-based companies, companies that were making discoveries in the human genome, assuming that the drugs would follow.
>
> Fred knew more about how these companies were going to succeed or fail than anybody else. He constantly said, "It's all very nice to have the technology, but you need to have a product." He would use as an example the stock price of Genentech—which of course generated huge excitement when it went IPO even without having a product. The stock rose tremendously and then plummeted because everybody was waiting for the products to emerge. Fred kept saying at the time: "A company will succeed or fail based on its product."
>
> And it was clear at the time that the technology base of the industry was undergoing a radical shift. People hunting down genes were the most important people who existed; they raised huge sums of money. There's an apocryphal tale, I'm not sure that it's true, that Bill Haseltine, the CEO of Human Genome Sciences, on his roadshow way back then had a single slide which showed three things on it. One was the word gene. The second was the equal sign. The third was the dollar sign. Fred was constantly saying, "Genes need to equal value."

HUMAN GENOME SCIENCES: THE SAGA
OF BILL HASELTINE AND CRAIG VENTER

One of those high-flying, highly volatile companies during this period was Human Genome Sciences (HGS), which Fred helped foster and get funded when it was launched in 1992. The company was developed by venture capitalists Wally Steinberg and Alan Walton. They took their idea of starting a new genomics-based company to a brilliant young scientist at the NIH who had recently run afoul of the first director of the Human Genome Project, James Watson, the Nobel Laureate who co-discovered the double-helix shape of DNA back in 1953.

The energetic and headstrong Craig Venter had butted heads with the equally obdurate Watson when the younger scientist championed a technique for sequencing DNA called shotgun sequencing, a method that many scientists dismissed as being less accurate than the more traditional Sanger sequencing method, named for British geneticist Fred Sanger, who helped perfect it. But Venter's method was much faster and proved to be accurate enough that even traditionalists eventually adopted it, even if purists like Watson derided it at the time as being bad science. Venter also had developed a new method for tagging genes called Expressed Sequence Tags (ESTs). Specifically, these were short sub-sequences of complementary DNA that scientists were able to produce quickly using shotgun-expressed messenger RNA sequencing. The sub-sequences could then be used to identify gene transcripts, which helped speed up the discovery of new genes.

Despite the rejection by Watson and many mainstream geneticists, Venter's techniques attracted attention in the private sector as a possible means of speeding up gene discovery and drug development. This led to a flurry of offers from entrepreneurs and investors who wanted Venter to leave the NIH to start or join a commercial effort around his new technology. These suitors included Steinberg and Walton.

Venter, however, at the time did not want to be a CEO or run a company. He told Steinberg and Walton that he was more interested in heading up a well-funded research effort that would set out to make molecular discoveries that might prove to be commercially viable. Steinberg and Walton liked this idea and went to Fred to broker a deal that would create and fund an effort that included both a commercial company and an affiliated research institute. This is where the idea came from that ended up creating Human Genome Sciences and The Institute for Genomic Research (TIGR), headed up by Venter.

To run HGS, Steinberg and Walton turned to William A. Haseltine, a famed Harvard researcher and entrepreneur working in oncology and HIV/AIDS. At Harvard, Haseltine had used the latest findings and techniques in molecular biology to develop powerful antiretroviral therapies to combat AIDS and to treat certain cancers, methods that Haseltine wanted to use to power the science at HGS.

With Haseltine on board as CEO, Fred helped organize the financing of the company and to provide around $70 million to fund TIGR, which was required under the deal to offer HGS any commercially useful molecular discoveries made by Venter and his scientists. HGS would then have six months, or in some cases a year, to file patents and begin development before TIGR could publish its sequencing results in the public domain. "It was a most inventive and unusual arrangement at the time," recalled Fred, "allying a leading academic research group with a commercially oriented company."

Fred had known Bill Haseltine since 1983, when one of Haseltine's earlier companies, Cambridge Bioscience, went public. Haseltine remembers:

> I believe Fred came to Cambridge Bioscience when we were talking
> to another company about something. He was representing them or
> something. I liked Fred immediately, and he took us public, so I've

known Fred for almost thirty years. He's been involved with every one of my IPOs—that's about seven or eight IPOs.

Like Venter at his institute, Bill Haseltine's aspirations at HGS were not modest. He aimed to create a huge company that would dominate molecular biology, a goal that later became the subject of a 2013 case study published in the *Journal of Commercial Biotechnology*, written by Laura M. McNamee and Fred D. Ledley of Bentley University. They wrote that:

> Human Genome Sciences was not a company with normal ambi-
> tions. At its founding in 1992, HGS aspired to dominate the newly
> emergent field of genomics by being the first to sequence and patent
> all of the genes expressed from the human genome and develop a
> pipeline of therapeutic and diagnostic products based on their genes.
> The company's outsized ambitions were advertised in elaborate annual
> reports, which featured Greek gods and saints as metaphors for the
> company's search for knowledge and fight against the disease.[22]

For a time, the TIGR/HGS partnership worked. Excitement over the hybrid commercial-research approach helped secure a deal in 1993 with SmithKline Beecham to gain access to both TIGR's gene sequences and HGS's rights. This sort of collaboration between Big Pharma and biotech, even after the Roche-Genentech deal, remained unusual at the time, coming in part from Haseltine's belief that HGS should actively collaborate with other drug companies large and small. "I had this attitude anyway," Haseltine remembered, "but I'm sure that Fred encouraged it, since he knew about both worlds. He had talked for a long time about the need for biotech's innovative ability in research to be paired up with pharma's ability to develop and sell drugs."

In April 1993, Fred helped coordinate the deal with SmithKline

Beecham to invest $125 million in HGS's genomic discovery platform, then the largest funding ever provided by Big Pharma to a start-up biotechnology company. The key player at SmithKline Beecham was its head of R&D, George Poste, an early and earnest advocate of Big Pharma doing deals with biotech companies as a means to bring innovation to the drug giants. "George was terrific in this," remembered Haseltine. "He immediately wanted to do the deal. I think he wanted SmithKline to get into diagnostics. He wanted to direct that effort, and he thought he could do it through HGS, and eventually he did."

Fred remembered a key moment in the negotiations:

> There were a lot of high-tempered, truly brilliant people in the room. There were also a lot of complicated issues: What intellectual property belonged to TIGR, what to HGS, what rights SmithKline would have, tension over funding to TIGR versus HGS. Things were getting out of hand, in a deal that everybody wanted to do, and I finally did something I almost never do. I started pounding my hand on the table and shouting that everybody should sit down and calm down. And we got the deal done, in the end, very cordially.

A year later, HGS and SmithKline Beecham divided another $320 million raised by selling access to HGS's discovery tools to other drug companies around the world, including Merck in Germany, Schering Plough in the US, Sanofi in France, and Takeda in Japan. HGS went public in 1993. Fred noted the cooperative spirit of the members of the distinct companies:

> In all of these transactions for HGS, one of the remarkable things was the incredible degree of integration into the research efforts of these Big Pharma companies. This included newly introduced computer interfaces and regular team meetings held electronically.

These were not traditional licensing collaborations; they were true partnerships in discovery, reflecting the importance of this new technology.

Both Bill Haseltine and Fred agreed from the very beginning that HGS would be not just an information services company—a temptation given the pile of genetic and other molecular data they were producing—but a pharmaceutical and diagnostic product–development company. Another company that ended up adopting a genome-based drug discovery platform in this era was Millennium Pharmaceuticals, while others, like Incyte Pharmaceuticals, focused more on providing genomic and other molecular data and analysis. Bill Haseltine explained his vision for HGS:

> HGS set out to be a pharmaceutical company, not an information services company, because an information services company would be quickly out of business. There would be too many competitors.

Despite the early success with SmithKline Beecham, the tensions between Venter's research-oriented approach at TIGR and the commercialization objectives of Haseltine and HGS caused friction between the two entities. The two men also were big personalities who could be abrasive and didn't always get along with others. These strains became pronounced when Venter embarked on a series of projects at TIGR that had little possibility of becoming commercially viable, and were therefore of little use to HGS. These included an exciting project that used new sequencing techniques to sequence an entire microbe for the first time ever, the tiny *Mycoplasma genitalium*. This attention-attracting feat of pure research foreshadowed some of the difficulties that business-minded collaborators would have with Craig Venter, first at HGS, and later at Celera, a company he founded in 1998 to challenge the public Human Genome Project in sequencing the entire human genome—which turned out to be a breathtaking feat of science, but less of a success as a business.

By 1997, the misalignment of objectives between HGS and TIGR culminated in a separation of the two entities, with HGS continuing to raise huge sums of money and develop their genomic-based drug pipeline during the high-technology boom in the nineties and beyond. Bill Haseltine recalled what was happening during this heady time as the company went IPO in 1993 in a deal led by Fred, and then raised more money:

> So in 1998, 1999, and 2000 we pulled in almost $2 billion. I remember the last offering we did was about $900 million and it was just before the 2000 election. I was terrified that the election would close down the wide-open window for raising money at the time. But everything was fine—in fact, the roadshow opened on and closed at $900 million on the next Thursday. We closed it, and then of course the election came, the dot-com bubble burst, and the whole market went down and then later recovered.

At the same time HGS was raking in cash, Craig Venter was having a huge success with his new company, Celera. Founded in 1998, shortly after Venter left HGS, Celera also raised billions of dollars and famously went on to compete in the race to sequence the human genome against a US government effort funded by the NIH and the US Department of Energy. Geneticist and future director of the National Institutes of Health Francis Collins led the public initiative for the NIH and its partners in the International Human Genome Sequencing Consortium (HGSC). The HGSC included research institutes from around the world, and particularly from the United Kingdom, including the Wellcome Trust.

Both the government initiative and Celera, after a sometimes contentious rivalry, published preliminary maps of the human genome in 2000 and a "final" (but still not entirely complete) version in 2003. Celera and Venter shook things up during this so-called "race" by using the shotgun sequencing technique he had continued to improve on since leaving the NIH. At first, the NIH-led public effort resisted shotgun sequencing in favor of the slower, more traditional Sanger method, although eventually they, too, adopted shotgun sequencing. Venter claimed that Celera's approach required in the end only about $300 million of private funding, whereas the intergovernmental approach cost about $3 billion.

The public-private rivalry resulted in the completion of two rough drafts of the human genome in 2000, which Venter and Collins and other scientists announced on March 15, 2000, in a White House ceremony with President Bill Clinton and Prime Minister Tony Blair of the United Kingdom attending by video conference. This was scientifically exciting news, although the announcement was accompanied by a promise from Clinton, Blair, and the government scientists that the data being released "should be made freely available to scientists everywhere."[23] This pronouncement that did not sit well with investors and companies, including Celera, which had been hoping to patent parts of the genome. The idea that they might not be able to own genes that might be valuable in developing drugs and other treatments—coming just as the bull market was peaking and was poised to begin its precipitous fall—led to an enormous sell-off of genomics and biotechnology company stocks. Some genomics companies lost between 20 percent and 40 percent of their market capitalization, wiping out billions of dollars in shareholder value.

Later, the White House said that it had not intended to prejudice the intellectual property rights of Celera or other biotech companies, but the damage would never be repaired. Fred recalled the issues involved:

> It was always clear from the beginning of the genomic age that there would be terrific frictions between the Celera human genome

project and the intergovernmental project, and that the question of patenting genomic sequences, actual genes, would be a ferocious debate—which still goes on to this day. But it was an exciting time, and my team at Lehman and I were heavily involved. Unfortunately, the questions of what was patentable and what was not cratered the biotech market at that time.

ANOTHER NON-PHARMA DEAL: NIELSEN'S RATINGS

The other big non-bio deal Fred did during these years was the merger of A.C. Nielsen, the marketing research company, and Dun & Bradstreet in May 1994. Fred had first met Art Nielsen in 1959 when he was still at Smith, Barney, and there he had helped to underwrite the company's IPO in 1958. Over the years he had kept up with Nielsen, offering advice and counsel.

Fred related one example from the early seventies about the sort of advice he proffered to Nielsen—and to others—in this case by calling a meeting with Art Nielsen at the company's headquarters in Chicago.

> One day I called up Art and asked him if I could come out and meet with him and his senior team. He said, "Well, Fred, what do you want to talk about?" I said, "I can't tell you." He said, "Well, how can I have a meeting?" And I said, "Art, you're the CEO, just have a meeting and I'll come."
>
> So I went out there. Art was always very gracious. He said to the team out there of about nine people, "Fred asked me to have this meeting, and I have no idea what the subject is, but we've had a long relationship with Fred, so here's the meeting. Fred, it's your meeting."

I said, "Look, I have a hypothesis that I want to share with you. You and Nielsen have only increased your prices to your clients twice in the last twelve years, and they were modest increases. My hypothesis is that the US is going to go through a period of hyperinflation, and you are going to get killed by that because you can't pass on prices that quickly at those levels. So I think what you should put in your contracts is that your prices will increase with the CPI (consumer price index). Nobody will complain about that; they'll understand that you have higher costs. If you increase only to the equivalent of the CPI index, that's being fair."

Inflation was very low at the time, less than 3 percent, so this turned into a great debate. The sales guys were all against it. The finance guys and the management were all in favor of it, and eventually they did it. And I'll tell you, that made a huge difference in the continued success of A.C. Nielsen, because we did in fact go through hyperinflation, and that protected their revenue and growth.

This sort of advice and attention over the years meant that Nielsen turned to Fred and Lehman when the company was considering a merger with Dun & Bradstreet. Fred remembered Nielsen's conveniently timed phone call:

Art Nielsen Jr. called me up one day and said, "Fred, it's very urgent that I see you. Is there any possibility you'd come out and see me tomorrow in Chicago?" I said: "All right, but why wait until tomorrow? I could see you today at lunchtime." This was at 10:30 in the morning, Chicago time. He said, "How can you do that?" And I said, "I'm in downtown Chicago, by coincidence."

I went out to see him, and that was when they'd been approached by Dun & Bradstreet to acquire the company. And he asked me to represent them and work with him on this.

Fred had a long conversation with Art about whether a merger was right for Nielsen. "It was an emotion thing, of course, because this was a family company," said Fred. "But there was a compelling case for the merger." Fred recalled how he explained it:

> I put together a time chart that said, OK, you went public here and now we are about here. Wall Street's expectation is [that] you are going to go like this, and the fact you are on this curve [means] you are going have a decelerating rate of growth. Right now, you are selling at a very high price/earnings ratio. If this happens that ratio is going to get killed. If your P/E ratio goes from 40 to 20 and your earnings are up less than 15 percent a year, your stock price is going to go down. I think this is the ideal opportunity for you to do this deal with Dun & Bradstreet.
>
> Nielsen said, "I want your help on this plus your advice because it's a very emotional issue, you know. I inherited the business from my father, so I have got a terrible moral issue here." So we had a long talk, and I represented them in this deal with Dun & Bradstreet in 1994. It ended up being worth slightly over a billion dollars, which in those days was a pretty big deal.

Mary Tanner recalled Fred's foresight about the business-services category and answered a common question about Nielsen's growth potential:

> The interesting thing about Nielsen was that Fred had this vision about business services and business-services models. One question that was always asked about Nielsen, who sold data to everybody, was how they could ever grow? Because they already sold everything to every consumer product company in the world. People used to ask how Nielsen would grow, but they underestimated new services to the same clients. And Nielsen itself innovated new ways to charge

so that you didn't just charge once for the data, you charged per task for the data.

Fred understood early on that the business-services model was shifting, because I remember an associate talking to him about these things, and he explained it to me. There were not a lot of business-services companies like that at the time.

Today, business-services models are ubiquitous and even larger than before because of the Internet. But it wasn't well understood in those days.

MARY MAKES A MOVE

In 1999, Mary left Lehman and joined Bear Stearns in 2000, another venerable Wall Street company that had started out in 1923 as a small firm and survived the 1929 crash without firing a single employee. By 2006 it had grown into a publicly traded, global colossus with more than 15,000 employees and hundreds of billions of dollars in assets. It was the seventh-largest securities firm in terms of total capital; Lehman had close to twice this capital, although by 2006–2007, both firms were leveraged at what turned out to be unsustainable levels—which we will get into in the next chapter. Mary recalled her move to Bear-Stearns:

> I had intended to retire and spend more time with our son. So initially I set up a small consulting firm, but I quickly became bored, missed investment banking. Bear Stearns recruited me, and I had a good time there, mostly doing mergers and acquisitions. We represented Pfizer in acquiring Pharmacia in 2003 for $60 billion and Amgen in acquiring Immunex in 2002 for $10 billion. But I soon left Bear Stearns. It did not have the same investment banking culture that Lehman had, and I didn't fit there. The firm was driven

by its mortgage business and trading. When the legendary [Alan] Ace Greenberg was pushed out of the firm, I left, in part because I thought his firm hand would be missed. And of course, it was missed, as the firm collapsed later during the financial crash in 2008–2009.

THE TURN OF THE MILLENNIUM AND THE DOT-COM BUBBLE

As the year 2000 approached, global stock markets were reaching the height of the dot-com frenzy. Companies promised to use the Internet to revolutionize everything from travel, search, and buying pet food to ordering wine, stiletto heels, and concrete online and were getting crazy valuations with vague business plans and no products as money flew in all directions. The boom also impacted biotech and pharma, with companies sprouting up (many with vague business plans and no products) and getting funded at an unprecedented rate.

Then came April 14, 2000, when the NASDAQ Composite Index fell 9 percent, capping a week in which it fell a whopping 25 percent as the roaring nineties ended in a spectacular and disastrous fashion. By November of that year, Internet stocks had dropped at least 80 percent, and many had ceased operations. The crash lasted until the autumn of 2002, with the loss in market capitalization since the peak of the boom totaling well over $5 trillion, a drop of almost 78 percent from the peak in March 2000.

"These were dark days after a wild decade," said Fred. "The crash and contracting markets killed the IPO market and really the mergers and acquisitions market, too. I don't remember any deals that got cancelled, but a lot of deals that might have happened never did."

Curiously, this abrupt and shattering end to the go-go years didn't slow down Fred in the least, even during the worst period between April

2000 and October 2002. "We soldiered on," he said. "It was a difficult time," Fred added, "but in biotech the underlying science and breakthroughs continued, so I knew that the future would remain promising."

Fred was right. Even during the crash his deals kept coming, including one that became notorious.

IMCLONE, MARTHA STEWART, AND BRISTOL-MYERS

In September 2001, even as world markets were cratering, Fred negotiated on behalf of Bristol-Myers a co-development, co-promotion agreement with ImClone Systems regarding Erbitux, a then-novel monoclonal antibody drug to treat refractory colorectal carcinoma. Erbitux was then in late-stage clinical development and had been fast-tracked for approval by the FDA. Bristol-Myers paid ImClone $1 billion for a near 20 percent stake in the company, in addition to receiving a significant share of product revenues.

Everyone expected the product to achieve rapid approval and to become a blockbuster out of the gate. Then the FDA shocked everyone by turning down the application to approve Erbitux at the end of 2001, a mere three months after the closing of the Bristol-Myers deal. The circumstances surrounding the product were complicated by an ensuing insider trading scandal involving ImClone's CEO Sam Waksal, his family, and celebrity homemaking entrepreneur Martha Stewart, all of whom sold ImClone shares prior to the FDA's bad news, which landed Waksal and Stewart in prison.

The FDA eventually approved the drug in February 2004, and Carl Icahn, of Icahn Enterprises holding company, purchased a majority of the ImClone shares in October 2006. The drug went on to success, and a takeover battle ensued between Bristol-Myers and Eli Lilly for the roughly 50 percent of the drug's profitability that ImClone had retained in the original Bristol-Myers deal. In October 2008, after several offers, Lilly succeeded in purchasing ImClone for $72 per share or approximately $6.5 billion. Fred remembered:

> It was a remarkable saga. But the product did succeed. Bristol-Myers's original judgment was correct. At the time of the Lilly acquisition, Erbitux's sales were $1.3 billion, large for an oncology product at that time. It became an important product for both Bristol-Myers and Eli Lilly in cancer, as they shared economics. I wasn't involved in the final resolution, and frankly, after all the angst, I was relieved not to be. And I didn't want to be between two clients of the firm in the very bitter battle that ensued.

As Fred continued to make deals even at the lowest point after the 2001–2002 crash, economic and market forces were realigning for what would be a surprisingly robust revival. A boom would follow, prompting another period of free-for-all risk-taking and profit-making as the new century began, and the uncanny ability of people to forget what happens when overexuberance and greed drives markets was about to play out yet again in the twenty-aughts.

CHAPTER 7

A New Century

BOOMS AND BUSTS, LEHMAN'S FALL, AND THE AFTERMATH, 2002–2020

Unless the continuity of the old and the new, the linkage of past and future, are brought into the focus of current opinion, it will betray itself into action without the protection of contemplation.

—Fred Frank, 1970

After October 2002, the economy began a slow recovery but remained volatile. The Dow Jones Industrial Average bottomed out at 7286.27 on September 27, 2002, and then began to increase—slowly at first, then quickly as the economy revved up again and came roaring back in the period between 2002 and 2007, almost as if the party during the dot-com era had never ended, although the profits this time came more from mega-offerings, mergers and acquisitions, and real estate. By 2007, the Dow would double and venture money would rise to $31 billion, compared to $15.8 billion in 2002.

In what might be called the Bank Boom of 2002–2007, the biggest banks went from huge to colossal, with JPMorgan Chase and Bank of America both reporting for the first time in history assets of over $1 trillion, and several other banks became so large and influential in the movement and management of vast sums of money that they would later be deemed "too big to fail." This meant that should any of them teeter or fail, the repercussions would dramatically impact not just the bank or Wall Street, but entire national economies, and possibly the global economy as well—something that few people in the thick of the swelling economy during this half-decade considered possible.

The upswell of markets and investment capital in the early aughts came about in part as a reaction to the partial deregulation of the banking industry late in the Clinton administration. This included the 1999 Gramm-Leach-Bliley Act, also known as the Financial Services Modernization Act, the legislation that repealed President Franklin Roosevelt's key initiatives back in the thirties to end certain financial practices contributing to the crash of 1929 and the Great Depression. As mentioned, the primary Roosevelt-era initiative that was axed was the 1933 Glass-Steagall Act, which mandated that investment banks—which primarily organize the initial sale of stocks and other financial instruments, facilitate mergers and acquisitions, and operate hedge funds—be separated from retail banks that took deposits, managed checking accounts, and made loans. By separating the two, the legislation had forbidden retail banks from using their depositors' funds for risky investments. Glass-Steagall also created the Federal Deposit Insurance Corporation and other agencies and protective mechanisms to protect depositors and keep the banking system from engaging in risky and speculative behavior. Now these safeguards were gone. As Arthur Fleischer pointed out, "Once you begin spending other people's money, the whole risk-reward ratio changes."

Fred doesn't mince words when expressing how he felt about these banking "reforms" and about another banking trend in the 1980s and 1990s, when one bank after another transformed itself from a small firm in which partners invested their own capital into a publicly traded company. He said:

> Well, we broke the Glass-Steagall Act. Huge mistake. Number two mistake was allowing investment banking firms to become corporations, because when you're in partnerships, you don't play with your own and your partners' money the way you might with somebody else's money. And it's worse than that. It's not only somebody else's money, it's somebody else's money leveraged forty times. So, what happened was, these young guys in the banks, they treated it like they were gambling, like going to Las Vegas.

For Fred, much of the frenzy that resulted from deregulation and all of the folderol around derivatives, hedge funds, and subprime loans in the early aughts was more or less background noise as he continued to do deals. One huge change, however, was that the deals—including purchase prices for acquisitions—were much larger in pharma and biotech than before, in part fueled by all of the capital available thanks to deregulation. Fred assessed the impact on his business:

> As always, when general markets crash, like they did when the dot-com bubble burst, the high-risk/high-reward sectors of the market suffer the greatest. But the power of the technology and emerging companies was such that biotech snapped back pretty fast after 2002, until the second crash in 2008.

BIOTECH BECOMES BIG BIOTECH
AS DRUG PIPELINES SPUTTER

During the period from 2002 to 2008, several of the larger and more successful (and in some cases luckier) companies that had been start-ups in the eighties and nineties now rivaled Big Pharma, at least in market cap, earning billions of dollars a year in revenues. In 2006, Amgen revenues were $14 billion, which placed it eleventh among the top twenty pharma companies that year.[1] Genentech's revenues in 2006 were $5.5 billion, which was more than Japan's Daiichi Sankyo, and just slightly less than Bayer AG on the top twenty pharma list of 2006.

These years were also marked by a very different regulatory environment for pharmaceuticals than what existed for banking. Indeed, even as Congress was loosening rules for banks they were tightening them around the approval of new drugs. In part, this came from revelations that some physicians and researchers were not fully disclosing their financial ties to drug companies whose compounds they were testing, and also that some companies were lavishing physicians who might prescribe their drugs with trips and other perks, practices that were later banned. Then in 2004 researchers testing Merck's popular painkiller Vioxx, which had sales of $2.5 billion in 2003 and had already been prescribed to 4 million Americans, revealed that the company had suppressed evidence of a dangerous side effect. Apparently, the drug in clinical trials had caused an increased risk of heart attack and stroke in patients with heart conditions, and allegedly had caused up to 140,000 heart attacks and 80,000 deaths.[2]

The period was also marked by a stubborn and, as the decade wore on, distressing rate of failure for drug candidates. In 1996, a high-water mark for FDA drug approvals, fifty-three new drugs were approved compared to only seventeen in 2002. This number popped up to thirty-six drugs approved in 2004, but for most years between 2002 and 2010 the number of new approvals at the FDA did not top twenty-five. This was a small number considering the thousands of drug candidates in clinical trials and the soaring costs of R&D. In part this came as Big Pharma companies were also finding their pipelines sputtering in terms of new and successful ideas for drugs, even as their R&D expenditures nearly tripled between 1995 and 2008.

Meanwhile, as biotech companies became larger, some, like Amgen and Genentech, dared to dream of becoming a fully integrated pharmaceutical company, with sales, R&D, marketing, and an active pipeline of potential new products all done in-house. However, the long time frames and the enormous investment required to make this dream come true was formidable for most, if not impossible. Peter J. Tanous, a longtime friend of Fred's dating back to the Smith, Barney days, wrote a book called *Investment Visionaries* that included a chapter about Fred that touches on the idea of Big Biotech wannabes. In the book, Tanous quoted Fred:

> What was the sequence to commercial success? If you want to become a FIPCO [Fully Integrated Pharmaceutical Company], you start with being a JITCO, a just-in-time provider of lead compounds to pharmaceutical companies, which will market them, manufacture them, and pay you royalties. If you license them compounds that in fact become successful, you go from being a JITCO to a RITCO, a royalty income trust company. Then if you receive enough royalties, you can afford to keep your subsequent research products and develop them yourself, because you have dependable cash flow. You won't have to go to the capital markets, which are very unpredictable. That's the way you go from being a JITCO to a RITCO to a FIPCO. I say to these companies, if you don't follow that sequence, you'll become a SHITCO . . . You've got to learn the sequence. The marketplace is fickle. This is an industry that is highly capital intensive.[3]

Despite this, researchers in the trenches at biotech companies large and small kept at it, working to develop new drugs. Their tenacity was something that Fred said he always has admired, particularly given that the vast majority of even the top researchers were, and still are, far more likely to fail than succeed at developing a new drug. Fred commented:

> You know that's one of the marvelous things about this industry if you think about it. People at the research side of it, they work for thirty, forty years, and never come up with a product. Think what dedication that is. It's not like you have constant reaffirmation of what you're doing. These people have come out of academia having worked for a long time. They have MD and PhD degrees. They're very talented people. They work forever and a day, and they may never come up with anything commercially successful, although their work may very well have advanced the science and our fundamental knowledge that will lead, in fact, to new drug discoveries.

ROCHE SETTLES A DISPUTE WITH IGEN BY BUYING IT

Despite the tumult in drug pipelines, the deals kept coming as the markets rallied in the early 2000s. In 2003, Fred worked with Maryland-based Igen, a medical diagnostics company that had a long relationship with Roche. This had begun in 1997 when Roche acquired Corange Ltd., a Bermuda-based holding company of the German drug giant Boehringer Mannheim Group, for approximately $11 billion, which resulted in Roche becoming the largest diagnostics company in the world at that time. Some of Boehringer Mannheim's diagnostics business, however, operated under a license from Igen International. This included a perpetual license to use Igen's patented amino acid–based technology in its diagnostic tests. Roche had some

$370 million in annual revenue from diagnostic products based on that technology.

The companies, however, became embittered over a dispute about intellectual property, what royalties might be due, and other facets of the licensing agreement. This resulted in extensive litigation between the two companies and a long legal battle between Igen and Roche. Igen won a $505 million judgment against Roche in 2003. An appeals court then reduced the award to about $19 million, but also gave Igen the right to cancel the license to Roche. This solution was certainly not optimal for either company, as Igen technology was by then deeply embedded in Roche's diagnostics business, and Igen could not easily duplicate the scope and applications of Roche's use of Igen's technology on its own. Fred recalled how, once again, business relationships he'd cultivated helped come up with the solution to have Roche buy Igen.

> It was sort of an existential transaction for both parties, who had also, understandably on both sides, become extremely embittered. I think because I knew both CEOs, Franz Humer of Roche and Sam Wohlstadter of Igen, and I believe each trusted me as a valued advisor, I was able to intervene to help them settle the matter.

The purchase price Roche agreed to pay, in July of 2003, was $47.25 a share, a premium of more than 20 percent over Igen's closing price of $37.20 at that time. There were other aspects to the agreement, including working capital financing for Igen, and a spin out of certain technology that at that time Roche did not want. Counting the working capital payment and other aspects, the transaction was approximately $1.4 billion, some 56 percent more than Igen's market capitalization at that time.

OTHER BIG DEALS BETWEEN CRASHES

The deals once again kept flowing during the 2002–2008 period even as the markets soared and began to overheat. Much of the action was in mergers and acquisitions as large companies wanted to be even larger by acquiring smaller outfits with proven products and expertise in new or complementary areas. For instance, in 2003, Fred represented Centerpulse, a Swiss-based dental-product company in the dental orthopedics and dental implants space. The company was trying to fend off a hostile takeover from Smith + Nephew, a London-based medical device company, when white knight Zimmer, headquartered in Indiana, appeared to beat Smith + Nephew's offer. Zimmer ended up paying 3.342 billion Swiss francs for the deal, which was one of a half-dozen acquisitions by Zimmer during this heady mergers and acquisitions period. Zimmer itself later merged with Biomet to become Zimmer Biomet, and has kept buying smaller companies ever since.

In another mega-deal, Fred represented Fujisawa Pharmaceutical Company in April 2005 when it merged with Yamanouchi Pharmaceuticals to form Astellas Pharmaceuticals, creating the second-largest pharmaceutical company in Japan in a deal worth $5.89 billion. A year later, Pfizer acquired privately held Rinat Neuroscience for $500 million, with Fred on the Rinat side. "This represented Pfizer's decision to finally get involved in the biotechnology sector," said Fred.

The deals kept coming for Fred, with another large one completed even in the midst of the 2008–2009 crash, in April of 2009. That's when CV Therapeutics, which made the cardiovascular drug Ranexa, was acquired for $1.4 billion by Gilead, then known mostly for its HIV drugs.[4] This was another white knight deal, with Gilead beating out Japanese pharma giant Astellas. "This enabled Gilead to diversify its product portfolio," said Fred. "I represented CV Therapeutics, having previously led their very successful $98.3 million common stock offering in 2006."

FRED FOSTERS AND GROWS BIOTECH START-UPS

Fred has always followed start-ups and early-stage companies, which is unusual for a Wall Street banker known for mega-deals. It's part of what he has enjoyed most throughout his career, starting back in the late fifties when high technology was just getting underway in a number of fields. "This is where the fresh ideas come from," he said. "Sometimes they work brilliantly, sometimes not, and often the reasons are not related to the quality of the technology or dedication of the management team. But they are an essential part of the ecosystem of biotech and of my love for this industry. Biotech investing is not for the faint of heart. But when it does work, the alpha for investors can be extraordinary, and the benefits to patients and mankind equally remarkable."

One example of Fred keeping track of new ideas emerging in the start-up space was Genomic Health, a cancer diagnostics company founded in 2000 by biochemist and entrepreneur Randy Scott. Previously, Scott was the CEO of Incyte, a company that initially did database service business in genomics during the human genome boom, before converting to a product strategy. Later, Scott founded Invitae, a genetic testing company, and Genome Medical, a clinical genetic specialists' practice.

Genomic Health went public in 2005, with Fred at Lehman Brothers and JPMorgan as co-leads and co-book runners. Investors at the time already included Versant Ventures and Kleiner Perkins Caufield & Byers, two of the most prestigious venture investors. On September 29, 2005, the company was listed on the NASDAQ with the symbol GHDX with the initial share price of $12, having filed in a range of $12 to $14 per share, or $60.2 million. The market value of the entire company was about $292 million after the offering.

The novel idea of Genomic Health was that the genomics of a patient's cancer tumor could predict, if tested, the recurrence of breast cancer and guide physicians and patients about whether or not to initiate chemotherapy. It was well known at the time that, although most patients were treated with chemotherapy after surgery, not all benefited from the treatment. These very toxic drugs, intended to eliminate any cancer cells that remained after surgery, also hurt normal cells. The question was: In which patients would cancer recur and why?

Genomic Health came up with an answer in the form of their lead product, Oncotype DX, a test that assessed gene expression in a patient's tumor that the company called an "oncotype." According to company literature, "When an oncotype is correlated with known clinical outcomes, it can be useful in predicting the likelihood of an individual patient's tumor behavior." The original Oncotype DX for breast cancer utilized a twenty-one-gene panel whose composite gene expression profile was represented by a single quantitative score, called a Recurrence Score, which the company vigorously tested clinically to ensure its accuracy. The higher the recurrence score, the company's research indicated, the more aggressive the tumor and the more likely it is to recur and, therefore, the more likely it is that a patient should have immediate chemotherapy after surgery. Fred remembered that the company's technology was at first viewed with suspicion:

> It was a tough offering, as no one at the time believed either that tumor genetic analysis could indeed project five- or ten-year recurrence outcomes or that oncology professionals would accept the idea. But it was one of those revolutionary ideas that biotech and molecular genetics could offer.
>
> Genomic Health went on to ever more rigorous clinical trials, began work on additional cancers such as prostate cancer, and became one of the most successful diagnostic companies of all time, originating the idea that molecular and genetic analysis of tumors and deep, serious trials could indeed predict recurrence and outcomes and guide clinical practice.

After a highly successful run of almost twenty years, Genomic Health was sold to Exact Sciences molecular diagnostics company in 2019 for $2.8 billion. Genomic Health's success spawned an entire new diagnostic segment of the industry, in which tumor samples (and now biomarkers as well) are used to predict outcomes of therapy and determine definitive diagnoses.

Genomic Health cofounder Randy Scott told a story about his early years, long before Genomic Health, when he first met Fred:

> In the late 1980s, I was the head of research for Invitron, a contract manufacturing company spun out of Monsanto in the mid-1980s that Fred had taken public right before the market crash of 1987. The company had a beautiful (and expensive) state-of-the-art manu-facturing plant for recombinant proteins and monoclonal antibodies in St. Louis close to Monsanto. Unfortunately, the business was fail-ing, as most of the biotech products of the eighties failed in clinical trials. The company was headed for collapse, but management was reluctant to change the business model that had taken the company public. As the young head of research, based in California, I had been encouraging the company to shut down manufacturing and invest in our exciting early research products.
>
> We went to Fred for advice in his New York office, and I was brought along by the CEO to present the research portfolio. In less than an hour of listening to the core business presentation followed by a short presentation of our research, Fred turned to the CEO of the company and said without hesitation, "That manufacturing plant is like a Tiffany's in Laredo, Texas. It may be a beautiful diamond but nobody's gonna buy it. You should mothball the plant and put all your money into research."
>
> The CEO declined, and within a year the company was on a path to liquidation for cents on the dollar. The research group, inspired by Fred's words, eventually spun out of Invitron to become Incyte

Pharmaceuticals, which went on to become one of the leading genomics companies of the 1990s and today is a $20 billion market cap biopharmaceutical company. Fred was right. In less than an hour he figured out the right path for the company . . . in stark contrast to a management team who spent years afraid to change course, leading to the company's demise.

Fred taught me a Wall Street lesson I would never forget: It doesn't matter where you've been, it matters where you're going. That belief in the power of research and the future of biotech helped launch my career with not only Incyte but also the future of Genomic Health, Invitae, and Genome Medical. Fred and Lehman Brothers played a significant role in inspiring me to take the leap into entrepreneurship.

PHYSIOME SCIENCES

Another start-up Fred championed in the early 2000s was Physiome Sciences, a company headed for a time by Jeremy Levin. Physiome, partnering with IBM, set out to create computer simulations of what happens in organs and cells. The hope was that this sort of in silico modeling might help test drugs in a computer before putting them into humans, an idea that remains elusive even today, although many have tried to capture the complexity and dynamism of what happens in the human body, and models are continually improving. Levin recalled the objectives behind the company and Fred's involvement:

The goal at Physiome was to radically reduce animal testing and improve the chances of a drug coming to market by being able to run millions of simulations in a computer. At that time there were just a few companies set up in this area. It's a very tough area, with very high risk.

Fred said, "Look, if it works, it's going to be one of the great game changers of the industry, and it's worth the effort." He agreed to be chairman. Together we raised enough money to get it going and a little bit beyond, and the technology showed tremendous promise. But at the end of the day, it did not do what we wanted it to do. Not because of its failing, but because the pharmaceutical industry is really conservative, and they were anxious to follow the FDA processes rather than try something new. We realized that we could not keep raising money while the pharmaceutical industry was not prepared to experiment with the technology.

Levin remembered that Physiome was an unusual proposition for Fred to work on, but he was happy that Fred took on the role he did:

I thought that Fred had great wisdom. I wanted him to come on board to help steer the company as chairman. I felt that the board was driven too much by venture capitalists and less by people who truly understood the industry, and Fred was more than prepared to do that. At that stage, he had largely stepped away from active IPOs, and Lehman had given him the latitude to do it. So he was very instrumental in capital formation. Physiome wasn't ready to go public, so it clearly wasn't really his type of work.

Levin departed Physiome in 2003, which merged in 2004 with Predix Pharmaceuticals, another company that specialized in computational expertise and biological modeling. The company tried to leverage its in silico modeling to create a successful drug development platform but struggled and was forced to shut down in 2009, in part a victim of the recession and the evaporation of funding.

2007–2008: THE GREAT MELTDOWN AND THE FALL OF LEHMAN

On October 9, 2007, the Dow Jones Industrial Average reached a then-heady 14,164.53, having nearly doubled in the five years since the low point following the dot-com crash in September 2002. This half-decade-long upward momentum was about to come to a screeching halt, however, as the markets began to tumble—and tumble and tumble. This time, the cause was not a dot-com and high-tech bubble, but a different sort of speculation. It started with the wave of new banking deregulation in the late nineties, which now allowed banks to offer mortgages to almost anyone, with little or nothing down, low interest rates, and little or no monthly payments for the first few months or years. These below-prime loans fueled an extraordinary real estate boom. Housing prices soared and mortgage-backed loans proliferated as people borrowed against the rising value of their homes. Mortgage-backed securities were then bundled and sold—and then rebundled and resold, sometimes dozens of times. Everything depended on mortgage holders making their payments when they came due, and on housing prices continuing to rise, or at least stay stable.

Inevitably, mortgage payments came due for millions of property owners who, it turned out, could not afford them once the "balloon" payments came due. Housing values plummeted and the whole edifice began to collapse. As John Cassidy wrote years later in the *New Yorker*, looking back on the crash of 2008:

> American authorities all but ignored the madness developing in the housing market and on Wall Street, where bankers were slicing and dicing millions of garbage-quality housing loans and selling them on to investors in the form of mortgage-backed securities. By 2006, this was the case for seven out of every ten new mortgages.[5]

Early indications of the coming disaster came in late 2006 as mortgage defaults rose sharply. Then in early 2007 came the bankruptcy of several medium-sized mortgage-lending companies and the bailout of a moderate-sized British bank, Northern Rock, on September 14, 2007. The Bank of England did the bailing, which caused a run on banks around the world. Smaller and then larger banks began to collapse too, and markets crashed as government banks around the world and the Federal Reserve in the US attempted to stabilize things, to no avail. On March 17, 2007, the Federal Reserve was forced to bail out a heavily leveraged Bear Stearns from bankruptcy by covering its bad loans so it could be sold to JPMorgan for a fraction of what it was worth just a few weeks earlier. Amid the crashes and failures, central-bank and government attempts to staunch the gathering cataclysm kept the system from complete collapse. But the downward spiral continued, bringing us to Sunday, September 14, 2008, when Fred and Mary were at home in New York following the news.

"I remember hearing that Lehman was planning to file for bankruptcy the next day," said Mary, who was sure, like many people, that the Federal Reserve would step in to save what was then the fourth-largest investment bank in the world by backing their bad loans, like it had done for Bear Stearns. The Fed, however, did not step in, instead allowing Lehman to fail. This precipitated a 504-point drop in the Dow, the worst decline in seven years, as Lehman's collapse triggered a seismic shock to the entire global financial system. The global money markets froze. Banks and insurance companies in most of the developed world suddenly found they could not borrow either. It took central banks lending on a colossal scale to prevent a cascade of financial sector bankruptcies of institutions even bigger than Lehman. It was a situation that the Federal Reserve chairman at the time, Ben Bernanke, called "the worst financial crisis in global history."

Mary recalled the Lehman disaster unfolding the night of September 14:

I think Fred was in denial that a firm of Lehman's stature—where he had worked since 1969, and had seen grow from 330 employees to 28,000 employees by 2008—was wiped out.

Fred recalled meeting with the CEO of Lehman, Dick Fuld, in the months leading up to September 2008:

I used to meet Dick Fuld once a month for breakfast, and I continually exhorted him during this period, saying that the leverage level on Lehman's equity (approaching 40 to 1) was excessive and could lead, potentially, to catastrophe if financial markets changed. But Dick told me I was old-fashioned.

In any case, I had never been interested in the upper echelons of governance at Lehman, only in new technologies, new businesses, innovation, meritorious deals, and using the great Lehman franchise for the advancement of new companies. This was the legacy of Lehman, from the days of Bobbie Lehman, when the firm financed the first airlines—Pan Am and TWA—and Radio Corporation of America, and so many others. This was Lehman's legacy, and what I was trying to do in the life sciences, biotechnology, and health services. And Dick told me to keep doing that. Perhaps I should have put my foot down fiercely, but I don't think it would have made any difference.

On September 15, 2008, Lehman did indeed file for Chapter 11 bankruptcy protection following the massive exodus of most of its clients, drastic losses in its stock, and devaluation of its assets by credit rating agencies. The filing marked the largest bankruptcy in US history and was the biggest disruption to the teetering global financial system yet. The following day, Barclays announced its agreement to purchase Lehman along with its New York City headquarters building. That Sunday, when Lehman announced it was going to file for bankruptcy, Mary remembered calling the headmaster at her son Frederick's school:

Frederick had just left for his first year of boarding school at Hotchkiss, his father's school, where Fred had been on the board for a decade, and was chairman. Plus, poor kid, his beloved golden retriever, Star, was dying of doggy lymphoma. I didn't want to exacerbate the situation, but I didn't want Frederick to be afraid that, first of all, we were broke or that something really horrible would happen—although at that point Fred and I didn't know if top executives at Lehman would be sued.

I called the headmaster of Hotchkiss and said, "Watch out, please, for our son, but while you're watching out for my son, watch out for the whole school. Because there are a lot of students whose parents are at AIG [American International Group, a finance and insurance company], which is part of this disaster, and many families may be wiped out at AIG, Bear Stearns, and other financial institutions."

Sandy Robertson recalled meeting Fred in New York for breakfast a couple of days after Lehman filed:

I said, "Fred, I'm really sorry to hear about this. You must've lost a lot of money in your stock." He said, "No, every time I got an allocation of stock, I shorted it against the box. So, I'm just fine. I've sold stock whenever I could over the years, shorted it against the box, and covered the short when it came."

Fred was very apolitical, he didn't get involved. He just wanted to do deals. He was vice chairman. He generated millions of dollars' worth of fees in the pharmaceutical area. He was on one side or the other of most pharmaceutical mergers. So he said, "Just let me run my own business and stay out of my way. I don't care about the politics of who's doing what to whom in the firm."

He had a great platform with a great old name, and he could do business there. I'm kind of surprised that someone else didn't come and drag him into their firm to do the same thing for them and bring Mary along at that point.

Mary summed up the fall of Lehman and shared a bit of the firm's lingering lore:

> The final demise of Lehman was the last of the firm's many near-death experiences. The first was when Lew Glucksman in the seventies tanked the balance sheet in a bad bet on Treasury bonds, which brought Pete Peterson in to run the firm. The second was in 1984, when a bad bet in a bad market led to the purchase of Lehman by Shearson and American Express. There were the bad bets made on RJR Nabisco and other deals that led American Express to rescue the firm but then eventually spin it out in May 1994.
>
> After Lehman was spun out of Shearson, it flourished for a while but then succumbed to what some have called the "Lehman disease" and finally went under. There is a legend about Lehman. That is, that Bobbie swore that no one would ever run the firm as well as he had. Many old Lehmanites tell me this is fantasy, and probably it is. Maybe it's just the changes in financial markets, the fact that brokerages/banks are now global enterprises. But there is the fact that governance at Lehman was never good, and ultimately, it couldn't survive in the new world of finance.

Looking back, Fred believes that the fall of Lehman was "unnecessary":

> The politics of the financial crisis determined that Merrill Lynch had to be saved and Lehman could go down. It was emotionally a difficult time for both me and Mary, as we had so loyally served the firm for over forty years, and its tradition of innovating new companies and new industries was not what drove it under. It was the relentless search for large fees, the mortgage disaster, the excessive level of leverage Lehman had, and the fact that Lehman waited too long to sell itself.

There was some unfairness there as well, as Lehman tried to convert itself into a federally/state-authorized bank early so as to borrow from the Federal Reserve "window," which is allowed only to authorized banks, and was denied, although Goldman and others later achieved that status as the crisis accelerated. Equally telling were the hubris of the CEO and the board who turned down several offers, as they were not "rich enough."

I was involved in helping to found the biotech industry, which today employs approximately 290,000 directly, and many more indirectly. Lehman never cared about this. The firm was only interested in the large pharma and other large transactions Mary and I did, with big fees and recurring transactions. So Lehman died, burdened by its leverage and poor governance. But my life's work, biotech, has not just survived but flourished.

AFTER THE CRASH OF 2008

Despite obvious warning signs, the 2008 crash was a shocker to many people and the repercussions brutal. This was especially true for how it impacted high-risk, capital-intensive industries with long time frames such as pharmaceuticals and biotech. A downturn like that in 2008 creates a major challenge in funding the biotech industry's voracious need for ever-increasing capital as research projects wind their way through development, testing, clinical trials, and the regulatory pathway. Fred described what happened:

> The impact on the smaller, earlier-stage companies was especially severe, and the IPO market came to a screeching halt. A consequence of this readjustment in valuations and capital access is a heightened interest by Big Pharma in effecting collaborations,

acquisitions, and product licensing opportunities with the struggling biotech companies. This confluence of factors is especially
severe for the specialty small investment banking firms that only
thrive during a robust capital cycle.

Of course, I find a rather sad aspect to the acquisition cycle—that
we lost our iconic biotech companies around this time, too: Genentech, Genzyme, Chiron, Cetus, and CV Therapeutics to name a few.
All of which Mary and I were intimately involved with throughout
their history.

AFTERMATH AND LEGACY

After Barclays' acquisition of the remnants of Lehman's banking business, Fred stayed on at Barclays for two years. After that, he joined a
series of boutique investment advisory firms. This was a slow period for
Fred and for biotech and pharma, particularly since none of the smaller
firms Fred worked with had equity underwriting franchises.

"I greatly missed the IPO business, which was moribund for a
while after the crash," said Fred. "I missed the many years of spon-
soring new companies in the public markets. However, mergers and
acquisitions and licensing as well as venture capital remained major
sources of financing for biotech, and I kept my head in that, mostly as
an advisor."

In 2014, Fred and Mary created their own firm, Evolution Life
Science Partners. Fred described the firm's niche:

Our focus is on companies that are still too early for IPOs, but we
look for companies with breakthrough science that need strategic
advice or a Big Pharma or Big Biotech partner for research and development. These kinds of companies can attract venture capital but are

often a bit deserted by even the boutique underwriting banks, who need immediate transactions to support the enormous costs of sales, trading, and research.

Today, a dozen-plus years after the fall of Lehman, Fred and Mary remain actively engaged as advisors to young, breakthrough companies looking for advice. Fred continues to look for "alpha" companies, those that will lead and produce something big in terms of both impact and returns.

Fred and Mary also have been relentless philanthropists, supporting or advising programs at Yale University and the Yale School of Management, the Johns Hopkins Bloomberg School of Public Health, the Harvard School of Public Health, the Salk Institute, Stanford University, and the Hotchkiss School, among others. To read more about Fred and Mary's philanthropy, check the afterword, which was written by Fred.

In the end, Fred is perhaps most proud of his efforts to engage in the sort of decency and loyalty that sometimes seems quaint on a Wall Street dominated these days by massive movements of money and, too often, the placing of transactions and profits over people and genuine innovation. Paul Abrams, a former NIH researcher, executive chairman of Geneius Biotechnology, and a serial biotech entrepreneur, described Fred and Mary like this:

> Fred Frank, along with Mary, has stood as a beacon of honor, character, loyalty, and integrity on a Street and in a world in which those features are in rapidly diminishing supply, and increasingly less valued. Over a lifetime, however, they are the only things that really matter.
>
> Fred and Mary treat you the same whether your career is flying high or experiencing a glitch. Although masters of creative financial and business transactions themselves, their interactions are personal and non-transactional. They are always there when one calls,

regardless of the circumstances. It is a relationship that I—and count-less others I know in the field and outside of it—treasure, and one that I have tried to emulate. Those in the earlier parts of their careers, in whatever field, would do well to model their lives after Fred and Mary.

Another legacy of Fred Frank's decades of deals and interactions has been to treat banking and finance—and the unyielding push to support innovation—as an endeavor that's every bit as creative as, say, writing a book that crackles with originality, or designing a building to create an original and inspiring space that will last. Here's how Fred put it:

> After all these years, there is almost no area or clinical trial or devel-opment that I haven't seen. And sometimes I have fallen on my sword about a new idea that didn't work. But the inventiveness of major sci-ence, the depth and knowledge of investors now in this industry, still provides the possibility of "alpha"—excess returns over the average market returns, and a product that benefits people and changes how we live. Ultimately this is driven by the human body, which doesn't give up its mysteries easily—it is forever young, and "alpha."

Fred has been a consummate risk-taker with an almost uncanny instinct for picking successful companies and promulgating inventive deals, which over the years he has combined with a work ethic that nearly everyone who knows him comments on. Fred reflected on this:

> I believe that, in addition to hard work and constancy, one of my skills is being able to look quickly at situations and see the likely outcome and success pathway. One of the elderly partners at Smith, Barney, when I was a new and green research analyst, said to me, "Fred, stocks are like the Madison Avenue bus here in New York City. Miss one, and another will be along very shortly."

So, it has been not only in therapeutics but in all the other areas that align with it, such as instrumentation. This includes the early work we did with Lee Hood at Applied Biosystems, which created the first DNA analyzer and synthesizers; and also Affymetrix, which introduced the first "biochip" system; and Qiagen, which first rationalized the labor intensive and complex matter of sample preparation; and finally Illumina, which has made genome analysis rapid and affordable; and many more. I also have been willing to act and bring my long history and reputation to some of these efforts when others were hesitant.

Fred Frank represents the type of investor who exemplifies what journalist Matt Taibbi once referred to as "long-term greed,"[6] the idea that capitalism can be used to build things that last and can also make money. This is opposed to "short-term greed," the sort of get-rich-quick ethos that sunk Lehman and so many others in 2007–2008, and continues to be too much of what predominates on Wall Street and beyond today. Short-term greed is the antithesis of what Fred has attempted to help build: companies and industries that make things that will not only make money, but will also benefit society and people in the long run.

Fred isn't happy that the pharmaceutical industry and, in some cases, larger companies in the biotech industry, has become so focused on short-term greed. He said it's been hard to watch this shift since he started out on Wall Street as a young man who discovered pharma when people thought of it as producing miracle vaccines and treatments, a time when the industry was one of the most trusted in the world. Americans in a 2019 Gallup poll placed pharma as the worst of 25 industries, with twice as many people surveyed giving pharma negative rather than a positive rating—58 percent to 27 percent.[7] Fred commented:

One sadness, given my lifelong devotion to the pharmaceutical and biopharma industry, in all its interesting segments, has been watching the reputation of the industry sink from once being among the most admired industries in the US, indeed in the world, to a status like natural resource extraction companies and the tobacco industry.

The reasons for this plunge in public trust are many, said Fred. They include not only an obsession for outsized profits—which averaged 16.5 percent in net profits for the top 35 pharmaceutical companies between 2000 and 2018, according to an analysis in the *Journal of the American Medical Association*[8]—but also the rise of excessive salaries for executives, plus a direct-to-consumer advertising push that often promotes expensive, patented versions of drugs at the expense of cheaper, but equally efficacious generics. Another major source of declining trust is a pricing system for treatments that seems untethered to the reality of what is actually happening in the economy—as measured, say, by rises in the consumer price index (CPI). The CPI for US cities rose between 0.1 percent and 4.1 percent between 2000 and 2018, with an average of around 1.8 percent,[9] while drug prices tripled between 2007 and 2018[10] and rose by almost 6 percent in 2020.[11] Of course Fred recognizes that researching and developing drugs is phenomenally capital-intensive and high risk, and that prices need to reflect that, but "the gap has grown too large and is probably unsustainable when pricing increases are so much more than the CPI," he said.

Fred wonders if the pandemic of 2020–21 might be an opportunity for the drug industry to work for the common good in a less profit-driven way as scientists and pharma have labored to come up with treatments and vaccines for COVID-19. In the spring of 2021 Fred said:

I'm hoping that the outpouring of immense effort by therapeutic and vaccine companies now, in the context of the COVID pandemic, will help restore a sense of respect for science and for a system that emphasizes people over profits. With science recently under assault, mostly for political reasons, it's time for the industry I have spent so much time in to regain the trust of people by continuing post-pandemic to restore a reasonable balance between pricing and what people and the economy can bear.

I consider it a positive development that regular news reports, even from non-scientific and TV sources, are talking during the pandemic about T cells and innate immunity and cytokine storms and why they happen and the effects on patients with COVID. The pandemic has been a horrifying experience for us all, but perhaps it will lead to a better, more positive attitude by people and the press about the basic value of the biomedical enterprise.

On the other hand, Fred wonders if the general state of the economy coming out of the pandemic will put a damper on the bull market of the past few years for financing companies that want to commercialize the latest round of new discoveries and technologies—from gene-editing tools like CRISPR to AI and biomedicine to new generations of wearables and consumer health companies, and more. Fred also worries that because so many companies in recent years were funded during the long period of ebullient markets that a slow-down in the markets will mean these young efforts will be starved of follow-on financing, and will die on the vine. Fred said:

I'm very concerned that we have too many new upstart companies funded over the past three or four years when so much capital was available. It may be impossible to further finance all these companies to becoming product and selling, marketing, and manufacturing entities as capital slows down.

For one thing, we have too many companies today that are public which really shouldn't be public. They're too early. They don't have enough capability. But it's been so easy to raise money that they've been smart and opportunistic in doing it. And we've told a number of companies that they should take advantage of the extraordinary opportunity.

But there is not enough money in the world to fund to late stage product development or commercialization for all the companies that have gone public in the last three years. When the market turns down, it's going to be a real challenge for this industry, for younger companies to raise capital to move their research projects forward.

Both Fred and Mary fear there may be a biotech-pharma "nuclear winter" approaching as the pandemic economy plays out. "The risk is great that the markets for fledgling companies will blow up and go dark, possibly for years, like they did in the 2000–02 and the 2008–12 periods," said Mary. Still, Fred and Mary remain optimistic even as they hole up like so many people during the COVID pandemic—in their case in a house in upstate New York, where they recently offered a few final thoughts in the spring of 2021 about where their thinking about life sciences, finance, and the state of the world is right now. Speaking one afternoon on Zoom during a shelter-in-place moment during the pandemic, Fred talked about the future, with Mary sitting beside him:

> One of the things that struck me from my early entry into this business over sixty years ago was that the goal of the best of the companies in biomedicine is to improve the longevity and quality of life. And that is still the underlying thesis on which Mary and I are working. And there's no end in sight to what can be done to improve the quality of life and the longevity of life. That's why the future holds great promise, because we're so far away from exploiting all the opportunities that exist to accomplish that mission.

Mary added:

And that's what drives us.

At this point, Fred and Mary on Zoom started talking fast and almost finishing each other's sentences, something that many who have worked with them have experienced:

FRED: Look at what's happened recently, there have been some really important and game-changing breakthroughs, like CRISPR. This was not expected. And it's probably been more useful for research than therapeutics so far, but it's still a huge game-changer.

MARY: These massive tectonic plate shifts happen not very often, but they do happen—like with the incredibly fast development of vaccines for the COVID-19 virus. And they happen not only in the science but also in business models.

FRED: And there is no end to the need. We have lifespans that keep extending so that people get older, and now we have a lot of diseases I call "diseases of medical progress." We didn't have those diseases before because people didn't live long enough to get them. Alzheimer's is a classic example.

MARY: Solving those problems also spins out all sorts of other businesses. Like a whole industry that has emerged around wearable devices—for instance, the continuous glucose monitor from Google for diabetes. Fred's grandfather nearly died of diabetes in the 1920s. Then came insulin and synthetic insulin and one product after another, but it took a long time.

FRED: It always does, which people need to remember. They also need to know and appreciate that this isn't easy. It's possibly the most difficult thing people have ever tried, to understand how the human organism works, and to try to make our lives better.

Financing the Future

A MASTER DEALMAKER PROVIDES HIS THOUGHTS AND REFLECTIONS ABOUT A SIXTY-PLUS-YEAR CAREER, 2009–PRESENT

"IT'S DÉJÀ VU ALL OVER AGAIN."

Among my favorite American pundits is the great Yankee baseball player Yogi Berra, famous for his malapropisms of speech. There are two quips that sum up my sixty-plus-year history in finance, still ongoing. These are: "It's déjà vu all over again," and "The future just ain't what it used to be." During my long career I have discovered that both are true, particularly for biotech.

There is a consistent trend in which breakthroughs emerge from academic medicine and science, which the financial community rapidly embraces by creating new companies to develop them. Each of these "Newcos" believes fervently that the "secret" or "cure" for human diseases, and "the answer we have been looking for" has arrived. This is followed by disillusionment when those companies do not succeed, at least at first. Because the best scientific breakthroughs keep coming back and often end up succeeding only over time.

An example that has loomed large in my career is antibodies, particularly monoclonal antibodies. While antibodies—which are specialized proteins the body uses to fend off pathogens and attack cancer cells, among other targets—have appeared in the scientific literature from 1881, with intense academic science development from the 1950s through the 1970s, most antibody therapies developed during that time proved to be maddeningly imprecise in fighting disease, making them less than useful as therapeutics. Then in a key development, Argentine biochemist César Milstein and German biologist Georges Köhler produced in 1975 the first hybridoma, which allows enormous quantities of completely identical (monoclonal) antibodies—which are highly specific to particular targets—to be produced. The news was published in the research journal *Nature* and Milstein and Köhler won a Nobel Prize for their accomplishment in 1984.

Milstein and Köhler's work on hybridomas and monoclonal antibodies and other advancements in the lab led to commercialization efforts in the space just as the biotech industry was emerging as an investment concept in the late 1970s and early 1980s—all of which failed, causing investors to completely desert the field.

For instance, when I took Cetus public in 1981, one of its products, invented by Dr. Stanley Cohen, was a monoclonal antibody. This molecule hooked to a segmented, nontoxic portion of the deadly toxin ricin, and was intended for use as a warhead-loaded monoclonal against targeted cancer cells. The product did not succeed, as the chemical linkers between the monoclonal and ricin fragment were not durable enough for consistent therapeutic treatment. Yet other companies kept at it, most of whom also did not succeed, until finally in 2011 Seattle Genetics introduced the first warhead-loaded monoclonal anticancer antibody, with Roche introducing a second one in 2013.

In the years since hybridoma technology emerged and has continued to make progress, investment in monoclonal technology has accelerated. Today the pharmaceutical industry has more than $20 billion of monoclonal antibodies sold by numerous companies, including treatments for COVID-19 developed by Eli Lilly and Regeneron, both authorized for emergency use by the FDA in November 2020. Diverse and robust research is also underway to produce biphasic and other monoclonals of different types with even better therapeutic possibilities.

The first really successful monoclonal licensed for use against cancer was Rituxin, invented by IDEC Pharmaceuticals, a second-generation biotech company that partnered with Genentech. Rituxin was originally licensed in 1997 by the FDA for non-Hodgkin's lymphoma, which afflicts approximately 77,000 people a year in the US. The licensor, Genentech, thought this drug would earn small revenues (compared to blockbuster drugs) of maybe $200–250 million, and based their offer of royalties to IDEC accordingly. So, I suggested to IDEC, whom I was representing, that they accept this, with a caveat that if the revenues went over a certain level, as IDEC expected, much higher royalties would apply. It was a relatively unusual set of terms in licensing, especially in an as-yet barely successful field like antibodies. Such terms are now common, but not in those days. Rituxin's label was expanded through additional clinical trials over time and went on to have peak sales of $7.32 billion in 2015 and 2016, when the primary patents expired.

Another novel science that has come and gone several times is gene therapy, the editing of mutant genes that cause disease. First conceived of in 1972, this science did not reach the clinic until 1990. The idea of permanently treating a genetically caused disease with a one-time repair has enormous clinical and investment appeal. Extensive clinical trials by companies working in the area failed during the 1980s and early 1990s, and again initial investment enthusiasm faded. The inherent attractiveness of the technology led to continuing investment, however, albeit at a lower level than the initial burst. In 2017, Spark Therapeutics' Luxturna (for treatment of RPE65 mutation-induced blindness) was the FDA's first approved gene therapy to enter the market. Since that time, drugs such as Novartis's Zolgensma (for treatment of spinal muscular atrophy) and Alnylam's Patisiran (hereditary transthyretin-mediated amyloidosis therapy) have also received FDA approval, and dozens more are on their way.

Cell therapy has the same history—early enthusiasm, early failed companies—yet today several cell therapy drugs are on the market, and many more are coming.

In my long career, I have probably led hundreds of initial public offerings and countless mergers and acquisitions and financings. All of them were, in their time, strategic and critical to my clients. Indeed, one of the pleasures of my business is being a critical participant at a moment in a company's history when the stakes for it are existential. Numerous important transactions stand out in my mind, including my associations with Genentech and Roche, my participation in major pharmaceutical transactions in the early 1990s, discussed earlier in this book, and my willingness to vociferously support the initial offerings of early-stage companies.

There are also many transactions I did which were small, often pro bono, but some of these made a difference. For instance, I helped with the merger of the two original organizations representing biotechnology in government—the Industrial Biotechnology Association (IBA), representing larger established companies, and the Association of Biotechnology Companies (ABC), which represented emerging companies and universities and focused on technology transfer issues, conferences, meetings, and other initiatives to help its members develop products. It was clear that the industry needed to speak with a single voice in front of its Washington and regulatory constituencies. In 1993, I assisted the leaders of both in overcoming fears that the interests of the smaller companies might be lost in a merger. It's fair to say that the combined entity, the Biotechnology Innovation Organization (BIO), has flourished.

From a small cottage industry in the late 1970s and early 1980s, with products and ideas emerging out of academia and championed by a handful of scientists and a few brilliant venture capitalists, the life sciences industry, broadly defined, today has grown to include more than 4,000 public companies listed on major exchanges and NASDAQ and a public market value of approximately $34 trillion. This does not even account for the number of private venture companies and those listed on the pink sheets and bulletin boards. There are dozens of venture capital firms and investment partnerships that focus only on biotechnology, some specializing only in therapeutics and other newer entries in fields like health information technology and artificial intelligence in healthcare.

The industry has benefited greatly from the benevolent stock markets we have enjoyed since the recovery from the financial crash of 2008–09. With more than 850 IPOs since 1979,[1] the last three years (2018–20) have in particular been golden days in biotech, with over 140 IPOs.[2] This has been driven in part (as with the stock market as a whole) by the extraordinarily low interest rates we have had for more than five years. I have always said that a very meaningful indicator for biotech returns, in an industry where drug and device development can take ten years or more, is the rate on the 10 Year Treasury note. In an environment of very low interest rates and a vibrant general and biotech stock market, such as we have today, high-risk, alpha equities, like biotech, benefit greatly.

It has not always been so. One of the key aspects of the biotech and life sciences industry, and particularly biotechnology, is its volatility. That volatility is mostly driven by general capital markets, and in some periods, by the investment community's disappointment with cutting-edge technology that didn't initially pan out, per my preceding observations on antibodies and gene and cell therapies. The chart below demonstrates the periods of "nuclear winter" for biotech.

Historical Biotechnology Capital Market Conditions

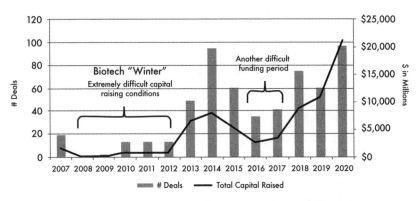

Courtesy of Gordian Investments, LLC and its division Evolution Life Sciences Partners

I would hope that, even if macroeconomic and stock market general conditions deteriorate, the biotech and life sciences industry will retain some vitality. This is because in the US we have developed an extraordinary "ecosystem" for the development of the industry. This ecosystem is the envy of the world, even as China, France, Germany, the UK, Singapore, India, and Malaysia try to duplicate the economic, employment, and health benefits our life sciences industry has brought to the US.

So what is that ecosystem? It begins and ends with the nature of US investors and our general cultural economy. US investors are prepared to absorb risks in exchange for returns. We all love the new. Few other countries, except now perhaps China, have that deep cultural attitude. But there is more to it.

Over the years that Mary and I conducted extensive business in Europe, we were always astounded that people regarded leaving a big, prestigious drug or life sciences company for a new start-up as a professional failure. This attitude meant that these places did not have the depth of the experienced managerial culture we do in the US. As our large pharma companies downsized and changed strategy, hundreds of experienced professionals left and ended up joining the emerging life sciences industry, bringing research, development, regulatory, and commercial skills to small companies, plus an enthusiasm for "making it work."

It was driven not only by the possibility of earning a lot of money from options. It was driven also by the fact that these professionals would have freedom to pursue their science and professionalism in a manner not possible in a big company. There was also the enduring fact that US academic science, fueled by NIH grants and philanthropy, has produced a remarkable outpouring of innovation. This combined with US venture firms and our investor base in the States made these new companies possible. Also, academic institutions signed on to technology transfer, enabling the development of companies, which is still not easy to do with academic institutions in Europe, although this is changing, especially at Oxford University in the UK.

The last and perhaps most important part of the ecosystem goes back to the beginnings of modern Wall Street and modern capital accumulation in the early twentieth century, when the US retail industry became the first to issue IPOs of breakthrough companies. Unheard of in other places, this was the start of large-scale public venture capital. Today, the biotech market is dominated by venture and professional investment institutions, but the willingness of public market investors makes the difference here.

More recently, new methods of financing the industry have also emerged. These include angel funds and private investors who have succeeded in life sciences and have reinvested in new ventures. These "angels" can provide the key early-stage investment needed to bring a company to the stage where a professional investor will enter. There are also new consumer and philanthropic forces with substantial resources and clout known as patient advocacy groups, and disease-specific foundations. These include entities such as the Juvenile Diabetes Research Foundation, with an annual budget of close to $200 million, and the Michael J. Fox Foundation, which spends $100 million a year to research and develop treatments for Parkinson's disease. Given the web and Internet economy, these groups can have a profound impact on FDA decisions, but are also a source of funding for early-stage companies.

Other countries are adopting some of the attitudes and techniques that have driven our US ecosystem to work so profoundly. The professional fear of leaving a big company for a small one is disappearing. There is more venture capital in Europe today than ever before. But there is not a group of public investors with the same risk absorption and understanding that we have here in the US, except perhaps in China and other parts of Asia. And in particular, there are not public investors of the same depth and knowledge that we have here. In fact, almost every foreign company Mary and I see has the ultimate goal of accessing US investors.

The unique relationship that the US venture and investment community has had with academic medicine is accelerating—including at my own beloved Yale. But other overseas institutions (notably Oxford and Toronto) are doing this as well, launching incubators funded by their schools and philanthropy.

Our risk here in the US is that foreign governments and foreign philanthropy are pouring enormous amounts of money into replicating or exceeding our US biotech ecosystem. The media has reported that China is dedicating $30 billion to this effort. We must fund the FDA and the NIH and its related agencies at a higher level. Despite some of the FDA's shortcomings—inadequate examinations of foreign manufacturers, the sources of active ingredients for drugs, and generic drugs generally, which are well documented in the recent book

Bottle of Lies: The Inside Story of the Generic Drug Boom by Katherine Eban[3]—it remains the best and most rigorous regulatory agency in the world, despite some challenges it faced during the Donald J. Trump administration over attempts to politicize its regulatory rigor. If we want to have safe drugs, sourced from all over the world, the FDA needs better funding.

There is no doubt that the rest of the world "free rides" on our research and the free market pricing we practice here in the US by charging lower prices for drugs that are often much more expensive in America. Impracticable proposals have been put forth to deal with this. Anyone who has read *Bottle of Lies* knows that sourcing drugs from overseas is not in the health interest of US patients. There are potential legislative solutions, such as limiting the amount of copays for US patients. But one thing is for sure: We need to increase the national investment we make in our biotech industry, lest we lose our lead, and the edge we bring in encouraging innovation, to others.

I have been privileged to know many brilliant scientists, venture capitalists, and entrepreneurs, many who have been serial entrepreneurs founding numerous companies. The list of these greats is too long to include here; I include many of the most important names in the acknowledgments in this book. During my very long career I also have been very fortunate in having the opportunity to be associated with many philanthropic and leading educational institutions. These associations also brought into my realm a broad array of extraordinarily successful, dedicated, talented individuals, broadening my horizons not only in science but also in the subtle work of making great institutions continue to flourish.

In the field of leading educational institutions, I have been on the advisory boards of the Yale School of Management, the Johns Hopkins Bloomberg School of Public Health, the Harvard T.H. Chan School of Public Health, and the Salk Institute. I had the privilege of knowing Jonas Salk, the creator of the polio vaccine. He died two years after I joined the Salk Institute Council. I have been chairman of the National Genetics Foundation, a member of the board of governors of the National Center for Genome Resources, and a member of the board of the *Journal of Life Sciences*. I have also been an advisor to Elm Street Ventures, an early-stage venture fund associated with Yale University, since 2005.

My greatest lifetime philanthropic interests have been Yale, my alma mater, class of 1954, and the Hotchkiss School, class of 1950. At Hotchkiss, I served on the board for the maximum allowable ten years, my last two as head of the board of trustees. I remain very active in the school, heading the 1891 Society, and I am now a trustee emeritus. Mary also created a Hotchkiss library fund as a birthday present for me. While everything is computerized today, books remain the staple of every library. Mary and I assisted the school in founding and progressing a summer music conservatory program, Hotchkiss Piano Portals, for students in grades seven through nine who play classical piano at a very high level but may never become professional musicians. The experience of high-level classical music study, master classes with visiting piano luminaries, and performance of classical music requires discipline and hard work, and that experience can be a valuable skill in any walk of life.

I have served on the Yale School of Management advisory board since 1975. In 1976, the school accepted its first master's degree class. President Richard Levin of Yale asked me to devote time and my Yale contributions to helping the newly started school establish itself as a leading, differentiated business school. I am still on the advisory board after forty-five years, and I marvel at what the school has achieved as a leading, globally oriented business school, now ranked in the top ten.

At the time I joined this effort for Yale's business school, Mary asked why I would do this, as I am a graduate of the Stanford Business School, to which I have also devoted philanthropic resources over the years. I told her that a major institution such as Yale was about to engage in an extraordinary entrepreneurial effort, founding a new, major graduate school almost out of raw, fertile earth, and I wanted to be a part of it. And I have been part of this school for more than forty-five years, funding two chair professorships, scholarship funds, and other initiatives, but I would like to think that my constant attention, guidance, and devotion of time has been of equal value to my financial contributions.

I was fortunate to be a member of the class of 1954 at Yale. By any standard, it is an exceptional class for the degree of bonding we all have and the sense of our Yale experience, which has led us to extraordinary philanthropic effort for the school. At our twenty-fifth reunion, in 1979, three of us, Joel Smilow, Richard Gilder, and I, set up the Yale 50/54 Fund with $75,000 each. The money was to be invested until our fiftieth reunion. By sheer coincidence, at our thirtieth reunion, we invited others in our class to contribute, which they did—another $300,000. We set up rules—only equity, no short positions, be as aggressive as possible. The money was invested by Joe McNay, Yale class of 1956, who later went on to found Essex Investment Management, which became an enormously successful money management firm. At our fiftieth reunion, in 2004, our class of 1954 gift to Yale was $120 million, which funded the new science building Yale so badly needed at that time. It remains the largest class gift in Yale's history. At our fiftieth reunion, we set the same goal, a fund for our class gift at our sixtieth reunion. At that reunion, our class gift was $220 million, and at our sixty-fifth, $165 million.

We'll see what happens for the seventieth reunion!

One just has to look at the Class of 1954 Field in the Yale Bowl stadium, the Smilow Field Center, the Smilow Cancer Hospital, and the Gilder Lehrman Institute for American History—plus the $20 million Gilder and his wife donated to help restore the Sterling Memorial Library, the gifts to the Yale School of Management, and many other significant gifts to the university. Charlie Johnson, from our class, has been an incredibly generous Yale philanthropist, whose recent gift of $250 million went toward the building of two new residential colleges. And he has funded many other programs at Yale and participated in many important committees and related activities for the school.

Another Yale initiative will, I hope, be part of my own legacy of service to Yale. In 1975, President Richard Levin asked me to head a university committee on how to expand and enhance entrepreneurship and more rapid technology transfer at Yale. Despite having more than 80 percent of Yale's research work concentrated in biomedical sciences, which is widely recognized as world leading, very few venture companies founded from these scientific developments stayed in New Haven. They moved to San Francisco or Cambridge, Massachusetts, where the scientific and venture ecosystem was more favorable.

Our committee interviewed potential faculty and administration for two years and produced a report suggesting, among other recommendations, that Yale both establish courses in venture finance and entrepreneurship at the Yale School of Management and elsewhere across the university, and establish a translational medicine fund to invest small amounts in faculty projects. These amounts were intended to bring their laboratory sciences to the point where the venture community would embrace them. Thanks to the generosity of a number of donors, all of this has happened.

The Blavatnik Fund for Innovation, generously endowed with $25 million from the Blavatnik Family Foundation, is now in its fourth year of operation, with a number of notable successes not only in the acceleration of venture funding for Yale science, but also in the willingness of companies to stay in New Haven. The transformational effect on the faculty of Yale has been remarkable, and undergraduate enthusiasm for entrepreneurial training is high.

I have been honored by many awards during the sixty-plus years of my career. In 2004, I received the Albert Einstein Award from the Weizmann Institute of Science in Israel for acting as a senior advisor to the Prime Minister. In 2019, I was given the Richard J. Bolte Sr. Award for Supporting Industries from the Science History Institute for my role "in shaping the modern global biotechnology industry from its infancy [with] strategic guidance in hundreds of financings, strategic alliances, and merger and acquisition transactions." I received the Award for Excellence from the American Liver Foundation's Northern California Division in 2007 and the "Salute to Excellence," the Biotech Hall of Fame Award at the Annual Biotech Meeting in Laguna Niguel in 1997, as one the key founders of the industry. And I received the Gilda's Club of New York City Visionary Award in 2006 and was named among Reed Elsevier's "Top 100 Living Contributors to Biotechnology." I have served as an advisor or board member to many early-stage biotechnology companies. Currently, I serve as senior advisor to Pure-Tech, a London Stock Exchange–listed biotechnology company, and Coherus Biosciences, Inc.

Today Mary and I are still active in the biotech industry. We run a boutique investment bank, Evolution Life Science Partners, which specializes in early- to mid-stage biotech, diagnostic, research tools, and related life-science companies. Every day we receive calls and e-mails from new companies that have been referred to us. Sometimes we will look at these and say to ourselves, "This is déjà vu all over again"—the market is too crowded already, the area is out of favor with the financial community (for now). But sometimes we see something cross our desks that causes us to say, "The future just ain't what it used to be," meaning that I fundamentally believe that for the life sciences industry, it will be a better future.

This is because science is always young. It renews itself endlessly, always getting better. It is my continuing love for this renewal effect of science, the fountain of youth, that has kept me in this industry for more than sixty years. And it will keep me in it, I fervently hope, for many years to come.

—Fred Frank, 2021

Acknowledgments

From Fred Frank:

I am grateful to David Ewing Duncan, our author. That a science writer of his stature would write a biography of me is a great honor, and I thank him not only for this book, but for his long personal history with Mary and me. I am also very grateful to the Science History Institute, not only for the awards they have given me, but for the marvelous oral histories that their Life Sciences Foundation has collected about me and many early founders of the biotech industry who figure in this book. Without this archive, the extraordinary history of the biotech industry might have been lost.

I have been privileged to know many brilliant scientists, venture capitalists, and entrepreneurs, many who have been serial entrepreneurs founding numerous companies. The list of these greats is too long to include here, but I particularly want to mention Dr. Lee Hood, Dr. Arie Belldegrun, Dr. William Haseltine, Dr. George Poste, Dr. Stanley Cohen, Dr. Joseph Schlessinger, Dr. Roger Perlmutter, Dr. Stanley Crooke, the great venture capitalist Brook Byers, and David Swensen, with whom I have enjoyed a long association, during which he worked for me at Lehman, and then went on to brilliantly run the celebrated Yale Endowment. My thanks to all those who contributed our mutual stories and accolades to me in this book, including those mentioned above and my lifelong friends Sandy Robertson and Arthur Fleischer.

Also, special thanks to Fabio Witkowski, head of the Hotchkiss Arts & Music Department, who edited and enhanced the photographic quality of many of the photos herein. Special thanks to the Karsh Family Foundation, who granted us permission to use the Karsh photographs of me on the front cover and in the book. How very special it was to be photographed by Yousuf Karsh, who was the renowned photographer who took iconic photos that we all recognize of Winston Churchill, Nelson Mandela, George Bernard Shaw, Martin Luther King, Fidel Castro, Princess Grace, Jacqueline Kennedy, and Ernest Hemingway. There are so many others to thank that the list would be too long for this context.

My lifetime thanks also to my many clients, who entrusted me with transactions, moments in their lives, personal and corporate, which were existential to them.

I also thank my wife and forty-year business partner, Mary Tanner, for her dedication to me, to our joint business, and to our family and our charities, and for the efforts Mary put into this book. And I thank Mary, my children, Jenny, Laura, and Frederick, and grandchildren, Gregory and Emma, for their devotion to me.

From David Ewing Duncan:

I want to thank Fred Frank and Mary Tanner for sharing their stories and truly fascinating and exceptional lives with me. I share Fred's appreciation for all of the many people who shared their stories and recollections to me for this book. I'd also like to thank J.D. Beltran for her sharp and precise fact-checking (aided by Mary, whose ability to parse a manuscript for the tiniest of details is exceptional). And deep thanks to friends and family who heard me talking about this project for years and remained patient and supportive throughout.

Notes

Chapter 1

1. Find a Grave memorial page 32434811, Arthur Frank (1873–1953), created by Judie Latshaw Huff, citing B'nai Israel Cemetery, Salt Lake City, Utah, accessed January 25, 2021, http://www.findagrave.com

2. *Salt Lake Tribune*, April 4, 1953; excerpted in Stone, Eileen Hallet, *A Homeland in the West: Utah Jews Remember* (Salt Lake City: The University of Utah Press, 2001), 130–131.

3. Pusey, Roger, "Arthur Frank Stores in Utah Will Close," *Deseret News*, November 13, 1992, https://www.deseret.com/1992/11/13/19016019/arthur-frank-stores-in-utah-will-close

4. Stone, *A Homeland in the West: Utah Jews Remember*, 127–132.

5. Ibid.

6. Pusey, "Arthur Frank Stores in Utah Will Close."

Chapter 2

1. Watson, J.D. and Crick, F.H.C., "A Structure for Deoxyribose Nucleic Acid," *Nature* 171 (1953): 737–738.

2. Winslow, Ward, *Palo Alto: a Centennial History* (Palo Alto, CA: Palo Alto Historical Association, 1993), 5.

Chapter 3

1. From Frank, Frederick, *Investment Thoughts: The Ferment of Change* (New York: Lehman Brothers Report, November-December 1970).
2. Mikulic, Matej, "Prescription drug expenditure in the United States 1960–2020," Statista, June 12, 2020, https://www.statista.com/statistics/184914/prescription-drug-expenditures-in-the-us-since-1960/
3. Geisst, Charles R., *Wall Street: A History* Updated Edition (New York: Oxford University Press, 2012), 274.
4. Ibid.
5. Ways, Max, "Antitrust in an Era of Radical Change," *Fortune* 75, no. 3 (March 1967).

Chapter 4

1. Robbins-Roth, Cynthia, *From Alchemy to IPO* (New York: Basic Books, 2000), 20.
2. Ibid.
3. Miller, Devin and Kiggen, Cassie Ann, "US Venture Capital Investment Surpasses $130 Billion in 2019 for Second Consecutive Year," NVCA, January 14, 2020, https://nvca.org/pressreleases/us-venture-capital-investment-surpasses-130-billion-in-2019-for-second-consecutive-year/
4. Bugos, Glenn E., "Kleiner Perkins, Venture Capital, and the Chairmanship of Genentech, 1976–1995," Thomas J. Perkins interview conducted in 2001, Program in the History of the Biological Sciences and Biotechnology, Regional Oral History Office, the Bancroft Library, University of California at Berkeley, 2002.
5. "The Ubiquitous Frederick Frank," *Life Sciences Foundation* magazine, Summer 2012, 11. In 2015, The Life Sciences Foundation merged with the Chemical Heritage Foundation to become the Science History Institute. https://www.sciencehistory.org/lsf
6. Ibid, 10.
7. Ritter, Jay R., "Initial Public Offerings, Updated Statistics," January 12, 2021, https://site.warrington.ufl.edu/ritter/files/IPO-Statistics.pdf
8. Wayne, Leslie, "Chrysler Sets Large Share Sale," *New York Times*, March 29, 1983.

Chapter 5

1. Auletta, Ken, *Greed and Glory on Wall Street: The Fall of the House of Lehman,* 4th ed. (New York: Random House, 1986).
2. Ibid.
3. Chapman, Peter, *The Last of the Imperious Rich: Lehman Brothers, 1844–2008* (New York: Portfolio/Penguin, 2012).

Chapter 6

1. "The Ubiquitous Frederick Frank," *Life Sciences Foundation* magazine, Summer 2012, 8–17.
2. Bugos, Glenn E., "Kleiner Perkins, Venture Capital, and the Chairmanship of Genentech, 1976–1995," Thomas J. Perkins interview conducted in 2001, Program in the History of the Biological Sciences and Biotechnology, Regional Oral History Office, the Bancroft Library, University of California at Berkeley, 2002.
3. *Life Sciences Foundation* magazine, "The Ubiquitous Frederick Frank," 13.
4. Ibid.
5. Ibid.
6. Bugos,"Kleiner Perkins, Venture Capital, and the Chairmanship of Genentech, 1976–1995," 36.
7. Ibid.
8. *Life Sciences Foundation* magazine, "The Ubiquitous Frederick Frank," 14.
9. Ibid.
10. Bugos, "Kleiner Perkins, Venture Capital, and the Chairmanship of Genentech, 1976–1995."
11. Ibid.
12. *Life Sciences Foundation* magazine, "The Ubiquitous Frederick Frank," 14.
13. Bugos, "Kleiner Perkins, Venture Capital, and the Chairmanship of Genentech, 1976–1995," 40.
14. Ibid, 38.
15. *Life Sciences Foundation* magazine, "The Ubiquitous Frederick Frank," 16.
16. Bugos, "Kleiner Perkins, Venture Capital, and the Chairmanship of Genentech, 1976–1995," 38.

17. Ibid, 37.

18. Fred has told certain stories multiple times with remarkable consistency. This quote was provided by Fred to the author; another source for Fred's remembrances of the Roche-Genentech deal is an oral history conducted by Mark Jones for the Science History Institute: Frederick Frank, interview by Mark Jones at Peter J. Solomon Company and by phone, New York, May 25, 2011, September 14, 2011, and August 16, 2013 (Philadelphia: Science History Institute, Oral History Transcript #1005).

19. *Life Sciences Foundation* magazine, "The Ubiquitous Frederick Frank," 12.

20. Bugos, "Kleiner Perkins, Venture Capital, and the Chairmanship of Genentech, 1976–1995," 17

21. Stroke (Activase); Cystic Fibrosis (Pulmozyme); Asthma (Xolair); and various forms of cancers (Rituxan, Herceptin, Avastin, and Tarceva).

22. McNamee, Laura M. and Ledley, Fred D., "Assessing the history and value of Human Genome Sciences," *The Journal of Commercial Biotechnology*, Vol 19 No 4 (2013), https://doi.org/10.5912/jcb619

23. Berenson, Alex and Wade, Nicholas, "Clinton-Blair Statement on Genome Leads to Big Sell-Off," *New York Times,* March 15, 2000.

Chapter 7

1. Roth, Gil, "2007 Top 20 Pharmaceutical Companies Report," Contract Pharma, August 19, 2007, accessed January 29, 2021. https://www.contractpharma.com/issues/2007-07/view_features/2007-top-20-pharmaceutical-companies-report/

2. "Vioxx," Drugwatch, accessed January 29, 2021. https://www.drugwatch.com/vioxx/#:~:text=At%20the%20time%20of%20its,60%2C000%20deaths%2C%20FDA%20investigator%20Graham

3. Tanous, Peter J., *Investment Visionaries: Lessons in Creating Wealth from the World's Greatest Risk Takers* (New York: Prentice Hall, 2003).

4. Reuters, "Gilead, a White Knight, to Buy CV Therapeutics," *New York Times*, March 12, 2009.

5. Cassidy, John, Packer, George, and Lemann, Nicholas, "The Real Cost of the 2008 Financial Crisis," *New Yorker*, September 17, 2018.

6. Taibbi, Matt, "Greed and Debt: The True Story of Mitt Romney and Bain Capital," *Rolling Stone,* August 29, 2012.

7. McCarthy, Justine, "Big Pharma Sinks to the Bottom of US Industry Rankings," Gallup Website, September 3, 2019, https://news.gallup.com /poll/266060/big-pharma-sinks-bottom-industry-rankings.aspx

8. Ledley, Fred D., McCoy, Sarah, Vaughan, Gregory, et al., "Profitability of Large Pharmaceutical Companies Compared With Other Large Public Companies," *Journal of the American Medical Association*, 323(9):834, March 3, 2020, accessed January 29, 2021.

9. US Bureau of Labor Statistics, "Consumer Price Index US City Average All Urban Consumers: 1990–2020," accessed on January 29, 2021. https://www.bls.gov/regions/midwest/data/consumerpriceindexhistorical_ us_table.pdf

10. Hernandez, Imaculata, et al., "Changes in List Prices, Net Prices, and Discounts for Branded Drugs in the US, 2007–2018," *Journal of the American Medical Association*, 323(9):854–862, March 3, 2020, https://jamanetwork.com/journals/jama/article-abstract/2762310

11. Hopkins, Jared, "Drug Prices Rise 5.8% on Average in 2020," Marketwatch, January 2, 2020, https://www.marketwatch.com/story /drug-prices-rise-58-on-average-in-2020-2020-01-02#:~:text=The%20 average%20increase%20was%205.8,doses%20for%20the%20same%20 drug.&text=The%20average%20is%20just%20below,%25%2C%20 according%20to%20the%20analysis

Afterword

1. For 1979–2018: "The MTS Biotech IPO Monitor – Edition 4: Q3 2018 Update – 2018 Looking to Beat the 2014 High Tide Mark For Biotech IPOs," MTS Health Partners, October 4, 2018, accessed January 29, 2021. https://www.mtspartners.com/news/the-mts-biotech-ipo-monitor-edition -4-q3-2018-update-2018-looking-to-beat-the-2014-high-tide-mark-for -biotech-ipos/

2. Glasner, Joanna, "Biotech IPOs Are On A Tear," Crunchbase, August 19, 2020, accessed January 29, 2021. https://news.crunchbase.com/news /biotech-ipos-are-on-a-tear/

3. Eban, Katherine, *Bottle of Lies: The Inside Story of the Generic Drug Boom* (Ecco, 2019).

About the Author

DAVID EWING DUNCAN is an award-winning, best-selling author of eleven books published in twenty-one languages, an award-winning journalist and broadcaster, and the cofounder and curator of Arc Fusion, a consulting, media, and events company. David writes for *Vanity Fair*, the *New York Times*, *The Atlantic*, *Wired*, *Fortune*, *National Geographic*, *Inc.*, *Fast Company*, *MIT Technology Review*, *Newsweek*, *Discover*, and many other publications. He is a former commentator for NPR's *Morning Edition* and formerly a special correspondent and producer for ABC's *Nightline* and *20/20*; a producer for Discovery Channel; and a correspondent for PBS NOVA's *ScienceNow!* He was the founding director of the Center of Life Science Policy at UC Berkeley and is a member of the faculty at Singularity University.

David's latest book is *Talking to Robots: Tales from Our Human Robot Futures* (Dutton-Penguin, 2019). Other recent books include *When I'm 164: The New Science of Radical Life Extension, and What Happens If It Succeeds* (TED Books), *Experimental Man: What One Man's Body Reveals about His Future, Your Health, and Our Toxic World* (Wiley), and the global best-seller *The Calendar: Humanity's Epic Quest to Determine a True and Accurate Year* (Harper-Collins). He is finishing a book co-authored by Craig Venter, *The Secret Lives of Earth's Smallest Creatures* (Harvard Press, 2021) about the microbiome of the Earth. He also is finishing his first novel, *The Cure*, a biomedical thriller.

David's awards include Magazine Story of the Year from the American Association for the Advancement of Science (AAAS). His articles have three times been nominated for National Magazine Awards, and his work has appeared twice in *The Best American Science and Nature Writing*. He also has served on a special committee at the National Academy of Sciences on science and communication.

He lives in San Francisco and is a member of the San Francisco Writers Grotto. His website is www.davidewingduncan.com.